Marx's Theory of Ideology

BHIKHU PAREKH

THE JOHNS HOPKINS UNIVERSITY PRESS
BALTIMORE AND LONDON

© 1982 Bhikhu Parekh
All rights reserved
First published in the United States of America, 1982, by
The Johns Hopkins University Press, Baltimore, Maryland 21218

First published in Great Britain, 1982 by
Croom Helm Ltd., 2-10 St. John's Road, London SW11

Library of Congress Catalog Card No.: 81-48079

    Parekh, Bhikhu
      Marx's Theory of Ideology.

    Baltimore: Johns Hopkins University
    Press/Croom Helm Ltd. Publishers

    300p
    8204   810915

    ISBN: 0-8018-2771-X

Printed and bound in Great Britain

CONTENTS

To Pramila

INTRODUCTION

Marx's theory of ideology charts a hitherto unexplored epistemological terrain. In the course of his study of such thinkers as Hegel, the young Hegelians and the classical economists, and the past and present societies, Marx discovered a distinct form of reasoning about man and society. It was ahistorical and universalistic in form, systematically biased in its orientation, justificatory in its implications, and involved distinct logical fallacies. Marx was struck by the fact that this pervasive and mistaken form of reasoning had never before been noticed and exposed. Following the contemporary usage he called it ideology, and characteristically invested the term with a new range of meanings. He analysed its logical structure, identified its characteristic fallacies and proposed an alternative form of reasoning about man and society. For him ideology was not an abusive slogan to be used to discredit the opponents, nor a general term describing any organised body of beliefs, but a theoretical concept, an epistemological category designed to conceptualise a specific form of thought.

Like all intellectual explorers Marx had great difficulty articulating his discovery in unambiguous terms. He formulated it in different idioms and gave conflicting accounts of it in different writings. He made exaggerated claims for it, and overlooked many a difficult problem raised by it. Above all he confused the phenomenon he had discovered with the others that looked like it, but were, in fact, very different.[1] As we shall see, throughout his life Marx used the term ideology to mean both idealism and apologia. He evidently thought that the two were logically connected, that idealism led to apologia and the latter required idealism as its necessary epistemological basis, but never clarified the nature of the connection. Similarly he thought that ideology and what has since come to be called the social determination of knowledge were closely connected, but remained unclear about the connection.

Since Marx did not offer an unambiguous statement of his theory of ideology, it has been interpreted in many different ways, some extremely dubious and implausible. For example, some commentators have maintained that for him, ideology refers to such things as illusory ideas, false ideas determined by class interests, class-conditioned thought, unfounded ideas manufactured at the prompting of an unconscious wish or interest, and a body of justificatory beliefs. Apart from the fact that there is little textual evidence to support these crude views, which generally rely on some careless remarks in the *German Ideology*, they reduce a highly complex theory to a slogan, and destroy its historical integrity. Since most criticisms of Marx's theory of ideology are based on such interpretations, they miss the target and are grossly unfair to him. Again, several commentators have argued that Marx was a relativist, rejected the concept of objective truth in favour of class truth, and inconsistently claimed to have offered an objective knowledge about the human history in general and capitalism in particular. Although the criticism is one of the commonest, there is little textual evidence to support it. What is more, Marx *cannot* be a relativist. Relativism is a form of absolutism. It singles out a specific factor and turns it into an absolute. Since Marx's theory of ideology was primarily designed to undermine all forms of absolutism, it can have nothing to do with relativism either.

My purpose in the book is to articulate the logical structure and epistemological basis of Marx's theory of ideology. Since Marx's theory of ideology is somewhat ambiguous and confused, an exposition of it is necessarily an interpretation, and any interpretation is necessarily a form of collaboration. In order to highlight its logical structure, I have felt it necessary to develop arguments he left inchoate, draw distinctions he only hinted at, and articulate his targets and presuppositions more fully than he did. This may sound arrogant, but it is not. Marx developed many fascinating ideas which he did not have the energy, will or time sufficiently to distinguish and defend. If his *Capital* were to be excluded, he has left behind little more than clusters of brilliant insights. Like Rousseau and Nietzsche, he never systematically worked them out, and tended to express them in striking epigrams and arresting casual remarks requiring sustained reflection in order to squeeze out their full philosophical significance. This may partly explain why the brief first part of the *German Ideology* and a couple of pages of *Theses on Feuerbach* have inspired a greater body of literature than the three bulky tomes of *Capital* put together. Like all creative writers Marx requires sympathy and help; sympathy in order to enter into his world of thought in its own terms, and help to enable him fully to articulate, refine and bring out the full theoretical power of his insights. Without either, a commentator is in danger of getting distracted by his ambiguities, confusions, inadequate arguments and exaggerated claims, and unfairly dismissing his whole system of thought as a 'philosophical farrago'.[2] A systematic critique and transcendence of Marx's thought is long overdue, but it cannot be undertaken without a full appreciation of both his greatness and limitations.

The structure of the book is dictated by the structure of its subject matter. The first chapter outlines and explains the two basic senses in which Marx uses the term ideology. Of the two the second, namely an apologetic body of thought, is of central interest to us, and the continuing concern of the rest of the book. Accordingly the second chapter examines the concept of apologia, elucidates its basic characteristics and assumptions, and specifies what Marx does and does not mean by ideology. The next three chapters outline Marx's analyses of the different ways in which the theorists of society became the apologists of the established social order; in the sixth, I collect together some of the important conclusions of Marx's analyses. In the next chapter I explore how, in Marx's view, he could avoid becoming an apologist, and assess the widespread view that he was able to do so by analysing the capitalist society from the proletarian point of view. In the eighth chapter I discuss some of the important ways in which he modified the traditional theories of truth, and outline the basic features of his own. In the final chapter I briefly and somewhat tentatively sketch some of the fundamental insights and limitations of Marx's theory of ideology.

To avoid misunderstanding I might make three points. First, I am primarily interested in exploring the ways in which, in Marx's view, the social *theorists* become ideologists, and only incidentally in his account of the way an ideology gains dominance in society. That the ordinary men should entertain ideological beliefs is explained with relative ease. The difficult and puzzling question is why, in Marx's view, the ideas of such highly sophisticated thinkers as Hegel and the classical economists retained an ideological dimension. Second, I am not concerned to attack or defend, but simply to understand Marx's theory of ideology. The theory has created considerable upheaval, especially in the disciplines relating to man and society. It is therefore worth exploring what it meant to its creator, and how he himself proposed to deal with its disturbing implications. Accordingly I have concentrated on laying bare its logical structure and basic assumptions as sympathetically as possible, and avoided commenting on them. Third, since I am only interested in Marx, I have generally avoided Engels's writings except when necessary to illuminate the obscure points in his friend's thought. This is not because I share the view that he misunderstood or vulgarised Marx, but solely because I am interested in what Marx himself thought and wrote.

Introduction

In the composition of the book, I have incurred many debts. The first draft of it, with a slightly different focus, was prepared some years ago. I am most grateful to Professor David McLellan and Dr R.N. Berki for commenting on it and making most valuable suggestions. I have greatly benefited from my years of discussions with them. I am grateful also to Sir Isaiah Berlin, Professor Joseph O'Malley, Dr John Gray and the late and much missed John Rees for discussing with me several parts of it and offering most helpful comments. Finally, I am grateful to Mr David Croom for bearing with the slow progress of the book with considerable understanding and patience.

Bhikhu Parekh

1 IDEOLOGY: IDEALISM AND APOLOGIA

Marx used the term ideology in two interrelated senses: first, idealism and second, an apologetic body of thought.[1] He used it in both senses all through his life, although he generally tended to use it in the first sense in his earlier, and in the second in his later writings. We shall examine each usage in turn.

I

Even when as a young man Marx felt drawn to Hegel's philosophy, he found the latter's idealism unacceptable. He ridiculed it in a letter to his father and subjected it to a systematic critique in the *Contribution to the Critique of Hegel's Philosophy of Right*.[2] In the *Holy Family* he turned his attention to the Young Hegelians. He traced their limitations to their idealism, and subjected it to a mixture of criticism and ridicule.[3]

In the *German Ideology* Marx continued his attack on the idealism of Hegel and the Young Hegelians with the significant difference that he now called them ideologists rather than idealists, and their systems of thought ideology rather than idealism. In the *Critique* he had invariably called Hegel an idealist; in the *German Ideology* he calls him both an idealist and an ideologist, and uses the terms interchangeably. In Chapter VI of the *Holy Family* Marx had criticised Bruno Bauer for his speculative idealism; in the *German Ideology* he criticises him for being an ideologist. The charge is the same, only the name is different. In other words the *German Ideology* carries on under a different banner a battle that Marx had begun in his first critique of Hegel and the *Holy Family*.[4]

Marx's preference for the new name was not inadvertent. He was familiar with de Tracy's work and referred to him in the *Holy Family*.[5] He was also aware of Napoleon's 'scorn of ideologists'. In his view the science of ideology developed by de Tracy and his colleagues rested on the idealist assumptions, and so did the philosophy of the German philosophers. Accordingly he took over the term ideology, used it to mean idealism and called the thought of Hegel and the Young Hegelians 'German Ideology'. As he put it in a crossed-out paragraph in the *German Ideology*,[6]

There is no specific difference between German idealism and the ideology of all the other nations. The latter too regards the world as dominated by ideas, ideas and concepts as the determining principles, and certain notions as the mystery of the material world accessible to the philosophers.

Marx's usage is basically the same as that of the French ideologists. For both ideology refers to a systematic and self-contained study of ideas, the crucial differences being that while the French ideologists regarded it as a wholly legitimate inquiry, Marx took the opposite view.

II

Marx uses the term idealism in a somewhat unusual sense. For him it refers not to a particular philosophical doctrine about the nature of knowledge, but to a general theory about the nature of consciousness. His meaning will become clearer as we proceed. For the present a few words should suffice.

In Marx's view the Western philosophy has been dominated by a highly questionable form of dualism.[7] In one form or another most philosophers have invoked the twin principles of nature or matter, on the one hand, and spirit, God, Ego, etc., on the other, to explain man and nature. In their view nature cannot be explained in its own terms, and accordingly they argued that it is created, constituted and/or somehow sustained by a supernatural or transcendental being. They also understood man in dualist terms. For them man is a bipartite being. Part of him belongs to the world of nature or what is also called matter, and part of him to the world of spirit. His body makes him a member of the natural world, whereas *qua* spirit he is a transcendental or supernatural being. Of the two the spirit represents his essence. It constitutes his *real* self, whereas the body is an incidental appendage. According to the dualist view thought, especially the theoretical thought, is the characteristic activity of the spirit, and the interaction with nature that of the body. Thus intellectual, moral, artistic, and such other activities are considered to be characteristic of the spirit, and hence spiritual in nature, whereas eating, drinking, the sexual activity and material production, etc. are characteristic of the body, and hence material in nature.

For Marx idealism is a logical corollary of the bipartite view of man.[8] Since consciousness is deemed to be the property of the spirit, and since the spirit transcends the natural and social world, the philosophers have argued, or more often simply assumed, that human consciousness is autonomous, free, self-determining, independent, inhabiting a realm of its own, guided and governed by its own principles and capable of being studied in its own terms. Marx gives the name idealism to such a view of the nature of consciousness. Idealism stands for the view that consciousness can be detached from its concrete, embodied and socially situated human subjects, and that ideas, theories, beliefs, human conduct and its other 'products' can be analysed and understood without reference to the natural and social contexts of the men who produce them. For Marx idealism has dominated a good deal of traditional ontology, epistemology, methodology, ethics, political theory, historiography, etc., and given rise to misleading theories.

Idealism assumes that the spirit or consciousness is conceptually and, for some, even temporally prior to matter. For it matter is not and *cannot* be the ultimate reality, and *cannot* generate and explain consciousness. Accordingly idealism refuses seriously to countenance the possibility that the natural world could be self-sufficient, and explains it in terms of such a transcendental and supernatural being or principle as God, the Absolute, *Geist*, Ideas, Substance or Ego. Some idealist philosophers go further and maintain that the transcendental principle not only creates but also constitutes the material world. They deny matter not only ontological primacy, but also any form of ontological reality or 'being'.

Marx argues that, given his view of the nature of consciousness, the idealist is led to hypostatise or reify abstract ideas. He regards them as independent entities possessing a distinct and autonomous nature of their own, which it is his task to comprehend. For the idealist abstract ideas are not only the legitimate, but the only legitimate, objects of investigation. And hence he inquires into the 'real' or 'true' nature of such concepts as man, property, law, liberty, justice and the state. Marx takes a different view. For him general ideas are designed to conceptualise specific social relations or experiences. Since the latter vary from one historical epoch to another, the general ideas have different contents and meanings in different historical epochs, and cannot be discussed in the abstract.

Marx takes the concept of property.[9] For him it conceptualises the social relation of property, which is differently constituted and defined in different societies. In some societies property implies absolute individual ownership; in some others the joint ownership by the individual and the community; in yet others it implies a right to use but not own an object; and so on. Since it has no universally common definition or mode of organisation, the only way to understand it is to examine in detail such distinctive forms of property as the Asiatic, the classical, the feudal and the bourgeois. Having analysed these we may abstract their common features. In Marx's view there is no *a priori* guarantee that we will find such common features. Even if we do, what we would have learnt is limited in value. The general features are necessarily trivial and lack content; at best they have only a classific-atory value; they depend for their validity upon the concrete historical analyses of the specific forms of property; they cannot be used either to infer what forms of property prevail in specific societies or to explain why they have developed these and not other types of property; and they only tell us something about the shared features of the differ-ent forms of property, but nothing about property 'as such' or the real nature and essence of property 'in general'. As Marx once put it in a different context, we can at best have a general theory of property, but not a theory of property in general.[10]

Marx contends that the idealist does not see this. He is convinced that 'what is property' is a substantive and significant question de-signed to illuminate the essence of property as such, that it must be answered first before we can undertake historical investigation into specific forms of property, and that our knowledge of the essence of 'property as such' enables us to explain why it 'takes' a particular form in a particular society. In Marx's view property as such is an 'empty phrase'. No social reality corresponds to it, and therefore it cannot be an object of investigation. It is not a concept at all, but a mere word lacking content and concrete reference. Further, to say that property 'takes' certain forms in specific societies is to turn a word into a spectre enjoying an ethereal existence and giving itself worldly incarnations. What is more, such a language implies the un-tenable thesis that property in general is more real than its specific forms, and that our primary concern must be to understand it rather than its forms. For Marx only the historical forms are real; the concept of property is an abstraction summarising their common features; and property *as such* is a fiction. It is not abstracted from any social reality, and therefore an illegitimate abstraction.

Since property as such, man as such and liberty as such, are all illegitimate abstractions, Marx argues that the philosophers engaged in analysing them have no real subject matter, and are only concerned with 'empty' words. Hence they have no alternative but to define them as they please, and invest them with whatever meanings seem 'proper' or 'appropriate' to them. They do the same with other such abstractions, connect them in terms of their 'internal' logic, construct logically coherent systems of ideas, and use them to explain the world. Since the philosophers in question do not care to study the 'real connections' between the social relations, 'they can without difficulty construct some fantastic relationship', and build up a wholly arbitrary system of thought.[11] For Marx the whole exercise, concerned as it is with an illegitimate object of inquiry, is totally illegitimate. The resulting body of thought, which consists of arbitrarily constructed and defined abstractions, has little relation to the actual world and can in no way explain or illuminate it.[12] Not surprisingly the debates between such systems are inherently trivial. Since each ultimately rests on the 'arbitrary' definitions of words, their debates are ultimately verbal, not amenable to empirical check, irresoluble and pointless.[13]

For Marx idealism has shaped a good deal of moral philosophy as well. Moral philosophers have devoted their energies to investigating and defining the nature of goodness, right, justice, morality, etc. without noticing that, for the reasons stated above, such abstractions cannot be independent objects of investigation. Besides, they have attempted to lay down the timeless and universally valid moral principles, without realising that men are not pure spirits, and moral principles do not connect with the world unless they are grounded in specific human needs and social relationships. Further, the moral philosophers have rested their systems on such historically invariant notions as man's innate sense of dignity, pride, humanity, fellow-feeling and self-respect without noticing that these are not at all natural to man and only emerge at specific stages of historical development. Again, they have freely constructed their conception of a 'normal', 'rational' or 'truly' human being on the basis of their analyses of the nature of man as such, without realising that these are all subjective standards grounded in arbitrary definitions.[14]

For Marx idealism has generated a distinctive theory of human action, including moral and political actions.[15] Even as the idealist takes the ideas to be independent objects of investigation, he takes them to be the independent bases of human conduct. In his view men act in certain ways because they hold certain ideas and beliefs, and the social reality and indeed reality in general *is* what men think it to be and can be changed by changing their thoughts or interpretations of it. Further, the idealist conceives the human agent as a transcendental spirit freely forming his beliefs, exploring the alternative courses of action, willing one of them, and then coming down to the earth to incarnate or 'translate' his will into action. Accordingly he holds the individual solely responsible and praises and blames him for his beliefs and actions.

For Marx such an account of human conduct is totally misleading. It ignores the fact that man is an integral part of society, occupies a specific position in it, is shaped and circumscribed by the dominant patterns of relationship, has a limited range of alternatives available to him, and is profoundly constrained by the ideological, social, economic and other pressures. A materially advantaged man finds it much easier to act in a desirable manner than one who is grossly disadvantaged and frustrated, has had no opportunities to cultivate good habits, was not, as a child, sheltered from temptations and unhealthy influences, or was, for all too familiar reasons, unable to build up pride and self-respect. What for the former may not even require a moment's thought may require a superhuman effort of will from the latter. Part of the responsibility for their good or bad actions therefore lies with their circumstances and social positions. An individual does not act or will in the abstract, but always within a specific social context. His social context or being is an integral part of him; he, *taken together with it*, constitutes an individual. No man can therefore be detached from his social being and judged in the abstract, except on the basis of an ideologically biased theory of individuation.

In Marx's view it is wrong to believe that an action is adequately explained when traced to an agent's intentions. This is not even the first step towards explaining it, for to say that a particular behaviour is an action *is* to say that the agent involved intended and willed it. To observe that a man did a particular thing because he intended it or believed it to be right is therefore to utter a tautology. One needs to show why he entertained specific beliefs, how he developed them in the course of coming to terms with his experiences, how these experiences occurred within the framework of his relations with others, how his beliefs were encouraged by the fact that his society is structured in a certain manner, and so on. Similarly the human intentions are not formed in a vacuum. As we saw they are formed by an agent *within* his specific social context, which must therefore be taken into account. The human agent is not a pure spirit forming intentions at will. He is socially situated, possesses a certain personality, holds specific beliefs, entertains certain fears, anxieties, insecurities, historical memories, and so on, all of which are to a considerable extent socially shaped. And unless one takes account of these, one is forced to treat his intentions as mysterious and inexplicable entities freely created by the spirit *ex nihilo*.

For Marx idealism has also shaped the writing of history.[16] The historians of ideas have treated them as if they were independent and self-determining entities freely travelling through historical time, following their own 'nature' and striking up friendships, alliances and hostilities as their temperament dictated. They have more or less completely ignored the human beings who developed the ideas, the social relationships which the ideas were designed to conceptualise, the social environment within which they were developed, and so on. Further, the historians have rarely explored why different forms of inquiry and knowledge come into being at particular times and in particular societies, rest on specific bodies of assumptions, undergo stagnation or accelerated development during certain historical periods, run into crises at certain times and merge into other disciplines, disappear altogether or are subjected to a radical reappraisal. They have either seen all this as unproblematic, or explained it away in terms of the mysterious movements of the human spirit. As we shall see, Marx takes the view that these questions are best answered in terms of the social contexts of the forms of inquiry and knowledge in question.

For Marx, then, idealism refers to the belief that human consciousness is autonomous, self-sufficient and capable of being studied and explained in its own terms. As he uses the term, idealism is a theory about the nature of consciousness, and covers not only what is generally called idealism but also empiricism. For Marx empiricism challenges idealism at the epistemological but not at the deeper level, and continues to share its basic view of the nature of consciousness. As such it is a form of idealism. Like the idealists, the empiricists detach consciousness from its socially situated human subject, and study ideas and sensations in an asocial and ahistorical manner. Hence Marx's conclusion that the basic assumptions of de Tracy and the other empiricists were the same as those of the German philosophers.

III

As observed earlier Marx uses the term ideology to mean idealism in the sense outlined above. For him ideology refers to the idealist view of the nature of consciousness, and entails the characteristically idealist 'method of approach' and 'mode of analysis'. Since he took the view that man's social being and consciousness are inseparable, he thought that ideology presented reality in 'a topsy-turvy manner'. Instead of seeing ideas as human products, ideology imagines that they are transcendental and independent entities, which human beings 'perceive', 'grasp' and 'live up to' in different degrees in different historical epochs. Since ideology inverts the relationship between the human subject and consciousness, and rests on a totally false assumption, Marx calls it 'an illusory form of consciousness' and observes that 'in all ideology men and their circumstances appear upside down as in a *camera obscura'*.

At various places in the *German Ideology* Marx lists law, philosophy, religion, jurisprudence, theology, morality, etc. as ideologies. In each case his reason is that the form of inquiry or the activity concerned treats consciousness as an autonomous entity. Religion is an ideology because it regards consciousness as conceptually and temporally prior to the material world. Morality is an ideology because it detaches the agent from his social being, takes a voluntaristic view of his action, and believes that bad conduct is a product of false beliefs or the lack of will power. Philosophy is an ideology because it detaches abstract concepts from the concrete relations they are designed to conceptualise, and treats them as independent and autonomous objects of investigation. It is grounded in the untenable distinction between the general and the particular or the universal and the historical, concentrates on the universally common features and ignores their divergent historical forms and content. For example, the philosopher does not 'dirty' his hands studying the distinctive modes of perception characteristic of the different historical epochs or societies, and fastens his attention on elucidating the features of human perception 'as such'. Marx argues that since perception as such, like production as such, is a 'myth', the philosopher ends up producing a banal epistemology which throws no light on the perceptual process of any concrete and recognisable human being or society. His account of perception 'as such' only applies to man 'as such'; and since no living man corresponds to man 'as such', his account has no explanatory power and is entirely 'worthless'.

For Marx, then, these and other disciplines and activities are ideologies because their existence is predicated upon the assumption that consciousness can be studied and judged independently of the social relations in which human beings are involved. Their questions, concepts, categories and the modes of argumentation are all based on this assumption, and cease to make sense once the assumption is rejected. For example, once a philosopher recognises that general ideas and concepts have social and historical roots, he can no longer study them in isolation. He needs to see them in a wider social context, and undertake a detailed sociological and historical analysis. As Marx puts it, he needs to 'leap out of it [philosophy] and devote [himself] to the study of actuality'.[17] When he does this, he 'leave[s] philosophy aside'. He is no longer a philosopher, at least in the traditional sense, for philosophy now becomes a moment of a more comprehensive inquiry and can no longer be pursued as an independent discipline. Again, when a jurist realises that he cannot analyse the legal categories and forms in the abstract, and must relate them first to the legal and then to the wider social relations, he is forced to undertake a historical and sociological analysis, and ceases to be a jurist in the traditional sense of the term.[18]

IV

As we observed earlier, Marx uses the term ideology to mean not only idealism but also apologia. Since we shall analyse the complex concept of apologia later, a few words should suffice.

Marx's second usage grows out of the first. As we saw the ideologist investigates general and abstract ideas. Since the general ideas are 'empty' and have no content, he has to supply one himself. The content can only be derived from experience, and the ideologist has his own experiences to draw upon. Accordingly he defines general ideas in terms of the content derived from his own experience. For example, he may want to examine the concept of property. As we saw, he does not analyse the primitive, feudal, bourgeois and other forms of property and abstract their common features. He is only interested in analysing the essence of property as such. Since property as such is an empty concept, the ideologist has no alternative but to give it some meaning and content. He is intimately familiar with the form of property obtaining in his own society which, for various reasons to be considered later, appears natural to him. Not surprisingly he ends up presenting the contemporary institution of property as property as such. For similar reasons he presents the contemporary man or forms of liberty or equality, as man, liberty or equality as such.

The idealist, then, universalises the ideas and experiences of his own class, society or historical epoch. He presents what seems normal, natural or self-evident *to him* as normal, natural or self-evident *sans phrase*. His ideas are conceptualisations of, and make sense within, the contexts of his own experiences as a member of a particular group or society. When he universalises the ideas, he universalises the underlying experiences and suggests that they are the only authentic forms of human experience, that only the society structured along these lines is fully human, that only a certain way of looking at man and society is rational, and so on. In suggesting this he presents the forms of thought, the categories of understanding, the values and interests of his group or society as universally valid. As Marx puts it, he becomes its apologist.

In the course of his investigations into the ideological (idealist) writings, Marx discovered that they were all apologetic in character. They had a universal form, but a particular social content, and did little more than articulate the experiences, modes of thought, values and interests of a particular group or society in an abstract and universal language. The idealists may or may not have wished to become apologists. Since they concentrated on abstract ideas, Marx contends that they had no alternative but to give the general ideas a historically specific content and become the apologists of the group from whose experiences the content was derived. Since the apologia seemed to Marx to be a necessary corollary of ideology (idealism), he extended the term ideology to mean apologia as well.

V

Marx, then, used the term ideology to mean both idealism and apologia. Contrary to the general impression he used it in the first sense throughout the *German Ideology*, the work in which he first introduced the term. It is true that the second sense is also present; however, the first dominates the text.[19] For Marx ideology *leads* to, but does not *mean*, apologia. The *German Ideology* is a remarkable text. Marx begins it by using the term in the sense of idealism. As the text proceeds the second sense begins to appear, but never succeeds in replacing the first or assuming dominance. Throughout the work Marx is struggling with idealism, his chief *bête noire*, and is far more interested in exposing its epistemological basis than its social and political consequences.

In the *German Ideology* Marx says that ideology represents an 'exclusive, systematic occupation with thoughts' and ascribes to 'conceptions, thoughts, ideas, in fact all the products of consciousness . . . an independent existence'.[20] He describes Hegel and, particularly, the Young Hegelians as the 'wholesale manufacturers of ideas, that is, the ideologists'.[21] In his view they 'abandoned the real historical basis and returned to that of ideology', gave ideas 'a theoretical independence', believed in the 'domination of the abstract ideas of ideology', treated ideas as 'independent beings' and 'inevitably put the thing upside down'.[22] He says that the German philosophers gave liberalism 'a petty bourgeois and at the same time highflown ideological form', clearly implying that its ideological character lay in its 'highflown' and abstract form and not its apologetic petty-bourgeois content.[23]

Marx uses the term ideology in the sense of idealism in the *Poverty of Philosophy* as well. He criticises Proudhon on two grounds: first, for detaching the economic categories from their social contexts and discussing them as if they were capable of autonomous and independent investigation; and second, for being an apologist of the petty bourgeoisie. Marx calls him an ideologist on the first ground, but not the second. He calls him an ideologist because he 'hold[s] things upside down like a true philosopher' and 'has not even gone far enough along the sideroad which an ideologist takes to reach the main road of history'.[24] This is precisely how Marx had defined ideology in the *German Ideology*: 'almost the whole ideology amounts either to a distorted conception of . . . history or to a complete abstraction from it'.[25]

In the works following the *German Ideology* and the *Poverty of Philosophy*, Marx's usage of the term ideology begins to change. He now takes apologia, which he had hitherto regarded as a *consequence* of ideology (understood as idealism), to be its *defining feature*. That is he defines ideology as an apologetic body of thought. In the *Class Struggles in France*, where he uses the term far more frequently than many other works, Marx generally uses it to mean apologia.[26] He talks about the 'ideological trimmings' of the French constitution, the 'ideologial demands' and the 'ideological representatives and spokesman' of the bourgeoisie, the 'republican ideology' and the hollow 'ideological formula' of constitutionalism, and comments on the reasons why the 'privileged interests had to bear ideologically disinterested names' in Louis Philippe's ministry.

In his later works too, especially the *Theories of Surplus Value* and *Capital*, Marx generally, but not always, uses the term ideology in the sense of apologia. He now refines the concept of apologia and draws an important distinction. He recognises that a man can be an apologist in one of two ways. He may be an open and unashamed advocate of a particular group, or he may be an honest and disinterested investigator who, for various reasons, may unintentionally end up becoming an apologist of a particular group. For Marx the two men are very different. The former is not a 'disinterested' and 'impartial' investigator, but a champion of a particular group in whose interest he distorts evidence, suppresses inconvenient facts and produces a justificatory body of ideas. By contrast the latter is scrupulous in his investigations and genuinely interested in the truth, although the body of thought he develops is systematically biased towards a particular group.

Although Marx recognised the difference between the two men and their bodies of ideas, and sometimes seems to wish to give them different names, he never settled upon an unambiguous nomenclature. He called the former 'vulgar' writers, 'vulgarians', 'sycophants', 'conscience-salvers', 'hired prize-fighters', and so on. As for the latter he had no distinct name. He generally referred to them as scientists, and added an adjective descriptive of the class towards which their ideas seemed to him to be biased. Thus he called the classical economists 'bourgeois economists' or 'bourgeois scientists'. It is striking that Marx wrote three volumes specifically dealing with the classical economists and three more discussing them *en passant*, and yet never developed a term specifically applicable to them.[27] He could have reserved the term ideologist for them, but did not, and used it to describe the vulgarians as well. He could have called one group conscious and the other unconscious apologists, but he did not.

Marx was, no doubt, acutely aware of the radical difference between the two groups of writers. However, the difference that he stressed related to the quality of their investigation, and not to the manner in which their ideas were biased. Thus he almost invariably called one group 'vulgar' or 'superficial' and the other 'scientific'. As for the ideological character of their thought, they were both alike ideologists and Marx does not seem to have considered the differences in the nature and origin of their ideological bias significant enough to warrant different names. There is no evidence to support the widely held view that Marx used or intended to confine the term ideology to refer to unconscious or unintended apologia. For him it referred to apologia, both intended and otherwise.

Although Marx increasingly used the term ideology to mean apologia, he did not stop using it in the original sense of idealism. In the course of discussing how social relations assume independence in the *Grundrisse*, he observes:[28]

The abstraction, or idea, however, is nothing more than the theoretical expression of those material relations which are their lord and master. Relations can be expressed, of course, only in ideas, and thus philosophers have determined the reign of ideas to be the peculiarity of the new age, and have identified the creation of free individuality with the overthrow of this reign. This error was all the more easily committed, from the ideological stand-point, as this reign exercised by the relations (this objective dependency, which, incidentally, turns into certain definite relations of personal dependency, but stripped of all illusions) appears within the consciousness of individuals as the reign of ideas . . .

Marx uses the term in this sense in *Capital* as well: [29]

The weak points in the abstract materialism of natural science, a materialism that excludes history and its process, are at once evident from the abstract and ideological conceptions of its spokesmen, whenever they venture beyond the bounds of their own speciality.

The context, the implied antithesis between ideology and materialism, and the juxtaposition of 'abstract' and 'ideological' make it clear that ideology in the above quote refers to idealism.

VI

It is sometimes suggested that Engels's usage of the term ideology is different from Marx's. There is no evidence to support the view. Like Marx, Engels used the term ideology all his life to mean *both* idealism and apologia. In *Anti-Duhring* he says that the 'old ideological method' is the same as 'the *a priori* method', and consists in abstracting ideas from 'the real social relationships' and treating them as independent objects of investigation. Again, in a letter to Schmidt he refers to the 'ideological outlook', which for him consists in detaching ideas from their social contexts and discussing them in the abstract. [30] In his letter to Mehring three years later he, again, observes that the ideologists believe in the autonomy and 'independent historical development' of ideas. [31] And in a letter to Borgius in 1894, he talks of 'pure abstract ideology'. [32]

There is also little evidence to support the contention that when Engels used the term ideology to mean apologia, he had only the unconscious apologia in mind. The following passage is usually cited in support of this view. [33]

Ideology is a process which is indeed accomplished consciously by the so-called thinker, but it is the wrong kind of consciousness. The real motive forces impelling him remain unknown to the thinker; otherwise it simply would not be an ideological process.

The remarkable thing about the passage is that Engels is here using the term ideology in the sense of idealism and *not* apologia, as becomes clear when one reads the lines that immediately follow it. Engels goes on:[34]

> Because it is a rational process he derives its form as well as its content from *pure reasoning*, either his own or that of his predecessors. He works *exclusively with thought material*, which he accepts without examination as something *produced by reasoning*, and does not investigate further for a more remote source *independent of* reason; indeed this is a matter of course to him, because, as all action is *mediated* by thought, it appears to him to be ultimately *based* upon thought.

Almost throughout the letter to Mehring, from which the usually quoted passage is abstracted, Engels uses the term ideology to mean idealism, and contrasts it with the historical approach.

VII

Marx (and Engels), then, used the term ideology to mean *both* idealism and apologia. Both usages appear more or less at the same time although, as we saw, the second sense does not become dominant until some years later. Of the two, apologia is a wider concept. For Marx idealism always leads to apologia, but not all apologias involve idealism. For this reason, as well as because we are primarily interested in investigating Marx's analysis of the nature and the logical structure of apologetic writings, we shall concentrate on his concept of apologia, and use the term ideology in that sense, in the rest of the book.

2 THE CONCEPT OF APOLOGIA

Strange as it may seem, Marx's concept of apologia bears a remarkable resemblance to, and can be best understood in the context of the traditional discussion of the nature and task of philosophy. Accordingly we shall begin with a brief outline of the latter.

I

Over the centuries philosophers have defined and distinguished philosophy from the other forms of inquiry in several different ways. One theme, however, has remained constant, namely that, unlike the others, philosophy is a self-conscious and radically self-critical form of inquiry.[1] The non-philosophical forms of inquiry rest on, and are constituted and defined by certain basic assumptions. For example, the scientific form of inquiry assumes that the world is an ordered whole, governed by laws, causally constituted, measurable, quantifiable and capable of being directly or indirectly perceived by the human senses. Theology assumes the existence of God, the possibility of knowing something about Him, and the veracity of the revealed Word. History assumes the reality of time and change, the possibility of dividing it into the past, the present and the future, the human capacity for initiative and free agency, and the internal coherence of human actions. These and other assumptions make possible the forms of inquiry in question, and constitute their theoretical conditions of existence. If the assumptions were to be challenged, the forms of inquiry concerned would lose their theoretical rationale and legitimacy. If, for example, the existence of God or the authenticity of Revelation were to be denied, the Christian theology, and indeed all forms of revealed theology, would lose their *raison d'être*. If the human capacity for freedom were to be questioned, and man were to be seen as no different from a natural object, history as a distinct form of inquiry would be rendered impossible and perhaps replaced by science.

According to the philosophers, when a form of inquiry rests on assumptions, its perception and interpretation of the world is necessarily mediated by them, and therefore inherently limited and distorted. Thanks to its basic assumptions, it abstracts certain aspects

15

of the world and ignores others, conceptualises its subject matter in a selective manner, asks certain questions and not others, employs certain methods of investigation and not others, and theorises about it in a specific manner. For example, a scientist concentrates on the quantifiable aspects of the world and ignores its qualitative or the so-called secondary features, uses such concepts as cause, effect, hypothesis, law, prediction and regularity, employs the methods of controlled observation and experiment, asks causal questions, and so on. History, theology and other forms of inquiry rest on very different assumptions, employ very different types of concepts and methods of investigation, and yield very different types of knowledge. Each form of inquiry operates within the framework of and the limits set by its basic assumptions, and offers an inherently inadequate account of the world.

The philosophers have argued that, since the non-philosophical forms of inquiry are not fully conscious of their assumptions, and therefore of their limitations, they have a constant tendency to claim universal validity and transgress into areas not their own. For example, a scientist *qua* scientist does not step out of his form of inquiry and investigate its nature and assumptions. The moment he asks what science is or its basic presuppositions or limits are, he is asking a philosophical not a scientific question. *Qua* scientist he lacks self-consciousness, and is unaware of the nature and limits of science. Consequently he tends to assume that its concepts and methods of investigation apply not only to the natural but also the social world, and that he can offer about the latter the same kind of knowledge as about the former. Such universalist claims were once made or are being made also by such other forms of inquiry as theology, aesthetics and history.

The philosphers have argued that unlike the others, philosophy is a radically critical and fully self-conscious form of inquiry. It aims to elucidate and criticise the assumptions underlying the other forms of inquiry; it also constantly turns on itself to elucidate and criticise its own basic assumptions. Unlike the other forms of inquiry which self-confidently study their subject matter, philosophy is constantly plagued by doubt. It wonders if its methods, concepts, questions and modes of investigation may not rest on unexamined assumptions, and directs its attention as much at itself as its subject matter. The investigation of the assumptions has been universally recognised by the philosophers to be one of their major preoccupations. And the criticism of a body of thought not in terms of its factual errors or inadequate supporting evidence, but its structural assumptions and limits has traditionally been recognised as the distinctively philosophical form of criticism.

While some philosophers, such as Kant, were content to maintain that the talent and task of philosophy lay in exposing and criticising the assumptions of the other forms of inquiry as well as its own, and that it was largely a formal and critical inquiry, others took a different view. For them the critical examination of assumptions only prepared the ground for its more important and substantive task of offering the uniquely undistorted knowledge of the world which is necessarily beyond the reach of the other forms of inquiry. Unlike them philosophy does not rest on unexamined assumptions; it analyses the world not from a narrow and abstract point of view, but from the 'standpoint of the whole' or the 'totality of experience'; it is not concerned with a specific aspect of the world, but aims to study it 'as a whole'; and so on. As such the knowledge it offers is not abstract, but concrete or un-abstracted; not conditional or limited by a framework of assumptions, but absolute; and not hypothetical or contingent upon the validity of its assumptions, but categorical.

Despite their considerable disagreements concerning the nature, methods and the ultimate objectives of philosophy, the philosophers have almost all been agreed on several basic doctrines of which two are relevant to our discussion. First, the assumptions underlying a form of inquiry limit and distort the knowledge offered by it. The undistorted knowledge of the world can only be offered by a form of inquiry which does not rest on assumptions. Second, the non-philosophical forms of inquiry have a tendency to advance illegitimate universalist claims. Since such claims can be best countered by demarcating and standing guard over their appropriate areas, it is hardly surprising that every major philosopher has in one form or another charted the field of knowledge and mapped out the boundaries of the prevailing forms of inquiry.

II

Marx's theory of ideology bears a striking resemblance to the traditional philosophical discussion of the nature of knowledge. Although he puts them to a novel use, he accepts the two basic doctrines mentioned above. He argues that human societies, his primary objects of interest, can be studied from different 'points of view' or what he also calls 'viewpoints' and 'standpoints'.[2] The points of view differ considerably in their ability to illuminate the social reality, and fall into two categories. A point of view may be 'narrow', and examine society from the standpoint of a specific 'part' of it. Or it may view society from what he calls the 'standpoint of the whole', and be fully self-conscious and self-critical.[3]

For Marx a narrow point of view rests on unexamined 'assumptions' or what he also calls 'presuppositions', 'premises' and 'postulates'.[4] Indeed it is constituted and defined by these, for a point of view is ultimately nothing but a way of looking at the subject matter through the prism of and within the limits set by a specific body of assumptions. To view society from a particular standpoint *is* to view it 'on the basis' or *within* the framework' of the relevant assumptions.[5] For Marx the assumptions of a point of view delimit its 'horizon' of thought; they set its 'bounds', 'boundary', 'limits' or 'barriers' within which it 'remains confined' or 'bounded', and which it simply cannot cross.[6] They determine how much of social reality it perceives, and in what manner. The more limited a point of view, the narrower is the segment of social reality 'perceived' by it, and the more 'abstract' and 'distorted' is its account of it. A point of view cannot transcend its conditions of existence any more than a man can leap out of his skin. Marx actually uses the metaphor of the skin to indicate that a narrow point of view is embodied within and 'inconceivable without' a specific body of assumptions.[7]

Thus far Marx's analysis is along familiar lines; he now introduces a radically new element. He argues that the assumptions underlying and constituting a point of view may be not only methodological, ontological and epistemological, but also *social*. Indeed he thinks that, so far as the study of man and society and even nature is concerned, the social assumptions are the most pervasive and important. A society is not a collection of individuals, but a system of positions.[8] A social position is constituted and defined by the distinct pattern of relationship in which it stands with respect to the rest of society. To be a member of a society is to occupy a prestructured social space and to find oneself already related to others in a certain manner. For example, to be a teacher is to be related to other teachers, the students, the school authorities and the wider society in a definite manner. These relations constitute and define the position of the teacher, and form his conditions of existence. They constitute his social predicament, which *qua* teacher he accepts as given. Since his relations with other positions are objectively structured in a determinate manner, so are his social experiences. They are acquired within a specific pattern of social relations, and therefore not chaotic but structured. Since his social experiences are structured, his forms of thought, the categories in terms of which he perceives and interprets the social world, are also structured. His distinct experiences require distinct forms of thought to make sense of them.[9]

For Marx, then, each social position is distinguished by specific conditions of existence, a specific set of social relations, and a specific body of social experiences and forms of thought. In each the totality of social relations come together and coalesce in a unique and distinct way. Hence each represents a distinctive 'point' or location from which to 'view' the social whole. Even as different physical locations offer different views of an object, the different social points of view offer different views of the social whole. According to Marx, under the influence of idealism, the traditional philosophy defined the knowing subject in transcendental and asocial terms, and failed to see that he is a socially situated being who brings to his study of society a body of unexamined social assumptions derived from the social position from which he experiences and views his society.

Marx argues that a narrow social point of view is by definition unaware of its assumptions. It can only become aware of them by stepping outside and examining itself in a larger context; and this it cannot do while remaining a narrow point of view. Since a narrow social point of view is necessarily unaware of its assumptions, it is unaware of its limits. Hence it has an inherent tendency to claim universal validity, and set itself up as an absolute. As we shall see, this is the crux of Marx's theory of ideology.

Like his philosophical predecessors, especially Hegel, Marx argues that a social theorist can offer an undistorted, concrete, categorical and objective knowledge of the social whole only by studying it from the standpoint of the whole. He must investigate not a specific part of society, but society as a whole. And he must do so not from the standpoint of a specific part or aspect of it, but from that of the whole. In short, he must investigate it as a whole, and from the standpoint of the whole. Marx argues that, in so doing, a social theorist is able not only to offer an undistorted knowledge of the social whole, but also to elucidate and criticise the assumptions and limitations of the narrow social points of view. Since he sees society as a whole, he is able to view them from the outside, and identify their conditions of existence and characteristic forms of experience and thought. As we saw, a narrow social point of view tends to claim universal validity. Its claims can only be deflated, and its proper limits determined from the wider standpoint of the social whole. Accordingly Marx suggests that a social theorist should elucidate and criticise the social or, what he also calls, material conditions of existence of the different social points of view and demarcate the areas within which their characteristic assumptions and forms of thought are valid. Such an inquiry is Marx's materialist counterpart to the traditional concept of philosophical critique. Just as the philosophers inquired into the basic theoretical presuppositions of the forms of experience and consciousness, Marx inquires into their material or social presuppositions. Like them, he too asks how, under what conditions, the particular forms of experience and consciousness are possible, and within what limits they are valid. As we shall see, Marx never systematically undertook such a materialist critique; the historical materialism still awaits its Kant.

III

According to Marx, then, a society is a system of positions. Men are parents, brothers, husbands, Christians, teachers, members of different associations, citizens, and so on.[10] Marx argues that of these, the class is the most important. This raises three questions. First, what does he mean by class? Second, why is the class so important? And third, how important is it? Does it 'determine' men? Or is its influence less stringent and deep? Marx's answers to these questions are rather sketchy and tentative. Since there is an extensive body of literature on the subject, a few words should suffice.

Marx does not offer a systematic analysis of the concept of class.[11] He embarked upon it towards the end of the third volume of *Capital*, but it was interrupted by ill health and death and does not proceed beyond a few lines. Marx's discussion of the concept of class is marred by several ambiguities. He says that the class is a modern phenomenon, and peculiar to the capitalist society. But he also says that the 'history of *all* hitherto existing societies is the history of class struggles'. Besides, he says that a class must be defined in terms of the relations of production. And yet the petty bourgeoisie, a class to which he devoted considerable attention in the political and philosophical but not his economic writings, does not occupy any recognisable place in the process of production and, with the exception of craftsmen, is largely confined to the process of circulation. Again, he uses such other concepts as the stratum and social group, but does not clearly distinguish them from the class. At times he treats what he calls the 'fractions' of a class as separate classes. Further, it is not clear whether such social groups as the lumpenproletariat constitute a class at all, and to which class the farm labourers and the hard-pressed and heavily indebted independent peasants belong. Again, sometimes he says that a class is defined in terms of the objectively shared conditions of existence; on other occasions he says that men must be conscious of themselves as belonging to a single group in order to constitute a class, and need another class to which their interests are opposed and in the course of struggling against which they can attain the necessary collective self-consciousness. It is almost impossible to formulate Marx's concept of class in precise and unambiguous terms. However, we can arrive at a working definition of it, and that is sufficient for our purpose.

Marx was primarily interested in the process of material production, that is the manner in which a society produces the necessary means of its sustenance. Here he distinguished 'three great classes', which he called the landlords, the capitalists and the wage labourers — the owners, respectively, of the large amounts of land, capital and labour-power, and whose respective source of income were ground rent, profit and wages. He was convinced that as the capitalist mode of production developed, land-ownership would increasingly be brought under the control of capital, thus leaving us two clearly separated and hostile classes. However, the three classes were the classes *par excellence* for him, and remained his theoretical frame of reference.

While concentrating on the process of material production, Marx also examined three other areas. First, he examined the realm of circulation of commodities, and noticed that it gave rise to its own distinctive groups, of which the petty bourgeoisie were the most important and easily identifiable. Although not involved in the process of material production, they are part of the economic structure of society. Second, Marx examined what he called the 'middle and intermediate' area, and noticed such groups as the doctors, lawyers, teachers and civil servants who serviced the social structure, especially the dominant class, by providing the technical expertise, training qualified men, administering society, and so on. Marx calls them 'ideological' professions. These groups are not engaged in material production; and unlike the petty bourgeoisie, they are not engaged in economic activity either. And third, Marx noticed men who were on the fringe of society, held no regular employment, were 'without a hearth or a home', 'living on the crumbs of society', providing a 'recruiting ground for thieves and criminals', and capable of becoming a 'mob'. He called them lumpenproletariat.

Although Marx sometimes seems keen to reserve the term 'class' for the three 'major' classes involved in material production, on other occasions he uses it to include the petty bourgeoisie as well, but not much beyond. Accordingly he calls the professional groups 'strata' or 'professions' and the various groups composing the capitalist class 'fractions'. However, he was not very careful in his usage, and from time to time followed the contemporary writers and used the term 'class' to refer to these two groups as well. Sometimes he preferred to use the less precise, but also less objectionable, term 'social group'.[12] Accordingly we shall follow him and use the terms 'social group' and 'class' interchangeably.

For Marx, then, the capitalist society consists of the following major groups; first, the landlords; second, the capitalists; third, the wage labourers; fourth, the petty bourgeoisie or what also he calls the 'lower middle class' or 'classes', and consists of such groups as the 'small tradespeople, shopkeepers, the handicraftsmen, and peasants'; fifth, the professional classes, which Marx also calls the 'middle class' or 'classes'; and sixth, the lumpenproletariat. The groups are fluid and, as the capitalist society develops, some may cease to exist. Their membership, too, is relatively fluid, and men may move from one class to another. Each group includes subgroups or fractions which, while fighting among themselves, share common interests. The subgroups may or may not be aware of belonging to a common group, although they objectively belong to it. The members of the group as a whole may not be aware of their collective identity, but do objectively share common interests and a common destiny. Basically, for Marx, his list of classes is a way of classifying the members of society. A class is a theoretical category, a concept, based on what Marx takes to be the important commonly shared features of a group of men.

This brings us to the crucial question as to what it is that the members of a class share in common. In Marx's view it is their 'conditions of life', 'conditions of existence', 'economic conditions', 'economic conditions of existence' or 'mode of existence'. Marx nowhere systematically analyses these expressions, nor the constitutive concepts of 'condition' (*Verhältnis*) and 'existence'. As he rightly says in the uncompleted passage in the third volume of *Capital*, the conditions of existence cannot be defined in terms of the 'identity' of the 'source' of income. The doctors and teachers have different sources of income, and yet, to Marx, they belong to the same social group. Nor can it be the way a group perceives itself, for this is too subjective, even idealistic, and denies the conceptual separation between the objective conditions and the forms of thought so necessary for Marx's historical materialism.

By the term 'conditions of existence', Marx seems to mean the constitutive characteristics and the basic presuppositions of the mode in which men exist or, what amounts to the same thing, the *manner* in which they earn their living. Earning a living is a social activity, and implies a social relationship. A *manner* of earning a living refers to and is constituted by, the pattern of relationship in which a group of men objectively stands with respect to the rest of society. As Marx repeatedly insists, a society is not a collection of individuals, but a system of relationship. Capital is not a thing, but a social relationship between one man and many others as mediated by his ownership of the means of production. Wage labour, interest, rent, etc. are also different forms of social relationship. In classifying the ways in which men earn their living or, what comes to the same thing, in dividing men into specific classes, Marx is interested in investigating the basic structures and presuppositions of the relationship to the rest of society implied in a particular manner of earning a living.

Let us take a couple of examples. To earn one's living as a worker is to be engaged in a specific type of social relation and to presuppose a specific type of social structure. To be a wage labourer is to be 'free' to alienate one's skills and activities to another, to work alongside a large number of other workers, to work under conditions determined by another, to produce commodities for sale, to be vulnerable to being replaced by a machine or another worker and declared redundant, and so on. To be a worker is also to presuppose a society in which private property is an established institution, men enjoy personal freedom, are free to enter into contracts, most men do not own the means of production, the latter can be bought and sold, and so on. Men may work in different factories, do different types of work and be employed by employers of vastly different character and temperament. Yet *qua* workers, they share in common a certain pattern of relationship to their fellow-workers and employers, and presuppose a certain type of society. In this sense they share their conditions of existence and belong to a common class. These conditions must exist in order for the workers *qua* workers to exist.

Again, the doctors, lawyers, accountants and architects do very different things, under different conditions, earn different amounts of money, and so on. Yet their modes of earning their living share certain basic features in common. They are not engaged in material production but in providing services, involved in mental rather than physical work, claim expertise in their respective areas, are relatively independent, free from constant supervision, work individually rather than in groups, earn a good income, enjoy leisure, establish certain types of relationship with each other. And they presuppose a relatively advanced society that produces surplus wealth, respects the monopoly of professional skills, institutionalises and upholds the distinction between the professional and the layman, and so on. In short their manner of earning their living involves a specific structure of relationship with other men, and presupposes a society organised in a specific manner. Marx's *list* of classes, that is his classification of the modes of earning a living, is somewhat crude, imprecise, narrow and unpersuasive. However, his attempt to identify and classify the basic features and presuppositions of the different forms of earning a living is not incoherent.

Having given some coherent meaning to Marx's concept of class, we may now turn to the second question as to why he thinks that it is of decisive importance. Marx did not give the question the attention it deserved. He was primarily interested in explaining why and how the relations of production shape the social, political, legal and other relations in society at large, but not in how and why they are decisive at the individual level. Basically he considers the manner of earning a living decisive for the following reasons.[13]

For Marx it is the most 'basic' or 'fundamental' activity in man's life, in the sense that no man can avoid it. In order to exist he must somehow earn his living, even if it only consists in depositing his money in the bank and living on its interest. As such it is of utmost and abiding interest to him and remains both the centre of his concern and the frame of reference of his other activities.

Further, the manner in which men earn their living shapes the quality and content of their lives. It determines the amount they earn, the number of hours they work, the conditions under which they work, the security of their job, the contingency of their livelihood, the amount of leisure they enjoy, the scope and interest they have to develop their capacities, their home environment, the education they can give and the time they can spend with their children, the physical risks they run, the diseases they are likely to develop, their longevity, and so on. Marx gives several examples of each. In these and other ways a man's manner of earning a living profoundly conditions his other activities.

Again, a man's manner of earning a living shapes the pattern of his relations with others. Most human relationships grow out of and centre around those a man encounters in the course of earning his living. As such it shapes the range and content of his social relations and experiences, and his conception of other men. It shapes also his 'personality' and his conception of himself. In Marx's view a worker who must 'sell' himself to the highest bidder, is confined to monotonous work, performs activities that do not result in the products he can recognise as his artefacts, is easily replaced by another worker or a machine and declared 'redundant', and never involved in planning, organising or even thinking about his work develops a sense of being an abstract, superfluous, unidimensional, highly fragmented, instrumental and largely physical being. Since his deeply scarred self-consciousness profoundly shapes his work-unrelated activities as well, his manner of *earning* a living shapes his manner of *living*. The social relations and experiences of the capitalist, the shopkeeper or the academic are very different; and so are their views of themselves and the world, and the way they live.

Finally, men engaged in a common manner of earning a living have common interests. They share in common their conditions of existence, and are related to and affected by the rest of society in a similar manner. Their common interests and experiences tend to generate a shared sense of identity, however indeterminate and inchoate it might be. Over the years they build up a shared body of ideas, feelings, attitudes, sentiments, conventional wisdom, and so on, which collectively constitute what Marx calls their 'historical tradition'. In belonging to a particular social group, an individual imbibes its tradition, and is initiated into a specific way of defining the world and his place in it, recognising some groups as his allies and some others as his enemies, and some political parties, policies and values as conducive and others as harmful to his interests. Marx puts the point well:[14]

> Upon the . . . social conditions of existence, rises an entire superstructure of distinct and peculiarly formed sentiments, illusions, modes of thought and views of life. The entire class creates and forms them out of its material foundations and out of the corresponding social relations. The single individual, who derives them through tradition and upbringing , may imagine that they form the real motives and the starting-point of his activity.

The nature of the relationship between the class and consciousness in Marx has been a subject of much controversy. Many of his critics ascribe to him a determinist thesis. Although Marx is ambiguous concerning the *precise* relationship between the class and consciousness, he says little to support the determinist interpretation.

First, he uses a variety of expressions, such as 'determine', 'condition', 'shape', 'mould' and 'form' to describe the relationship. It is therefore wrong to fasten on the term 'determine', which he uses only on a few occasions. Further, as we shall see, the term does not have, for him or for Hegel, the causal meaning that it has for us.

Second, the determinist thesis implies a passive view of the nature of consciousness. Those who interpret Marx as a determinist also, as a rule, ascribe to him a passive and reflectionist view of consciousness. There is little evidence to support the view that Marx thought of human consciousness in this way. He takes an activist view of man, and defines him in terms of the inherently active capacities and powers. Consciousness is a power, a power to explore, appropriate and recreate the world in thought. Marx invariably refers to thinking as an activity of 'producing' ideas, and the thinkers as 'producers' of ideas. For Marx an idea or a theory is 'veridical' if it 'corresponds to' or 'reflects' the social reality. He uses the term 'reflection' in a logical, not a causal, sense. To reflect reality is to be true to, correspond to, and not to be caused by it. The significance of the metaphor of mirror is that the mirror faithfully reflects the object in front of it, and constitutes the paradigm of the relation of correspondence.

Third, Marx freely acknowledges on many occasions that men can and do rise above their classes. As he says, the Chartist movement was led and supported by the middle classes whose interests would have greatly suffered if it had been successful. And he also remarks that, for various reasons, several sections of the bourgeoisie 'desert their own standpoint to place themselves at that of the proletariat'. Further, as we shall see, Marx rarely explains the ideas of Hegel, the classical economists and others in terms of their respective classes, and considers the influence of the social structure far more important.

Fourth, the terms 'determine' and even 'condition' belong to the mechanical-materialist tradition of thought, which is totally foreign to Marx and which he rejects. Marx thinks within the German, especially the Hegelian, philosophical tradition where the whole question of the relationship between man and the world is not posed as that between the crude abstractions of 'consciousness' and 'environment', but very differently. Even as Hegel was interested in elucidating the basic assumptions of the form of consciousness of an age, Marx was interested in exploring the basic assumptions of an individual's forms of thought. He was not interested in his specific ideas, but the underlying *forms* of thought. He aimed to explain not how his ideas are 'caused', but the general assumptions or limits within which his thought remains 'confined', 'bounded', 'restricted', 'shut up', and 'imprisoned'.

He was struck by the fact that men take certain general beliefs for granted and think within their framework, and wished to explore why this was so. No determinism is involved in saying that men mistake the familiar for the natural, and the limits of their world for the limits of the world itself. The best proof of Marx's rejection of determinism lies in the fact that he systematically explored how men can be made conscious of, and thereby helped to *rise above*, their basic assumptions. For Marx, if an individual is acutely aware of and deeply concerned to transcend his limiting assumptions, he *can* rise above them. If he is not, then he remains imprisoned within them. For Marx a fully self-conscious and self-critical man can transcend his assumptions, become a 'free agent of thought', and look at his society from *any* standpoint he chooses. As we shall see, Marx is guilty not of determinism but the opposite.

IV

For Marx, then, a society is a system of positions or social classes, each of which is constituted by its conditions of existence, has distinct interests and represents a distinct point of view. Since a narrow social point of view is encased within and constituted by a specific body of assumptions, it has three characteristics. First, it is 'biased'. It examines the social whole from the standpoint of one of its parts. Its view of it is therefore partial in both the senses of the term. It views the social whole from the standpoint of a part, and is therefore partial or limited. Further, it views the social whole within the framework of its unexamined assumptions, and therefore its view of it is partial to itself or biased. It does not examine the social whole in its own terms or with an open mind; being encased or 'imprisoned' within its assumptions, it cannot. Since it is already committed and predisposed to certain assumptions, the validity of which it takes for granted, its perception of the whole is filtered through them, and is inherently biased. For Marx every partial (limited) point of view is *necessarily* partial (biased).

Second, since a narrow point of view is biased, its view of the social whole is necessarily 'distorted'. Like bias, distortion is a crucial concept for Marx, and he nowhere analyses either. However, a coherent meaning can be given to his different usages of it. Marx uses such terms as 'distort', 'cover up', 'twist', 'block' (*Sparren*), 'veil' and 'mystify'. Although they are metaphorical expressions and signify different things, they represent Marx's attempt to highlight a specific relationship between a point of view and its perception of the world. As we saw, a narrow point of view rests on certain unexamined assumptions. It sees the world *through* them. Like a man who tries to fit a big, square object into a small, round box and cannot avoid distorting or mis-shaping it, the man with a narrow point of view tries to fit the totality of society into the narrow conceptual boxes dictated by the require-ments of his basic assumptions. In so doing he cannot avoid 'distorting' the social whole. The distortion takes many forms. He does not see certain aspects of the social whole. In this sense his assumptions 'block', 'veil' or 'cover up' the relevant aspects. Further, he misinter-prets those aspects of it that do fall within his view. He tries to trap the complex social whole within the narrow boxes of his assumptions, and necessarily gets its various aspects out of proportion. In other words his assumptions lead him to 'misperceive' and 'distort' them. Again, since all the parts of a social whole are interconnected whereas he sees only some parts of it, he is unable to give adequate accounts of the latter. His explanations sometimes become highly implausible, get the causal connections the wrong way round, and 'mystify' the social whole or set up 'illusory' causal agencies.

Third, since a narrow social point of view by definition lacks full self-consciousness, it is unaware of its assumptions, and therefore of its limits. Even as the scientist *qua* scientist does not know the limits of his basic assumptions, and both considers his forms of thought to be self-evident and extend them beyond their legitimate areas of applica-tion, every narrow social point of view has a tendency to take for granted its characteristic forms of thought, and make one or both of the following claims. First, it may claim 'universal' validity for them. The bourgeoisie, for example, think that society would be much better off if *everyone* defined himself as a bourgeois and pursued appropriate objectives. Second, it may claim *'eternal'* or *'absolute'* validity.[15] The bourgeoisie, for example, argue that every man is *by nature* possessive and greedy, and that the bourgeois society is *natural* to man. The second claim necessarily entails the first, for to say that a form of relationship or thought is natural to man *is* to say that it is universally valid. The first claim, however, does not entail the second, for one may claim that a particular form of relationship or thought is univers-ally valid without saying that it is natural to man, or only claim that it is valid within a specific historical period but not throughout history.

When Marx says that men unconsciously universalise or absolutise their ideas, he has in mind not some complicated Freudian mechanism, but their tendency to assume that what is natural and self-evident in their view is so *in fact*, that the limits of their world are the limits of the world itself. When men remain confined to the limited world of their social position, they cannot appreciate the limited nature and basis of their forms of experience and thought, and hence there is nothing to restrain them from claiming universal or absolute validity for them. To this familiar view, Marx adds a new element. He argues that men universalise their forms of thought not only because they find them self-evident and natural, but also because it is in their interest to do so. A social position is constituted by certain conditions of existence, and has specific interests which are best served if the whole society could be structured along the lines of its conditions of existence. For example, it suits the interests of the bourgeoisie if all fellow-citizens defined themselves as bourgeois and pursued appropriate goals. There would then be a universal consensus on the basic assumptions of their society, and no radical and subversive challenge to its structure.

For Marx, then, an individual's tendency to universalise or absolutise the conditions of existence and forms of thought of his social position has two different sources, between which he does not establish any clear relationship. As a result his writings reflect a deep ambiguity. We shall discuss the subject later. For the present three general points would suffice. First, Marx emphasises both sources, and not just the interests as some of his critics maintain. Second, when he discusses *theoretical* works, he almost never refers to their authors' material interests, and explains their universalisation of the specific forms of thought in terms of their tendency to assume that what seems self-evident and natural to them is in fact so. And third, even when Marx explains the dominant ideology in a society or the thoughts of *ordinary* men, the role he assigns to material interests is limited. As he puts it,[16]

one must not take the narrow view that the petty bourgeoisie explicitly sets out to assert its egoistic class interests. It rather believes that the *particular* conditions of its liberation are the only *general* conditions within which modern society can be saved.

V

Marx gives the name 'ideology' to a body of thought resulting from the universalisation of a partial and narrow social point of view. An ideology understands man and society within the framework of a set of assumptions characteristic of a specific social group or class. It reflects a systematic orientation of thought, a perspective, a standpoint, a point of view derived from the forms of thought and conditions of existence of a particular social class. As such it is necessarily biased towards it; it presents it in a favourable light, and explicitly or implicitly suggests that only a society structured in terms of its characteristic form of thought and in harmony with its conditions of existence is fully rational or consistent with human nature. As Marx puts it, an ideology 'defends', 'justifies', 'legitimises', 'speaks for' or is an 'apologia' for a particular social group. And its author is a 'defender', a 'spokesman' or an 'apologist' of the group in question. It reflects not some occasional and understandable personal predilections, blindspots or failure of imagination, but a systematic and pervasive bias. The bias is not accidental, but inherent in its basic assumptions, not detachable but structurally embedded, not sporadic but systematic. Since it is systematically biased, an ideology is necessarily led to 'distort', 'conceal', 'disguise', 'mystify' or 'misunderstand' its subject matter. We saw earlier what Marx means by the complex concepts of 'bias' and 'distortion'.

For Marx, then, an ideology is a body of ideas systematically biased towards a particular social group. Schematically it has the following features. First, it is a body of *ideas*. Although Marx sometimes refers to such professions as the medical and legal as ideological, he does not think that the social practices, professions and institutions can themselves be called ideologies; rather they *embody* an ideology.[17] They can be *ideological* in the sense of embodying a biased conception of their social role, and being so defined and structured that they are systematically biased towards and favour a particular social group; however, they are not *ideologies*.

Second, an ideology is a *biased* body of ideas. It is biased towards a specific social group from whose standpoint it views society. It views the social whole from the perspective of a specific part of it, and is therefore partial in both senses of the term. It universalises the conditions of existence and form of thought of a specific social group, and directly or indirectly recommends them as the only basis upon which a rational social order could be constructed.

Third, an ideology is a *systematically* biased body of ideas. Its bias springs not from its author's incorrect reasoning or misperception of facts, but his fundamental assumptions or point of view. The bias is embedded in the basic structure of his thought; and hence it is not superadded or confined to his conclusions, but permeates his perception and explanation of the world.

Fourth, an ideology is systematically biased towards a specific *social group*. It is true that Marx himself concentrated on the class-based ideology. However, it would be wrong to suggest, as is done by many commentators, that he intended to *confine* the term to the class-based ideology, especially if the term 'class' is understood in a narrow sense. As we saw, Marx uses the term 'class' to include every group characterised by a distinct manner of earning a living, and classifies the professional group as a distinct class. Further, he talks about the German ideology, says that Hegel was an ideologist of the contemporary German *society*, and that some of the Left Hegelians glorified the German *nation*. The group towards which an ideology may be biased need not therefore be a class in the narrow sense, and may include a professional group, a nation, a social order, a race or a subgroup within a class. Accordingly it would seem that, although a little too wide, the term 'social group', which Marx himself frequently used, better expresses what he has in mind than the term 'class'.

For Marx the history of India, Rome or Britain written respectively from the Brahmanic, the patrician or the aristocratic point of view, selecting, ignoring, emphasising and interpreting facts so as to show that in each case the country flourished under the leadership of the group in question, and declined when other groups acquired dominance is ideological in nature.[18] Likewise a philosopher who proposes to structure society on the model of the university, the political discussion on the model of the academic seminar, and assigns a leading role to the academics generalises the conditions of existence and the characteristic forms of thought of the academic, and is an ideologist. Since ideologies are biased towards specific social groups, Marx describes and classifies them according to the groups towards which they are biased. He calls them bourgeois, petty-bourgeois, feudal, German, etc., meaning in each case that the body of ideas concerned is systematically biased towards, and distorts the social reality *in favour of* the bourgeoisie, the petty bourgeoisie, the feudal society or Germany.

It is possible for a body of ideas to be systematically biased without being biased towards a social group. A writer may offer a highly pessimistic account of human existence, presenting it as painful, shallow, empty, and so on. His account is systematically biased, and ignores such experiences as the profound satisfaction offered by love, the contemplation of beauty and friendship. Unless he can be shown to reflect the forms of experience of a specific social group, his account is *not* ideological. Marx was not interested in the bias *per se*, but in a socially relevant bias, and wished to reserve the term ideology for it.[19] In the course of his study of social and political thought, he noticed that the allegedly objective bodies of ideas were, in fact, systematically biased towards specific social groups, and wished to give them a distinct name. There is something to be said for restricting the usage in this way. To equate ideology with bias *per se* is to imply that, since bias in some form is an unavoidable feature of human thought, ideology too is an inescapable human tendency, and that no theorist can be criticised for developing a socially biased body of ideas! To take this view is to emasculate the critical force and explanatory power of the concept of ideology.

Finally, since ideology is systematically biased, it necessarily *distorts* its subject matter. It analyses it from a specific point of view, and through the prism of its basic assumptions. As such it notices certain facts and not others, gets them out of proportion, establishes misleading connections between them, and so on. We saw earlier that distortion is a complex concept and covers a wide range of phenomena. We shall discuss it at length later. For the present we may only note that, for Marx, not every distortion is ideological. As we saw, a writer giving a highly distorted account of human existence is not necessarily an ideologist. Distortion is ideological when it reveals a systematic social bias. An idiosyncratic personal preference or a quirk of personality may lead a writer systematically to distort his subject matter. However, the resulting body of thought is not socially representative and biased, and hence not an ideology. The distinction is of crucial importance in the field of literature where a bias is fairly common, but is not always of a social nature.

For Marx, then, a society is a system of positions, each of which has a characteristic point of view which it tends to generalise. This means that every society is, in principle, characterised by a plurality of ideologies competing for the intellectual and political allegiance of its members. The plurality, however, is drastically emasculated by the fact that the social groups are not all equal. Some enjoy considerable economic power and have in-built advantages over others. They use their economic power to shape their society's political, social and other institutions in their own image. As a result they are able to institutionalise and enforce their forms of thought upon the rest of society. Further, their forms of thought enjoy a considerable measure of social respectability and have an attraction for others that far exceeds their intellectual cogency. For these and other reasons, more about which later, Marx argues that the conditions of existence of the dominant class provide the content of the dominant ideology.

For Marx a society is characterised by two types of ideology, namely the dominant and the subordinate. The dominant ideology articulates and generalises the forms of thought of the dominant social class. The subordinate ideologies articulate and generalise the forms of thought of the other social groups. For example, in the bourgeois society the dominant ideology universalises or absolutises the bourgeois forms of thought, and the subordinate ideologies universalise the points of view of the vestigial feudal classes, the petty bourgeoisie, the working classes, the professional groups and others. The subordinate ideologies exist on the periphery of society, lack a coherent expression, and are intellectually overwhelmed by and generally define themselves within the framework of the dominant ideology. Marx shows little interest in the relationship between the dominant and subordinate ideologies, and the way the latter are formed and preserve their intellectual integrity. He was primarily interested in showing how the dominant ideology comes into being and shapes the thoughts of both the ordinary men and sophisticated thinkers. Contrary to the general impression, Marx's basic concern is to show not how men are conditioned by their respective social classes, but the way they are shaped by the dominant ideology of their society.

VI

An ideology, then, is a systematically and socially biased body of thought. Ideologies differ greatly with respect to the groups they champion, the idioms in which they are articulated, the extent to which they are biased, their degrees of sophistication, the ways in which their bias permeates their various aspects, and so on. Marx argues that, despite these and other differences, all ideologies share an identifiable logical structure objectively dictated by their ideological character. Since they are all systematically biased towards specific social groups, they share several logical features in common. Although they are by no means the only ones, the following are, for Marx, the most important.

First, every ideology has an inescapable moral or prescriptive dimension.[20] By generalising the ideas of a particular social group and presenting them as the only valid or rational ways to think about man and society, it holds them up as the universally valid norms to which all other social groups are expected to conform. Every ideology represents an attempt to shape the whole of society in the image of a particular social group. Further, for the social group whose point of view it articulates, these ideas are faithful accounts of its experiences and represent the way it actually thinks and lives. For the other groups, whose experiences and forms of thought are different, they become norms. In other words an ideology turns what is a fact for one group into an 'ought' or 'ideal' for others. As Marx puts it, when a view is 'generalised' and 'addressed to every individual without distinction' and in disregard of their 'conditions of life', it gets 'transformed into an insipid and hypocritical *moral* doctrine'.[21] Marx argues that since an ideology generalises a narrow point of view beyond the limits of its validity, it is compelled by its very logic to 'moralise' and 'preach'. However much it may disavow such intentions, it cannot avoid becoming prescriptive and, indeed, 'telling others how to live'.

An ideology then has a dual character. It has an empirical basis in the conditions of existence of a specific social group; and it is *normative* so far as the rest of society is concerned. Its biggest problem is to effect the logical transition from what is a fact for one group to what is to be a norm for the others. The most common manoeuvre is the introduction of the mediating concepts of human nature and human condition or predicament. An ideology presents the ideas and experiences of a particular group as inherent in human nature, and its conditions of existence as the human condition or predicament; and then, from the human nature and condition so defined, it deduces appropriate moral recommendations. The ideologist employs several other devices as well, and each involves a logical fallacy. We shall later discuss these at length.

Second, in being biased *towards* a specific group, an ideology is necessarily biased *against* the other social groups, whose conditions of existence and forms of thought are opposed to or even at variance with those of the group whose standpoint it reflects. It turns the group's conditions of existence into universal norms, its needs and interests into the sole criteria of human well-being, its view of reason into the sole criterion of rationality, and so on. It therefore treats the other social groups as a mere means, and denies the integrity of their forms of experience and thought. It aims to shape the entire society in the image of a particular group, and to reduce it to the limited proportions of the latter's forms of thought. Since an ideology universalises a limited point of view, it is inherently assimilationist in orientation. It is impatient of diversity, and seeks either to eliminate it altogether or only permits it within the limits dictated by it. The bourgeois ideology consists in making everybody bourgeois, and the petty-bourgeois ideology recommends a 'world of hucksters in which everyone gets his advantage'. It is not often appreciated that a very strong pluralist undercurrent runs through Marx's thought. Marx is opposed to class domination and indeed all forms of domination because, among other things, they lead to the imposition of a single form of experience and thought upon the entire society, and stifle new forms of experience and thought, the development of the 'all-sided' and 'rich individuality' and the 'creative' release of individual 'energy' as an 'end in itself'.

Third, an ideology can never adequately defend itself.[22] It rests on assumptions which it has never critically examined or even explicitly formulated. It takes the forms of experience and thought of a specific social group as its point of departure, and constructs an elaborate theoretical system on their basis. Since it finds them self-evident, it takes them for granted. It is unable to distance itself from and critically examine them, and can hardly be expected to provide their satisfactory defence. In Marx's view it is one of the most striking features of an ideology that it is 'critical towards its adversary, but . . . uncritical towards itself'.[23] While it could be fiercely uncompromising in its exposure of the basic assumptions of others, it is almost entirely reticent about its own. Consequently it either never states its first principles, or makes a perfunctory case for them, keeps reiterating and reformulating them, elaborates on them in the name of critically examining them, and so on.

Fourth, for Marx the basic assumptions of an ideology are ultimately nothing more than the intellectual 'transcripts' of the conditions of existence of the social group whose point of view it reflects.[24] As we saw, every social position is in his view constituted and defined by a specific set of social relations. To occupy it is to find oneself already related to others in a certain manner. The relations constitute one's social predicament, something one accepts as given, unalterable and forming the existential boundary of one's daily existence. One therefore takes them as given for the intellectual purposes as well. An assumption is a belief which is taken for granted or imagined to be self-evident. When an individual in his day-to-day life experiences the world in a uniform manner, he takes his forms of experience for granted. He does not experience the world in any other way, and hence thinks about it within these limits. What a man does not transcend in reality, he cannot effectively transcend in thought either. The limits of his existence are the limits of his thought. His basic assumptions are therefore ultimately nothing but his conditions of existence 're-produced' in thought. The fundamental features of his social being or existence constitute the basic assumptions of his social thought. It is because Marx takes what one might call a materialist view of the nature of assumption that he asks such apparently curious questions as whether an assumption is 'true', if it does or 'does not exist' and under what conditions it 'could arise' or 'could have been made'.[25] We shall return to this later.

VII

For Marx an ideology universalises or absolutises the conditions of existence and forms of thought of a social group, turns its needs into the norms for the whole of society or mankind, rests on assumptions which are ultimately nothing more than the intellectual transcripts of its conditions of existence, and so on. Marx's point would become clearer if we took an example. The example is his; the detailed elaboration is mine.[26]

The bourgeois mode of production is geared to the production of commodities, that is, the production of goods with a view to exchange and the accumulation of value. Unlike the previous modes of production, the production of commodities is not marginal to it, but is its *telos* and organising principle. Consequently when it first appeared on the historical scene, it required a specific set of social conditions in order to grow and flourish, for example, personal freedom, the formal equality of all men, the alienability of labour and the means of production, the separation of the civil society and the state, a more or less centralised state, a body of clearly defined general rules, and a more or less absolute right to property. Since we cannot discuss all these, we shall take the interrelated ideas of individuality, personal freedom and equality — for Marx some of the most important conditions of existence of the bourgeois society.

The bourgeois mode of production required that men should be free to buy and sell both labour and the means of production. In order that they could sell their means of production and labour, men had to be so defined that these were not deemed to be an integral part of them. If the means of production were to be considered integral to the individual in the same way that his hands and feet are, he obviously would not be able to alienate them any more than he can alienate his hands and feet. Some past societies did so consider them, and declared them inalienable. In their view an individual's means of production were his 'inorganic body', and no different from his hands and feet; to take them away from him was to mutilate him. The bourgeois society obviously had to take a very different view.

Again, in order to argue that an individual could sell his labour to others, his physical and mental capacities and activities, of which his labour ultimately consists, must be considered alienable, and therefore not an integral and inseparable part of him. The classical Athenian believed that to render any form of service, especially the physical, to another man in return for money, even if only for a short time, was a form of slavery, and unacceptable to a free man. Since the bourgeois mode of production required that men should be free to sell their labour, that is their skills, capacities and activities to others, it had to define the individual so that these were not considered an integral and inseparable part of him. He had to be seen as somehow separate from and only contingently related to them, so that *he* is not believed to be sold when they are, and is doomed to remain free even when his activities and skills are no longer under his control. In order to say that his freedom is not compromised when his abilities, skills and activities are placed at another man's disposal, he had to be defined in the barest possible manner.

Since almost everything about an individual was considered alienable — his skills, capacities and activities — the crucial question arose as to what was to be considered *essential* to him, such that *its* alienation was *his* alienation and his loss of control over it amounted to his loss of freedom. The bourgeois society by and large located his essential humanity in the interrelated capacities of choice and will. For it they represented man's *differentia specifica*, and were the bases of human dignity. The individual was, above all, an agent. As long as he was not physically overpowered, hypnotised or otherwise deprived of his powers of choice and will, his actions were *uniquely* his, and therefore his *sole* responsibility. It did not matter how painful his alternatives were, how much his character had been distorted by his background and upbringing and how much his capacities of choice and will were debilitated by his circumstances. As long as he was able to choose, his choices were his responsibility. The individual was abstracted from his social background and circumstances, which could not be considered co-agents of and co-responsible for his actions. He stood alone, all by himself, stripped of his social relations, circumstances and background, in a word, his social being as Marx called it, facing the world in his sovereign isolation and, like God, exercising his unconditioned freedom of choice and will. In short their conditions of existence required the bourgeoisie to equate the individual with an abstract mental capacity, namely the capacity to choose and will, and to define him in asocial and 'idealist' terms. The facts that the concepts of will and choice should have acquired such an unprecedented importance in the thought of the late medieval nominalists, Hobbes, Locke, Rousseau, Bentham, Kant, J.S. Mill and others should not surprise us.

When the individual is so austerely conceived, the question arises as to how he is related to his alienable bodily and mental activities and powers. They cannot be conceived as his modes of being, the ways in which 'he' expresses himself and exists for himself and others; they can only be understood as something he *has* rather than he *is*. The bourgeois writers appropriately defined them as his *properties*, which in the legal language became his *possessions*. If 'he' referred to the totality of his being and not merely to the will or choice, his powers and activities would be seen as an integral part of him, as *constitutive* of him, and therefore not as his possessions which he could dispose of 'at will'. He would not be able to alienate them, any more than he could alienate his will or choice. And his so-called 'freedom' to sell his capacities and activities would appear not as freedom, but slavery. The lean and austere bourgeois definition of the individual had, of course, a very different implication.

The bourgeois mode of production then required a society of independent, sovereign, self-determining human agents defining their dignity in terms of the powers of choice and will, and freely competing with others to pursue their self-chosen activities with minimal interference by the government. Accordingly when the bourgeoisie became the dominant class, they successfully demanded that the existing legal, political, moral and other institutions should be so altered as to conduce to their development.[27] The law abolished the restrictive medieval corporations and guilds, made the austerely defined individual the subject of rights and obligations, and guaranteed his personal freedom, including and especially the freedom to dispose of his abilities and activities as he pleased. It abolished also the complex and customary restraints on property, and gave the individual an almost absolute right to his property. A single legal system consisting of general rules and enjoying jurisdiction over the entire country came into being. The political institutions were developed to safeguard the liberties of the citizens by limiting and separating the functions and powers of the government. The courts of law came to acquire considerable independence and authority.[28] Over the decades the social morality, too, underwent important changes, replacing the feudal morality of honour and personal obligations by the ethic of prudence, personal choice, economy, reciprocity, moderation and the rational calculation of interests.

Marx draws several important conclusions from the analysis sketched above. The conception of the individual enshrined in the practices and institutions of the bourgeois society is biased. The individual is not given by nature, but socially defined. Men are inseparably connected with other men and nature. To individuate a man is to demarcate him, to separate him from and draw a boundary between him and the other men and nature.[29] Now men can be individuated in many different ways. Some societies, among which Marx included the Asiatic, do not individuate them at all. Classical Athens was the first society to develop the idea of the individual. For in it a man lacked determinancy outside an established community and without an independent piece of land. Hence a man *together with* his land and political rights constituted the individual. In the feudal society, too, land was seen as 'the inorganic body' if its owner, and part of the definition of the individual.[30] Only the lord of the land was deemed to be the individual. His serfs were 'his men' who paid 'homage' to him as a symbol of having become *his* men.

For Marx himself man remains abstract and indeterminate without certain material and social conditions of existence. They are therefore not externally or contingently related to him, but an integral part of him. He is simply not an individual without them. When separated from them, he is merely a body, a physical entity, and not an individual. When others acquire control over his conditions of existence, his existence is no longer subject to his control. It is contingent and 'accidental', subject to the caprice of others. Not he but they decide whether he will live or die, where he will work, under what conditions, how long, what he will earn, the kind of life he and his family will live, and so on. Once he has chosen to work for an employer, he abdicates his will, forfeits his freedom, and becomes a 'slave' for at least part of the day all his life. Marx cannot see how a choice to become a slave can be called an act of freedom, for his freedom only relates to the initial choice. Further, the worker's initial choice is not a free choice, for the only alternative to 'wage slavery' is starvation and death, and such a stark choice, like the choice to shoot a man when the alternative is to be shot oneself, cannot at all be considered a free choice in any meaningful sense of the term. For Marx he who lacks access to and control over his conditions of existence is merely an object of others' actions, and not an independent subject or individual.

Men, then, can be individuated in several different ways, the bourgeois mode of individuation being one of them. It is therefore not the *only* way to define the individual as the bourgeois spokesmen maintain. What is more, since men can be individuated in different ways, the bourgeois mode of individuation must be shown to be better than the rest, and not 'merely assumed' to be obvious, self-evident and natural as the bourgeois spokesmen do. Further, the bourgeois definition is biased. If we were to individuate men differently, for example, in the manner of classical Athens or Marx, we would have to guarantee each individual those conditions without which he cannot live, flourish and become an individual. And this would obviously undermine the very basis of the bourgeois society. By contrast, the austere and minimalist conception of the individual, which entitles him to nothing save the relatively unhindered exercise of his formal capacity for choice and will, and allows him no claims upon others save forebearance, suits the bourgeois society well. It enables it to blame and punish its members for their actions on the ground that they have freely chosen and are accountable for them. At the same time, it releases society from the obligation to increase their range of real alternatives and give them greater control over their lives. In other words the bourgeois society defines the individual within the limits of and in a manner conducive to its conditions of existence.[31] Its definition is ideological.

Like its conception of the individual, the bourgeois society's conceptions of liberty, equality, right, justice, and so on are also biased. Liberty and equality, for example, can be defined in several different ways, depending on how we define the individual. If we defined the individual as forming an organic unity with his conditions of existence, so that not a man abstracted from but taken *together with* them constituted an individual, we would have to define freedom as an access to, a share in the control over and non-interference in his use of them.[32] And likewise we would have to define equality as an equal access to and control over these conditions as well as an equal opportunity to develop one's abilities. Since the bourgeois society defines the individual in minimalist terms, it defines liberty and equality too, in extremely narrow terms. For it liberty is the absence of interference by the government, equality is the formal equality of rights, a right is the capacity to do what one likes with one's own and justice is whatever is offered by the market.

As we saw the bourgeois definitions are not the only ways in which liberty, equality, etc. can be defined. They must therefore be defended, shown to be more satisfactory than their alternatives, and not simply assumed to be obvious and non-controversial. Further, the bourgeois definitions are biased. The bourgeoisie require that the government should not interfere with their activities. For them *this* freedom is the most important, it being one of their conditions of existence. Accordingly, they equate it with freedom as such, *define* freedom as non-interference by the government, and make their specific requirement a universal norm. In Marx's view the bourgeois society's definitions of equality, justice and right are equally biased and ideological, as they do little more than universalise and institutionalise the conditions of existence of the bourgeoisie. They generate demands which can be easily met, and can only be met within the bourgeois society. If we were to define them differently, they would entail demands that cannot be met within the framework of the bourgeois society. To accept the bourgeois society's definitions of liberty, equality, right, etc. is to remain within its bounds.

By embodying its minimalist conception of the individual in its legal, social, educational, moral, economic, political and other institutions, the bourgeois society enforces it upon all its members. It sets up the minimally defined individual, its own basic condition of existence, as the norm to which they are all required to conform. They are told that they lack dignity and are subhuman unless they stand on their own feet, make no claims on society, accept full responsibility for the consequences of their actions, however painful and stark the alternatives, bear their social misfortunes with dignity and blame none but themselves for them. The institutions and practices of the bourgeois society do little more than induce and compel the rest of society to become what the bourgeoisie want them to become. As we saw, Marx argues that, like the concept of the individual, the concepts of liberty, equality, justice and right as defined in the bourgeois society are also ideological. Inasmuch as the bourgeois legal, political, social and other institutions are structured in terms of these conceptions, Marx argues that they are all systematically biased against all but the bourgeoisie. His argument has profound implications, especially for the theories of authority and obligation, which we cannot here explore.

To avoid a very common misunderstanding, three important distinctions need to be drawn. First, when Marx says that liberty, equality, right, and so on are bourgeois concepts, he does not mean that the concepts themselves are bourgeois, but rather that the way they are defined by the bourgeois society is bourgeois. As we saw, they can be defined in the non-bourgeois manners as well. In his polemical remarks Marx often dismisses a concept itself when he really means to dismiss only the current manner of defining it.

Second, the bourgeois definitions of liberty, equality, etc. are bourgeois *not* because the bourgeoisie so define and champion them, but because they are biased towards them. That is, they are bourgeois not because of the social *origin* of the group defining and championing them, but because of their systematic social bias. We saw earlier how this is so.

Third, contrary to what is sometimes suggested, Marx does not wish to say that to understand liberty as non-interference by the government is to give a bourgeois definition of it.[33] There is nothing bourgeois about wanting to keep the government off one's back, nor is there anything Marxist about inviting it to run one's life. Many a pre-bourgeois society included, and Marx himself includes, non-interference by the government as *one* of the constituents of liberty. For Marx, not the non-interference by the government *per se*, but the non-interference of a certain kind and understood in a certain manner constitutes the essence of the bourgeois definition of liberty. As he puts it, it is the *absolutisation* of the non-interference by the government, the belief that it represents the 'absolute form of free individuality', that constitutes the ideological character of the bourgeois conception of liberty. The bourgeois society and writers *equate* non-interference with liberty, rather than see it as one of its several constituents. They conceive freedom negatively and narrowly, and not as the capacity to develop one's potentialities and enjoy access to the necessary conditions of it. They regard the non-interference by the government in the economic life as one of the most important liberties, and see no restriction of liberty involved in the considerable arbitrary power the employers exercise over their workers. They view the government as an alien and 'interfering' agency rather than an institution through which the community realises its collective aspirations and governs itself. Their conception of liberty rules out the government action designed to liberate men from the vicious and cumulative cycles of deprivation. They define self-help and self-reliance as the basis of human dignity, and thereby morally blackmail the weak into not pressing for collective action. They demarcate the *boundary* of interference in such a flexible way that it suits their interests, as when the strike by labour may be punished but not the one by capital. In short it is not the non-interference by the government *per se*, but the way it is defined and practised in the bourgeois society that is systematically *biased* towards the bourgeoisie, and hence ideological.

Marx argues that if we looked at the writings of many of the philosophers from the seventeenth century onwards, we would see that their conceptions of the individual, liberty, equality, justice, right, etc. are basically the same as those dominant in the bourgeois society.[34] Hobbes, Locke, Kant, Adam Smith, Bentham, Ricardo and others abstracted man from his conditions of existence, equated him with the will or the capacity to choose, and advanced an austere and minimalist conception of the individual, which they, no doubt, formulated and defended in different ways. Further, they too defined liberty as non-interference by the government, equality as the formal equality of rights, property as the more or less absolute right to use and dispose of an object as one pleased, and so on. Although they articulated their ideas in such different idioms as the contractualist, the utilitarian and the idealist, they all shared a common 'form of social consciousness'. Their philosophical definitions of the individual, liberty, etc. did little more than reiterate the definitions prevalent in the bourgeois society; in so doing they conceptually reproduced and legitimised its basic conditions of existence. The limits of its existence were the limits of their thought. As Marx sometimes puts it, its conditions of existence became their fundamental philosophical postulates. They never transcended the bourgeois horizon of thought or, what comes to the same thing, they analysed men and society from the bourgeois point of view. As Marx puts it,[35]

> their minds are restricted by the same barriers which the petty bourgeoisie fails to overcome in real life, and that they are therefore driven in theory to the same problems and solutions to which material interest and social situation drive the latter in practice. This is in general the relationship between the *political and literary representatives* of a class and the class which they represent.

Marx notes that the definitions of the individual, liberty, equality, etc. advanced by the philosophers and the economists were no different from those given by the ordinary man. No doubt, the philosophers presented their view in an elegant language, defended them with sophisticated arguments and developed impressive theoretical systems. However, when their philosophical forms are peeled away, the actual content and quality of their views is not very different from that of their simple-minded contemporaries. The philosophers' horizon of thought was co-extensive with that of the ordinary men. Both alike remained 'prisoners' of the dominant bourgeois ideology. Notwithstanding their considerable intelligence and powers of analysis, the philosophers were as ideological as their less gifted contemporaries.

In social and political matters, the philosophers *are* ordinary men, and just as prejudiced and apologetic.

VIII

For Marx, then, an ideology is a body of thought systematically biased towards a specific social group. To call a body of thought ideological is to say that it offers a systematically biased and distorted account of its subject matter, and to convict it of grave theoretical inadequacy. This means that a critic calling a body of thought ideological has an obligation to demonstrate by means of a patient and systematic analysis that it is biased towards a specific group, and that *as a result* it gives an inadequate account of its subject matter.[36] Marx calls such an analysis a *critique*. A critique of an ideology has a twofold objective. It aims to show that a body of thought gives a distorted and inadequate account of its subject matter and, second, it does so because of its basic social assumptions. At the first stage, the critic demonstrates that the body of thought systematically distorts its subject matter, and at the second, he explains the distortion in terms of its biased basic assumptions. For Marx, while the critic's own *investigation* begins with the first stage and proceeds to the second, he may *present* his critique differently. He may first state what he takes to be the biased basic assumptions of a body of thought, and then demonstrate how they lead it to offer a systematically distorted account of its subject matter.

After demonstrating the distortion and tracing it to the basic social assumptions of a body of thought, a critic is in a position to describe it as a characteristically bourgeois, petty-bourgeois, feudal or any other way of looking at its subject matter depending on the character of the underlying assumptions. For Marx such descriptions are not clichés or summary dismissals of social and political theories as they have become in the hands of some of his followers, but *theoretical* judgements based on careful analyses of the logical structures of the bodies of ideas concerned. They are intended to signify that the writers involved view their subject matter through the distorting prism of a specific body of assumptions, and offer misleading accounts of it. To call a body of thought bourgeois, feudal, etc, is to specify the social point of view from which its author analysed his subject matter, and to highlight both its unifying principle and its basic limitations.

Marx's own practice provides sufficient evidence of this. For example, in the *German Ideology* itself he never dismissed a writer's ideas on the basis of his social origin, and he devoted considerable attention to exposing the limitations of the Left Hegelians, especially Stirner, and the Utopian socialists.[37] In the *Poverty of Philosophy* and his letter to Annenkov, he offered a detailed critique of Proudhon. And only after demonstrating the pervasive structural bias of his thought did he call him petty-bourgeois. As he put it in a letter to Schweitzer, 'I declared this book to be the code of socialism of the petty-bourgeois and *proved this theoretically* . . .'[38] Again, in the *Theories of Surplus Value* he devoted many pages to examining the ideas of each of the major classical economists, demonstrated their basic biases, showed that these distorted their explanations of economic life, and *then* called them bourgeois ideologists.[39] One may criticise him for not being sufficiently rigorous or patient in his examination. However, there is no basis for the crude view that he did not take the ideas seriously, or was only interested in their social origins and not truth, or that he summarily dismissed them on the basis of their authors' class.

IX

Having demonstrated the ideological character of a body of thought, the critic may wish to go further. He may inquire *why* the thinker in question viewed his subject matter from a particular standpoint or, what comes to the same thing, why he made specific assumptions or found certain ideas obvious and self-evident. In the *German Ideology*, where he first outlined his theory of ideology, Marx sometimes remarks that the question is answered by tracing the social background of the thinker, and showing that a certain way of looking at his subject matter comes naturally to a person belonging to a particular group. In his later writings he moved away from such a simplistic and what he himself called a 'narrow view'. He appreciated that the thinkers and the social groups whose points of view they articulate may be 'poles apart' in 'their education and their individual situation'. Accordingly, he argued that a social theorist may adopt a group's point of view not because he belongs to it, but because of professional socialisation, the influence of the dominant ideology, or he is convinced of its validity. Since his point of view cannot be read off his class, Marx maintained that the explanation of his adoption of it involves an examination of the dominant ideology, the evolution and assumptions of his discipline, his own social background, and so on. Marx has no name for such an inquiry. We might call it a sociological inquiry or, following Mannheim and others, sociology of knowledge. Neither term adequately captures the complexity of the inquiry Marx has in mind. Since the latter has acquired unfortunate associations, we shall call it a sociological inquiry.

Marx's theory of ideology, then, involves two related but logically distinct types of inquiry, namely a critique or a critical and a sociological inquiry.[40] A critique aims to demonstrate that a body of thought is an ideology. The sociological inquiry aims to explain why its author made the assumptions involved, and failed to notice his bias. A critique is concerned with the theoretical content of a *body of thought*, which it critically examines and whose structural bias it exposes. The sociological inquiry is concerned with the *thinker*, and explains why he never became aware of and/or criticised his biased assumptions.

Of the two, the critical inquiry is central to Marx's theory of ideology, for one cannot call a body of thought ideological without showing that it is systematically biased. Although not entirely marginal, the sociological inquiry is not so central. Having demonstrated that a body of thought is ideological, one may *not* ask the further question why its author made specific assumptions; one may find such a question uninteresting, unanswerable or even mistaken. It is worth noting that in many of his writings, especially the *Theories of Surplus Value* and *Capital*, Marx is basically interested in the critical, and not the sociological inquiry. He demonstrates at length that the classical economists were biased, but has little interest in explaining *why* they were so biased.

If our analysis is correct, Marx's theory of ideology can be detached from the sociological inquiry with which it has so often been confused. The heart of his theory of ideology lies *not* in the view that a man's ideas are determined or conditioned by his class or society, but rather that an unself-critical writer produces a body of thought systematically biased towards a particular social group. Marx's theory of ideology is primarily logical, not sociological in nature, and advances a logical, not a sociological thesis. What it entails is a logical investigation into the structure of a body of thought with a view to articulating its basic social assumptions and demonstrating its bias.[41]

Marx's theory of ideology is therefore not damaged by showing that a man's class does not shape his thought. All it asserts is that, when carefully analysed, most bodies of thought turn out to be socially biased, and that the existence and influence of the bias can be objectively demonstrated. Whether their authors were so biased *because* they belonged to a particular class is irrelevant. Nor is Marx's theory damaged by showing that an individual belongs to several different social groups and works out a distinct point of view not reducible to any one of them. An individual may entertain a complex point of view that is uniquely his own. Yet he may write the history of the world from a white or a black man's point of view, analyse his society from a bourgeois point of view, and develop a political theory that generalises the uniquely English political experiences and forms of thought. However complex an individual's *total* view of the world might be, it is not difficult to imagine that he may approach a particular area of inquiry from a specific point of view. All that Marx's theory of ideology asserts is that a body of thought could be constructed from a narrow social point of view. The validity of *this* thesis is unaffected by the contention that human beings are far more self-determining and complex than he imagined.

Unfortunately Marx does not explicitly distinguish the two types of inquiry we have teased out of his writings. As a result he sometimes makes highly ambiguous and misleading remarks which have given rise to a good deal of misunderstanding and misplaced criticism. When he describes an individual as bourgeois or petty-bourgeois, he could mean one of two things which he never clearly distinguished. First, he could mean that the thought of the individual concerned systematically reflects and moves within the limits set by the social point of view characteristic of the bourgeoisie or the petty bourgeoisie. Second, he could mean that the thinker himself belongs to the class in question, and *hence* his thought is systematically biased towards it. Generally Marx means the first, not the second. Further, when he means the second, he intends it as an account of the *reasons* why the thinker concerned viewed his subject matter from a particular point of view, not as a basis for deducing or inferring the character of his thought.

X

In the light of our discussion it would be useful to spell out what ideology, for Marx, is not, especially since some commentators have attributed views to him for which there is little or limited textual evidence.

First, for Marx an ideology is systematically biased towards a social group, be it a class, a nation, a profession or a race.[42] It is therefore wrong to *define* it as a body of ideas biased towards a class. Such a definition is narrow, and ignores the fact that an ideology may be biased towards the other social groups as well.

Second, since an ideology could be biased towards any social group, it is wrong to define it as a body of ideas biased towards or legitimising the rule of the *dominant* class. A body of ideas legitimising the dominant class is a *dominant* ideology; and not all ideologies need be dominant. It is, of course, true that Marx was himself most interested in analysing the nature and mechanism of the dominant ideology. However, he never said that a non-dominant ideology is not an ideology. For him the Left Hegelians, Proudhon and others were all ideologists, although they were apologists of the petty bourgeoisie; Malthus was an ideologist, although an apologist of the feudal aristocracy, and Engels sometimes speaks of the 'ideological Left' as well.[43]

Third, for Marx not every body of ideas serving the interests of a social group is an ideology. The hippie doctrine of inner withdrawal or 'happy commune' serves the interests of the dominant class, but it does not legitimise or justify the latter and is therefore not an ideology. Further, a body of thought may champion the interests of a particular group without being an ideology, if it can show by means of an un-biased investigation that the group's interests deserve to be championed. Marx thought that although he championed the cause of the proletariat, he was nevertheless not an ideologist.

Fourth, although an ideology generally serves the interests of a social group, it is wrong to define it in terms of interest as is commonly done. Such a definition shifts the emphasis from the logical structure of a body of thought to its putative consequences. For Marx an ideology is essentially a body of thought giving a systematically biased and dis-torted account of its subject matter. That it also serves the interests of a particular social group is its important but derivative character-istic. Further, an ideology may confer social prestige and intellectual respectability upon a particular group, but not serve its material inter-ests in any obvious sense of the term. A history of ancient Rome which is systematically biased towards the patricians is ideological, but serves no obvious interests, for the patricians are a defunct group. It may, no doubt, be used to support the role of the privileged groups in general; however, it need not, and the historian concerned may make it clear that the patricians were a historically unique group without a modern counterpart.

Fifth, an ideology is not a body of false or incorrect ideas. A scien-tific theory may be false, but it is not an ideology. Besides, as we saw, an ideology is not entirely false, and contains enough grains of truth to make it plausible. Further, when it contains false ideas, their falsity has a specific character in that it arises from the social bias of the ideologist and displays a consistent pattern. In this connection it is worth noting that Marx generally contrasts ideology not with truth but objectivity. Unlike an ideologist who is partisan in his investigation and offers a biased body of knowledge, a scientist 'impartially' and 'critically' investigates his subject matter and aims to provide an 'unbiased' and 'disinterested' account of it.[44]

Sixth, an ideology is not a lie or a tissue of lies. It distorts its subject matter, but distortion is very different from lying. Further, a body of thought may contain deliberately false statements, yet not be an ideology. All that matters is whether it is systematically biased towards a particular social group. This may explain why Marx rarely attributes good or bad motives to its author.[45]

Seventh, it is wrong to say that for Marx ideology refers to class-determined, class-based or class-conditioned thought. As we saw, his account of human thought is much too complex to be captured by such expressions as class determinism and class conditioning. Besides, for Marx, whether or not a body of thought is ideological is determined by examining its basic categories and assumptions; its author's social class, relevant in other contexts, is totally irrelevant. Further, as we saw, Marx defines the term class widely to refer to many more social groups than the three major classes. Finally, as we saw, the class-conditioned thought is not by itself ideological but becomes one when it is universalised, and general validity is claimed for it.

Eighth, an ideology is not a body of illusions or false appearances. As we shall see fully later, Marx's concept of illusion or false appearance is highly complex. For the present we need only note that for him an ideology consists in *presenting* an illusion or appearance as reality. Although Marx occasionally uses the term ideology to *mean* illusion, the basic thrust of his argument is different. That the sun goes round the earth is an illusion, but not an ideology or an ideological illusion. For Marx an ideology is a body of *ideas*, and consists in interpreting and explaining an illusion in a biased manner. For example, in the capitalist society the individual *appears* to be the basic unit, although he is, in fact, class-mediated. And the worker *appears* to be, but is not, in fact, paid the full reward of his labour. The views that the individual is *really* the ultimate unit in the capitalist and indeed all societies, and that a worker is fully paid for his labour are ideological. An ideological illusion is one that conceals the social reality in the interest of a specific social group.

Ninth, for Marx not every body of justificatory ideas is an ideology. Ideology involves a particular type of justification. Marx justified capitalism as the most progressive mode of production in history, but was not its apologist. By contrast the classical economists were its apologists. Unlike Marx they not only justified, but *absolutised* it. They presented it as natural to man, the most rational mode of organising the economy ever likely to be discovered by man and to which there was no viable alternative. In so doing they distorted the historical truth, made false claims on its behalf, and offered a highly biased account of the non-capitalist modes of production.[46]

Finally, nearly all the interpretations of Marx's theory of ideology fall into one of three categories, namely the structural, the genetic and the consequentialist. According to the structural interpretations, ideology refers to a body of thought *structurally* and systematically *biased* towards a particular social group; according to the second, to a body of thought *conditioned or determined* by the thinker's social group, especially the class; and according to the third, to a body of thought serving the interests or promoting the cause of a social group, especially the dominant class. Despite some ambiguity, Marx defines ideology in structural terms. The genetic interpretation is mistaken because, as we saw, a thinker may generalise the viewpoint of a group without belonging to it; for example, a man may accept the dominant ideology without belonging to the dominant class. Further, a body of thought is an ideology not because it has its origin in a thinker's social group, but because it claims universal validity for the forms of experience and thought of the group concerned. Finally, as we saw, Marx's theory of ideology is conceptually detachable from his theory of the so-called social determination of knowledge. The consequentialist or functionalist interpretation is mistaken because, as we saw, an ideology does not always serve the interests of a social group, and conversely, a body of thought may serve its interests and yet not be an ideology.

XI

For Marx the apologetic or ideological writers are of two types. First, they may be patently partisan and not at all interested in the pursuit of truth. Second, they may be genuinely disinterested and impartial, and yet for various reasons end up developing the apologetic bodies of thought. Marx calls the first group of writers 'base', but has no name for the second. He divides the second group of writers into three groups or, what amounts to the same thing, he thinks that the writers may unwittingly develop apologetic systems of thought in one of three ways. First, by confining themselves to the surface of society; second, by studying abstract ideas rather than the social relations; and third, by studying the social relations in an ahistorical and uncritical manner. For Marx the vulgar writers represent the first; Hegel and the philosophers in general represent the second; and the classical economists the third. In the following chapter we shall outline his analyses of the base and vulgar writers; and in the next two, of Hegel and the classical economists respectively.

3 BASE AND VULGAR WRITERS

By a 'base' writer Marx means one who lacks professional integrity, is patently partisan, intellectually dishonest and only interested in reaching a particular conclusion. As he puts it, 'When a man seeks to accommodate science to a viewpoint which is derived not from science itself (however erroneous it may be) but from outside, from alien, external interests, then I call him base.'[1]

Although Marx does not put it this way, he seems to think that a base writer may belong to one of two types. First, he may have no intellectual convictions of his own and use his talents in the service of whoever offers him the highest reward; Marx calls him a 'hired prize-fighter', 'a bought advocate', or a 'sycophant'. Or secondly, a writer may entertain strong personal prejudices and use his writings to propagate them, freely distorting facts and arguments as they serve his purpose. In Marx's view Proudhon's book on Louis Bonaparte's *coup d'état* was of this type.[2] Despite their obvious differences, the two types of writer share several features in common. They lack intellectual integrity, are partisan and committed to a particular cause which they aim to propagate at all cost; and their writings, being 'merely catchpenny efforts', are justificatory in nature and have no explanatory content.[3] Marx brings out these features well in his contrast between Ricardo and Malthus.

According to Marx, Ricardo was 'scientifically honest'.[4] He believed in the increase of national wealth and the development of the productive forces, and did not care whom that benefited. As he put it, 'I shall greatly regret that considerations of any particular class are allowed to check the progress of the wealth and population of the country.' When the interests of the bourgeoisie coincided with those of production, he supported them; when they did not, he came out against them. Marx praised Ricardo's 'scientific impartiality'. He acknowledged that Ricardo treated the workers as beasts of burden, but thought that he did so not out of regard for class interest but for the development of production. In Marx's view this is evident in the fact that, when his theory led him to conclude that the increase in wages did not increase the price of commodities, Ricardo 'says so in a straightforward manner'. He was a philanthropist when this was possible 'without sinning against his science'.

In Marx's view Malthus was very different. He 'draws only such conclusions from the given scientific premises . . . as will be "agreeable" (useful) to the aristocracy against the bourgeoisie, and to both *against* the proletariat'. Malthus's very first book had 'the practical aim' of proving that the French revolutionary doctrines were Utopian and that the existing society was the best possible. In Marx's view Malthus's subsequent writing on the protective tariffs and the ground rent also intended to defend the landed aristocracy against the industrial bourgeoisie, and justify the poverty of the worker. Like Ricardo, he treated the workers as commodities on the ground that the interests of production required it. Since his argument was not biased towards any class, Marx raised no objection. However, when the same interests of production required that the landlord's rent and the church's tithe should be reduced, Malthus resisted and 'falsified science on behalf of these interests'. In Marx's view he did this in a number of books, not least *On Population*, for Marx a 'libel on the human race'. Malthus's primary loyalty was to the ruling classes, especially the landed aristocracy, and not to the development of the productive forces which, for Marx, coincided with the true interests of the human species. Marx observes:[5]

> Malthus does not sacrifice the particular interests to production but *seeks*, as far as he can, to sacrifice the demands of production to the particular interests of existing ruling classes or sections of classes. And to this end he *falsifies* his scientific conclusions. This is his *scientific* baseness, his sin against science . . . The scientific conclusions of Malthus are *'considerate'* towards the ruling classes in general and towards the reactionary elements of the ruling classes in particular; in other words he *falsifies* science for these interests. But his conclusions are *ruthless* as far as they concern the subjugated classes. He is not only *ruthless*; . . . he takes a cynical pleasure in it and *exaggerates* his conclusions . . . he was no *man of science*, but a bought advocate . . . a shameless sycophant of the ruling classes.

For Marx, then, the 'base' writers have no intellectual integrity. Their writings are exercises in special pleading, and necessarily apologetic. Although they may and, for obvious reasons, generally do insist that they are impartial investigators, Marx thinks that their apologetic intention is never difficult to uncover. It is evident in the way they ignore counterevidence, select some and suppress other facts, twist their arguments to reach the desired conclusions, and so on.

II

By a 'vulgar' writer Marx means one who is 'superficial', 'philistine', 'shallow', confined to the 'surface' of society and unwilling to probe deeper. The distinction between 'appearance' and 'essence', also expressed as that between the 'phenomenal forms' and their 'deeper connections', the 'merely apparent' and 'real' movement, the 'surface' and the 'disguised essence', the 'forms of appearance' and the 'inner interconnection', lies at the basis of Marx's theory of science. As he puts it, 'If there were no difference between essence and appearance, there would be no need for science.' And again, 'All science would be superfluous if the manifest form and the essence of things directly coincided.' Marx's distinction between the appearance and essence or between the surface and depth should be understood not in the Kantian demarcationist sense, but rather the Hegelian sense of structural mediation. The essence is not a thing-in-itself, but the inner constitution or structure, and the depth does not refer to some subterranean world, but the inherent and latent tendencies of the inner structure. As we shall see, Marx argues that the task of a scientist is to analyse the phenomenal forms of an entity, elucidate its essential nature and tendencies, and use the knowledge so acquired to explain its phenomenal behaviour.[6]

It is precisely this crucial distinction between the essence and appearance that the vulgar writer denies or overlooks. He mistakes the appearance for the essence and does not probe deeper. As Marx puts it:[7]

Vulgar economy feels particularly at home in the estranged outward appearances of economic relations . . . these relations seem the more self-evident the more their internal relationships are concealed from it.

The philistine's and vulgar economist's way of looking at things stems . . . from the fact that it is only the direct form of manifestation of relations that is reflected in their brains and not their inner connection.

. . . vulgar economy . . . deals with appearances only, ruminates without ceasing on the materials long since provided by scientific economy, and there seeks plausible explanations of the most obtrusive phenomena . . . but for the rest, confines itself to systematising in a pedantic way, and proclaiming for everlasting truths, the trite ideas held by the self-complacent bourgeoisie with regard to their own world, to them the best of all possible worlds.

Before analysing Marx's discussion of vulgar writers, two points need to be made. First, although Marx is somewhat ambiguous he seems to think that the term 'base' describes the professional character of a writer, and the term 'vulgar' his level of investigation. For Marx a base writer is almost invariably vulgar because, first he is only interested in reaching a particular conclusion and not in arriving at the truth, and second, he has the 'apologetic dread' that the truth might not turn out to be 'palatable' to him.[8] A vulgar writer, however, need not necessarily be base, although he might well be one.

Second, although Marx frequently used the term 'vulgar economy' to refer to the economists whose writings absolutised the bourgeois society, there is no evidence to suggest that he intended to confine the term to either the economists or the apologists of the bourgeois society. As we saw, he uses the term 'vulgar' to characterise a certain level of investigation. Further, he uses such expressions as 'a vulgarian', 'vulgarians', 'vulgar apologist' and 'vulgar socialism'.[9] It would seem, therefore, that in Marx's view the vulgar writers can be found not only among the economists but also among the philosophers, the historians, the political theorists and others, and further, that they may be not only conservative but also radical in their political biases.

Marx makes a number of perceptive comments on the logical structure of vulgar writing. We cannot discuss them all and shall concentrate on the one most relevant from our point of view, namely that a superficial student of society is compelled by the very logic of his inquiry to become its apologist. Even if he were critical of his society, his very level of investigation condemns him to becoming its apologist. Marx thinks that this is so because the surface of society is ideologically constituted, so that whoever remains confined to it can do little more than reproduce the underlying ideology.

III

Marx argues that in a class-divided society the dominant class needs to devise ways of consolidating and perpetuating its domination. Broadly speaking, it has two effective means at its disposal. It might rely on force, and/or win over the support and loyalty of the dominated class by somehow legitimising itself in its eyes.[10] Now force by itself is never enough. It might overcome the hostility of the dominated class in the short run, but it cannot subdue it permanently. Moreover, force is ultimately grounded in beliefs and loyalties, for one must first command the allegiance of the police and the army before one can use them to put down one's opponents. Again, while force can be effective in the primitive society which requires little more than a few basic services from the dominated class, it is useless in the industrialised society which requires the exercise of initiative and responsibility and depends upon the willing co-operation of its members.

Further, for Marx, men are rational beings who are aware of belonging to a common species. Thanks to their capacity to labour and manipulate nature, they are aware also of being superior to the rest of the natural world, and possess a sense of dignity, a feeling of fundamental moral equality with other men and a conception of what is due to them and others. The dominated class cannot, therefore, avoid asking why it is treated as an inferior *species* or a *beast of burden*, and demanding a 'justification' of its condition. The dominant class, too, does not consist of amoral monsters, but of human beings gifted with a 'conscience'. As such it seeks to convince itself that it is right to treat the dominated class the way it does. As Marx says, the member of a dominant class needs to 'silence his conscience' by reassuring himself that the misery of the dominated class is 'its own fault' and that his 'hard-heartedness' is morally right. Unless he can justify his actions to himself, he lacks the moral strength to watch human suffering 'as calmly as other natural events without bestirring himself', and cannot long sustain his 'enthusiasm' and morale.[11] It is because men are rational and moral beings that force alone cannot be the basis of their relationship. Marx's theory of ideology is grounded in and unintelligible without a reference to its underlying conception of man.

A class-divided society, then, must somehow legitimise itself to its members. It must get them all to agree on a common set of values, a common way of understanding man and society, a common view of what is and is not possible, ought and ought not to be desired, is and is not rational, proper, acceptable, moral, and so on. This common self-understanding should be such that it conduces to the basic conditions of existence of the dominant class. A class-divided society requires a body of beliefs which is *both* accepted by all its members and systematically biased towards the dominant class. In other words, it needs an ideology. Every society requires at least some commonly shared beliefs, as otherwise, it simply cannot exist as a single society. Only a class-divided society, however, needs an ideology; indeed, ideology is one of its necessary conditions of existence. A class-divided society operates under a fundamental constraint. It accepts the reality of class domination as given and unalterable, and defines its standards of rationality and morality *within the limits* set by this fundamental premise. The generally shared body of beliefs must therefore conform to the *a priori* demands of the social structure, and is by definition apologetic and ideological.

Marx maintains that since the need for ideology arises from the fact that a social order is exploitative, and since the nature of exploitation varies with the mode of production, the form and content of the dominant ideology vary with the mode of production. For example, in classical Athens ideology had a political, in the feudal society a religious, and in the bourgeois society it has a juridico-economic form and content. Despite these differences, however, all exploitative societies share certain formal features in common. Marx argues that the ideologies of all class-divided societies therefore display two basic characteristics: first, they 'obscure' or 'conceal' class conflicts; and second, they 'veil' the fact that the social order is historical and transient by presenting it as 'natural' and 'everlasting'.

An ideology must somehow obscure the fundamental conflicts of interest, and explain away the exploitative and antagonistic nature of society. This can be done in several different ways, some more effective than others. It may explain away social conflicts as products of false and mischievous doctrines propagated by the enemies of society. Such a conspiratorial theory, however, usually wears thin, particularly if it is frequently invoked. The ideologist of a social order may try to neutralise the class conflicts by the moralistic exhortations to love the country, trust and obey the authority, put the national before the personal interest, and the like. While such 'moralising' may have a desired effect, it cannot be invoked too often, and is easily seen through if, as is often the case, the dominant class itself appears to place its own interest above the nation's. In Marx's view the most effective strategy for the ideologist of the established order is to get its members to understand and conceptualise it in such a way that the conflict is made 'invisible', or so perceived that it can be resolved without significant structural alterations. Basically this consists in getting them all to define their human identity and interests in an identical manner, such that they all accept the existing social order as given and see themselves as engaged in a common enterprise whose successful prosecution is their common and overriding concern. The dominant way of understanding the modern society would seem to illustrate Marx's point well. The workers, employers, managers and others are all supposed to be primarily consumers having no other interest than to improve their material conditions. As such they all have a common interest, namely to increase the size of the national 'cake' of which each group is deemed to get the slice it deserves.

The second strategy of legitimisation consists in presenting the existing social order as natural. It is not enough to argue that the social order is basically good and worth preserving, for this leaves open the possibility that other forms of social organisation might be equally good or even better. Nor is it enough to argue that the prevailing social order is better than any other and indeed 'the best of all possible worlds', for even this entails an appeal to the principles independent of and external to the social order in question, and opens up the possibility of disagreement about the principles themselves or their application. The most effective way to legitimise a social order is to argue that it alone coheres with human nature, and is *natural*. Such an argument forecloses discussion and rests society on an apparently unshakable foundation, for just as one does not complain about such natural facts as having only two eyes or the earth's rotation round the sun, there is obvioulsy no point in evaluating the merits of and exploring the alternatives to a social order which is natural. We shall presently see how a social order can be presented as natural.

The logic of legitimisation, then, compels the ideologist of a social order to argue that it is essentially harmonious and natural. The two claims are closely connected. A society torn by internal conflicts can hardly be presented as natural, and hence its conflicts must be obscured. Conversely, social harmony can, in principle, be secured in a number of different ways, that achieved by the society in question being but one. One must therefore argue that *only* the type and degree of harmony attained in the present society accord with human nature, human condition, human predicament or whatever other limiting principle one cares to introduce.

For Marx the dominant ideology basically consists in generalising the ideas and forms of thought of the dominant class. As we saw earlier, the continued existence of the dominant class requires certain conditions. For example, the existence of the bourgeois society requires an austere and minimalist conception of the individual and the appropriate definitions of human dignity, liberty, equality, justice, rights, etc. When this way of thinking becomes widely accepted, and each individual defines and judges himself in terms of it, the bourgeois society gains legitimacy and consolidates its moral and material hold over its members. They judge it by its own standards and find that it conforms to them. They also judge themselves by its standards and set themselves appropriate goals. Once their deepest ambitions and aspirations become bourgeois in nature, a threat to the bourgeois society is felt by them as a threat to themselves. Once the bourgeois ideology strikes deep roots in the minds and hearts of its members, its 'moral domination' is complete, and its continued existence guaranteed.

The dominant ideology does not merely remain a body of beliefs. It permeates the totality of social relations, shapes the economic, social, political and other practices and institutions, and structures the entire society in its own image. It is embodied in the relations between the employers and the employees, the government and the citizens, the parents and children, the teachers and pupils, the husband and wife, between the neighbours, and so on. According to Marx it shapes also the language of social and public communication. It develops a distinct vocabulary, invests words with appropriate meanings and nuances, generates expressions that 'obscure' the unpleasant features of social life (for example, the national family), and embodies the social hierarchy in the language itself (for example, the wages v. salary, a profession v. an occupation). The dominant ideology so defines and structures the legal, educational, medical and other professions that they come to be narrowly conceived, do little more than attend to the social needs as defined by the dominant ideology, are barred from commenting upon the wider social and political issues, institutionalise the distinction between the expert and the 'lay' man, and preserve the professional monopoly of the relevant knowledge and skill. The professions reinforce and 'presuppose each other' and 'administer' the dominant ideology in their respective spheres of influence.[12]

In these and other ways, argues Marx, the dominant ideology does not remain merely 'ideal', but becomes part of the lived world and enjoys an objective or 'material' existence in the lives and relations of its members. It is not merely a body of beliefs, but a way of life. Its adherents do not merely hold, but live their beliefs. By structuring the entire society in its image, the dominant ideology establishes coherence between the beliefs and practices of its members. For example, in the bourgeois society men believe that the austerely defined individual is the basic moral unit. In their day-to-day practices and their legal and political institutions, only such an individual is recognised. Thus their beliefs correspond to and are confirmed and 'proved' by their practices, and appear to them to be obvious and self-evident.

Marx argues that in a society so structured and defined, only the ideas and forms of conduct compatible with the interests of the dominant class enjoy respectability, command attention and deliver results. For example, the workers asking for higher wages, healthier working conditions or longer lunch-breaks are taken seriously. The employer understands their demands and knows how to deal with them. If, however, they were to argue that their dignity as self-determining agents is violated by being made the objects of another man's will and power, and to propose that they should be allowed to hire his machines and even perhaps his services rather than be themselves hired by him, they would be met with sheer incomprehension, and treated as if they were men from Mars who did not know what an industrialised society was like. In principle, their demands in the second case are as sensible as the first. Thanks to the dominant ideology, the second type of demand is universally regarded as odd, irrational, irresponsible and falling outside the rules of the game. Since such demands are peremptorily dismissed, they are never made. By contrast, the first type of demand is taken seriously, negotiated and rewarded. The reformist demands work, the radical demands do not. Every success in securing the former, and every failure in securing the latter, strengthens the hold of the operative ideology, and encourages an ideologically acceptable style of negotiation and leadership. In these and other ways the social order brings the workers' beliefs into harmony with its practices. Since only the beliefs formulated within the framework of the dominant ideology are rewarded and confirmed by 'facts', they appear rational, responsible and realistic, and acquire the status of 'natural, self-evident modes of thought'.

What was said above about the nature of the industrial debate is equally true of the debates in other areas of life. In Marx's view the dominant ideology structures the realm of political debate, defines some but not other issues as political, some but not other views as responsible, some but not others as the appropriate functions for the government to undertake, and so on. In this way certain subjects never reach the public agenda or reach it in a highly emasculated form, and certain forms of experience never get articulated or are distorted beyond recognition.[13]

For Marx, then, the lived world in a class-divided society is ideologically constituted. It is structued in a systematically biased manner, and not only conceals the real world but presents it in a radically different manner. On the surface, the social order appears to be a single family happily living together and equitably sharing the national wealth; in actual fact, it is ridden with contradictions and conflicts. The social practices and institutions appear to be in harmony with human nature; in fact, they only accord with the human character as created by the social order in question. A large section of society appears inherently inferior and lacking drive, ambition and character; in actual fact, it has become so as a result of the centuries of deprivation and the lack of opportunities for growth. In short the social world as it is lived and experienced radically misrepresents its real nature.

This means that a student of society who remains confined to its surface cannot avoid becoming its apologist. The surface of society is so structured that he is rarely puzzled by it and provoked to probe deeper. His society appears to him to be a well-ordered, fundamentally sound and natural structure to which he sees no alternative. His beliefs conform to his experiences and seem self-evidently true. Besides, there is in normal times nothing in his experiences to lead him to sus-pect that the social reality might be very different. In short a vulgar student of society has no defence against its ideological claims, and is unable to resist their appeal. It is, of course, true that the surface of society is never wholly idyllic, and is marred by conflicts, inequality and suffering. However, the dominant ideology has ready explanations of these. Since they 'fit' into the ideologically shaped forms of thought and are 'confirmed' by experience, the vulgar theorist finds them persuasive. When, for example, he is told that some men are poor because they lack drive and energy, he has no reason to doubt the explanation, for he finds that the poor do, in fact, lack drive and energy. Lacking knowledge of the inner structure of society, he is unable to rejoin that the causal relationship is the other way round.

Contrary to what some of his commentators have said, Marx does not take the view that the dominant ideology is a solid mass of thoroughly integrated beliefs, articulated in a single idiom, blocks out all awareness of alternatives, and leaves no intellectual space for criti-cism. For Marx the dominant ideology consists of different kinds and levels of ideas drawn from different historical sources and contributed by such diverse groups as the vulgar writers, the philosophers, the journalists and the ordinary members of the dominant class. No doubt, this motley collection has some internal unity. However, no single individual has sat down to systematise it, and it retains large areas of incoherence. Its main unifying principle is the justification of the existing social order, and such a practical consideration is too nebulous and weak to achieve theoretical unity.

Further, the dominant ideology may be articulated in several different idioms. For example, in the bourgeois society it may be expressed in the language of natural rights, utilitarianism, idealism, radical scepticism, relativism, and so on. According to Marx, what makes all these doctrines bourgeois is the fact that, despite their 'multiplicity and variety', all these articulations rest on shared assumptions, 'move within certain common forms' and remain 'imprisoned' within the bourgeois horizon of thought. In Marx's view they all accept the austere and minimalist conceptions of the individual, liberty, equality, justice and right discussed earlier. As he sometimes puts it, although their contents and languages of expression vary, they all share the same 'forms of social consciousness'.[14]

In Marx's view the dominant ideology is rarely able to block out all awareness of the alternatives. Barring extreme cases, a dominant class is unlikely to have abolished all the classes of the previous social order. In the bourgeois society, for example, the landed aristocracy continued to survive for a long time, and so did the body of ideas associated with it. Further, sometimes the dominant class itself revives old ideologies as additional sources of its legitimisation, thereby opening the door to alternative modes of thought.

Just as the dominant ideology cannot entirely shut out the past, it can even less successfully shut the door to the future. A dominant class necessarily presupposes the dominated class, which is its historical twin. As the dominant class grows, the dominated class grows too, and acquires a cohesive sense of identity and a firm self-consciousness as a class. It has a distinct pool of experiences and interests which throws up novel questions and which the dominant ideology cannot easily answer.

In Marx's view, further, the dominant ideology contains an internal tension. It is universalistic in form, but particularistic in content. As such it is precariously structured, and can be subverted by providing its general form with a different content. For example, the dominant ideology in the bourgeois society invokes the principle of equality to legitimise the latter. Although it defines equality to mean the formal equality of rights, its critic may ask why it should be so narrowly conceived, and go on to define it broadly to include the equality of opportunity and even the equal right to live fulfilling lives. As Marx puts it, the bourgeois weapons can be 'turned against' the bourgeois society itself.

In Marx's view the dominant ideology contains an internal tension also because the dominant class cannot itself live up to it. He gives several examples. The dominant ideology talks of putting the national interest above the sectional; yet the bourgeoisie freely ignore the national interest when their own so requires it. Again, the dominant ideology talks of the minimal government and individual liberty; and yet the bourgeoisie clamour for a strong government and extensive restrictions on individual liberty when threatened by social unrest. Again, the dominant ideology preaches the virtues of a happy family; yet the bourgeoisie freely break up their own. And it glorifies the ethic of hard work; and yet the bourgeoisie themselves rarely abide by it. In Marx's view the ever-widening gap between the ideology and the conduct of the bourgeoisie eventually shows up the former for what it is, a form of 'cheap moralising', a body of allegedly universal principles which are only meant for others. Far from thinking that the dominant ideology is all-powerful as is sometimes argued by his commentators, Marx was misled by his dialectical logic and the materialist epistemology into believing that the dominant ideology is hollow and exposed with relative ease.[15] He could not understand how the bourgeois ideology could hold sway when the organised working class threatened its material supremacy. Having fiercely rejected 'idealism', Marx failed to appreciate fully the power of ideas not, or insufficiently, grounded in the material relations of production.

IV

Marx argues that in the capitalist society the hiatus between the lived and the real world widens considerably. This is so because, in addition to the ideological constitution of the lived world, the very character of the real world is such that even without the help of ideology it appears very different from what it really is. It is a universal feature of reality that a thing often is not what it appears to be. A stick appears bent in water, but in fact it is not. The sun appears to go round the earth, but the truth is the opposite. The air we breathe appears simple, but in reality consists of very different elements. For Marx what is true of the natural world is true also of the social.

The essence and appearance are not uniformly divergent in all societies. The pre-capitalist society had a greater degree of transparency. Under feudalism, for example, a serf worked on his lord's land for a specific period, and knew when he worked for himself and when for another man. The capitalist society is very different. It is so structured that the essence and appearance part company to a historically unprecedented degree. The phenomenal reality not only makes the inner reality 'invisible', but even presents it in a form 'the direct opposite' of what it really is. As Marx puts it,[16]

> The final pattern of economic relations as seen on the surface, in their real existence and consequently in the conceptions by which the bearers and agents of these relations seek to understand them, is very much different from, and indeed quite the reverse of, their inner but concealed essential pattern and the conception corresponding to it.

The capitalist society is characterised by several distinctive features, such as the commodity production, wage labour, competition and the absence of conscious social control over the process of production. Since the producers are separated and atomised they can only be related by the acts of exchange, that is by means of the commodities. Among the isolated men their products become their sole bonds. Since men do not collectively control them, the commodities acquire autonomy and behave like 'independent beings endowed with life' and capable of 'entering into relation with one another'.[17] The relations between men are mediated by the commodities, whereas those between the latter appear direct and unmediated by men. It appears therefore as if the exchange value of a commodity were its natural and not a socially derived property. Gold appears inherently more expensive than potatoes, and a table inherently worth a certain sum of money. In this way a definite social relation between men 'assumes in their eyes the fantastic form of a relation between things', and gives rise to what Marx calls commodity fetishism. The commodity fetishism 'has its origin . . . in the peculiar social character of the labour that produces them', and is inherent in capitalism. The reification occurs in the other areas as well. Rent seems to 'grow out of the soil', money seems to 'generate value and yield interest, much as it is an attribute of pear-trees to bear peas', the machines seem to have the miraculous property of producing wealth, and gold seems to have the natural ability to act as a universal medium of circulation.[18]

In Marx's view the rupture between the appearance and reality characterises also the wage contract between the capitalist and the worker, the basis of the capitalist society. The contract has 'three moments', namely 'the subjects', the 'objects' and the 'act' of exchange itself.[19] It appears as a relationship between two equally independent and self-determining individuals. Further, each 'serves the other in order to serve himself' and seems to be involved in a relationship of strict 'reciprocity'. Their relationship appears as an exchange of equivalent values in which no one seems to have taken a 'one-sided advantage' of another. Finally, it appears to be free and uncoerced. 'No one seizes hold of another's property by force. Each divests himself of his property voluntarily.'

All this occurs only on the surface, 'beneath which, however, in the depths entirely different processes go on, in which this apparent individual equality and liberty disappear'.[20] First, the two parties are not equal. One of them owns nothing and, unless he wishes to starve, is entirely at the mercy of the other. Second, there is no exchange of equivalents for, if the employer paid the full price of labour, he could make no profit. Their apparently equal relation 'extinguishes every trace of the division of the working day into necessary labour and surplus labour, into paid and unpaid labour'. The relation between the capitalist and the worker appears to be of exactly the same kind as that between the buyers and sellers of other commodities. In each case the buyer gives a certain sum of money, and the seller an article or a service. This apparent similarity of form hides the fact that the exchange between the capitalist and the worker is fundamentally unequal, and involves a net transfer of value from the latter to the former. Finally, the relations between the capitalist and the worker are neither voluntary nor between two individuals. They 'are in reality mediated' by the classes. They occur between those who own the means of production and those who own nothing but their labour power. To fail to see this 'basic precondition', which makes the acts of exchange necessary in the first instance and persists as their 'continuing presupposition' is to fail to grasp the real nature of these acts which 'conceived by themselves are pure abstractions'.[21] Further, the worker is forced to sell his labour because, thanks to his humble social origins, lack of education, etc. he has no other source of income. His *personal* limitations are derived from his social background; that is he is a worker because he belongs to a certain class and has specific 'class characteristics'. This is equally true of the captialist. Hence each meets the other not as a unique individual, but as 'an individual member of a class', as 'a class individual'.

The wage relation conceals the economic reality in other respects as well. The capitalist appears to pay for the worker's labour; in fact, he only pays for the use of his labour power. Again, the capitalist appears to pay the worker from his past savings. In actual fact, his variable capital from which he pays the worker is built up from the latter's own previous labour. Marx observed:[22]

It is his labour of last week, or of last year, that pays for his labour-power this week or this year. The illusion begotten by the intervention of money vanishes immediately if, instead of taking a single capitalist and a single labourer, we take the class of capitalists and the class of labourers as a whole. The capitalist class is constantly giving to the labouring class order-notes, in the form of money, on a portion of the commodities produced by the latter and appropriated by the former. The labourers give these order-notes back just as constantly to the capitalist class, and in this way get their share of their own product.

The surface of the capitalist society then conceals its real nature. The reality of the class is veiled by the appearance of discrete individuals going about the business of earning their living. The reality of exploitation is veiled by the appearance of the individuals exchanging equivalents. The fact that the worker has no choice but to sell his labour to a capitalist is concealed by his formal freedom not to sell his labour. The fact that he has no real choice of employer is concealed by his formal freedom to sell his power to the highest bidder.

The capitalist mode of production, then, necessarily creates a world of 'false appearances' and 'illusions'. Its 'form ... hides its inner core'.[23] And it is the form that is 'reflected in the imagination' of the people and generates inaccurate 'modes of thought'. To be sure, the false appearances and illusions are not deliberately created, but 'arise ... from the relations of production themselves'. Their emergence, however, is not an aberration resulting from a specific form of organising the capitalist society, but 'inevitable' and integral to its very essence. They do not all arise from some single feature of the capitalist mode of production. Some arise from the fact that the production occurs among the atomised and isolated individuals; some from the process of circulation; some from the universal use of money; and some others from the capitalist method of paying its workers. Whatever their sources and modes of origin, the false appearances arise not from subjective misperceptions, but the objective nature of the capitalist mode of production itself. As Maurice Godelier puts it, 'It is not the subject who deceives himself, but *reality* which deceives him.'

By its own dynamics, then, the capitalist society creates a world of 'false appearances'. Ideology is built into the very structure of the phenomenal reality, and is 'directly and spontaneously' reproduced into the human consciousness. This means that a writer who remains confined to the surface of the capitalist society studies only the appearances and misses their essence. Not knowing what causes, sustains and regulates the appearances, he does not know how to deal with them. Further, since he only knows the appearances, he mistakes them for reality and imagines that nothing can be done about them. One cannot criticise what one cannot transcend in thought. Again, he develops the categories of thought which seem to him to adequately conceptualise the 'obvious' and 'incontrovertible' facts of social life. Since these facts pertain to the world of deceptive appearances, his categories and modes of thought are inherently positivist and uncritical. They are as ideological as the appearances they conceptualise. As long as he continues to think in terms of them, he is unable to transcend and evaluate the social order.

Further, the vulgar writer sees around him men and women who define themselves as independent, equal and self-determining individuals engaged in free bargaining, exercising uncoerced choices, exchanging equivalent values and freely determining their lives. The individual *is* the basic unit on the surface of society, and hence the vulgar writer accepts it as the basic premise of his thought. As we saw, for Marx the minimalist conception of the individual is one of the most important vehicles of the capitalist ideology. As long as one accepts and thinks in terms of it, one cannot avoid the entire ideological vocabulary of choice, free bargaining, the equality of individuals, the exchange of equivalents, the minimal government, and so on, upon which the legitimisation of capitalism rests. Within the individualist framework one can, at best, ask for fair wages and social justice, and even these appear to detract from the dignity of the self-made man. In short Marx argues that a vulgar writer cannot avoid accepting the structurally embedded features of capitalism. And in accepting them, he remains firmly imprisoned within its horizon of thought. He not only cannot criticise the bourgeois society, but also cannot say anything that does not directly or indirectly legitimise it.

V

For Marx, then, an uncritical or vulgar student of society cannot avoid becoming its apologist. As we saw earlier, Marx goes further and argues that as long as he remains confined to the surface of society, even a critic cannot avoid becoming its apologist. A vulgar social theorist may be personally very critical of the established social order. However, since his level of inquiry is not sufficiently penetrating and critical, he is unable to realise his critical intentions. There is a hiatus between what he subjectively wishes to, and what his inquiry objectively allows him to say. Since his analysis of the social order is shallow, his criticism of it cannot but be shallow. It either leaves the social structure intact, or unwittingly ends up legitimising it. Marx takes the example of vulgar socialism to show how and why this is so.[24]

The vulgar socialists were deeply concerned about the misery and suffering of the working classes, and explored ways of ending it. Unlike the vulgar bourgeois apologists who interpreted the capitalist society from the bourgeois point of view, the vulgar socialists did so from the workers' point of view. Although their point of view was different, their level of investigation was the same. Like their bourgeois counterparts they remained confined to the surface, and did not probe the 'essence of capitalist production in any way'. Since they had no knowledge of the inner structure and dynamics of capitalism, they were unaware of the real causes of the poverty of the proletariat. They had neither a language in which to formulate a critique of capitalism, nor a clear conception of the alternatives. Not surprisingly they thought within the same framework of assumptions, reasoned in terms of the same categories of thought and deployed the same language of discourse as the bourgeois apologists. They remained 'completely within the bounds of the bourgeois horizon', and their 'whole criticism' was 'restricted within a narrow range'.[25]

In Marx's view their 'handicapped criticism' took one of three forms. First, some of them did little more than attack a particular aspect of capitalism that aroused their indignation, dislike or disapproval. Second, some thought that capitalism was not responsible for its poverty and suffering, and blamed a particular social institution or human failing for its malfunctioning. And third, some condemned and rejected capitalism altogether in favour of an allegedly idyllic primitive society.[26] Marx sometimes calls the first criticism shallow or superficial, the second dogmatic or doctrinaire, and the third abstract. Let us briefly outline each in turn.

Some vulgar socialists attributed the evils of capitalism to the use of money and demanded its abolition, without realising that it was a necessary product of the commodity production which they had left untouched.[27] Marx wryly commented that they were trying to 'retain Catholicism without the Pope'. Some other socialists attacked the financial or interest-bearing capital without, again, attacking the commodity production of which the financial capital was 'one of the consequences'. Marx finds it interesting that the demand for the abolition of the interest-bearing capital was also commonly made by the industrial capitalists and the petty bourgeoisie. In his view this form of vulgar socialism was basically a 'bourgeois' striving 'disguised as socialism'.[28] Some other socialists attacked the unfairness of capitalism and made fair wages their principal demand, but again did not attack the commodity production of which 'wage slavery' was an inseparable part. In Marx's view they were also wrong not to realise that capitalism cannot be regulated by the abstract and indeterminate concept of fairness, and that the demand for fair wages makes no difference to the plight of the ever-expanding army of the unemployed. Some other vulgar socialists attacked greed and class conflict and pleaded for altruism and class harmony, without realising that greed was a necessary product of the capitalist relations of production, and that class conflict was inherent in a society in which one class could promote its interests only by exploiting the other. Marx concludes that the 'superficial socialism' of the vulgar socialists 'hardly deserves the name'.[29] They were all apologists of capitalism not only in the negative sense that their impotent remedies left it intact, but also in the stronger and positive sense that their superficial analysis of it led them to attack not its very structure but only some particular and ultimately insignificant aspect of it.

In Marx's view some vulgar socialists offered what he calls metaphysical or dogmatic criticism of capitalism. They did not examine the actual operation of the capitalist mode of production. Instead, they abstracted specific aspects of it, formulated their concepts, related these in a logically proper manner, arrived at a 'truly rational' form of capitalism, and claimed that although 'in practice' it creates suffering, 'in principle' it was a most desirable economic arrangement. They explained the gap between the principle and the practice in terms of human irrationality, ignorance and the like. In Marx's view Proudhon's socialism was a paradigmatic example of such a metaphysical or idealist approach.

Proudhon was unhappy with the social consequences of capitalism, especially its institutions of competition, the division of labour and exchange. However, he did not examine the manner in which competition operated in the capitalist society, generated monopoly, and so on. Instead he analysed the *concept* of competition, praised its virtues and insisted that, since *logically* the competing men restrain one another, competition can *never* lead to monopoly. He knew that, in fact, the situation was very different, since competition leads to monopoly and does not, in practice, display its alleged theoretical virtues. However, this did not provoke Proudhon to reconsider his abstract approach. Instead he pleaded for 'real' and 'rational' competition, and blamed human ignorance for frustrating its 'true' nature. In more or less the same vein he abstracted the *concept* of the division of labour. He insisted that, in principle, it possessed the virtues of developing social interdependence and individual talents. When he found that, in reality, it crippled men and created an atomised, rather than a genuinely interdependent, society, he again called for a 'truly rational' division of labour and searched for scapegoats.

Marx argues that thanks to his 'wholly metaphysical method of procedure', Proudhon never really examined the reality of the capitalist mode of production. He analysed the abstract concepts of capitalist institutions, but not the institutions themselves. He established purely formal relations between the concepts, constructed an ahistorical image of capitalism, and imagined that he had understood its inner nature. His abstractions bore no relation to the historical reality, and could throw no light on it. As Marx says, Proudhon reduced political economy 'to the slender proportions of a scientific formula; he is the man in search of formulas'. Further, Proudhon's approach was disingenuous. He praised capitalism in the abstract, and ignored its actual consequences. He praised it for what it allegedly could be in principle, but which it never was, nor could be in practice. That is he praised the hypothetical essence of capitalism although, as he himself admitted, its historical existence never conformed to it. He approved of the *idea* of capitalism, and disingenuously extended the approval to the *reality* of it. Marx remarks that Proudhon constantly 'mixes up ideas and things'. Thanks to his idealist manner of analysis, Proudhon committed 'a mistake in method' and remained totally unable to explain capitalism.[30] What is more, since it abstracts and idealises its basic features, Proudhon's socialism does little more than 'eternalise' capitalism. Marx observes that[31]

> fundamentally it only idealises the existing society, takes a picture of it free of shadows and aspires to assert its ideal picture against the reality of this society.

Marx sums up Proudhon's limitations as follows:[32]

> M. Proudhon does not directly state that *bourgeois life* is for him an *eternal truth*; he states it indirectly by deifying the categories which express bourgeois relations in the form of thought . . . Accordingly he

does not rise above the bourgeois horizon . . .

Indeed he does what all good bourgeois do. They all assert that in principle, that is, considered as abstract ideas, competition, monopoly, etc., are the only basis of life, but that in practice they leave much to be desired. They all want competition without the pernicious effects of competition. They all want the impossible, namely, the conditions of bourgeois existence without the necessary consequences of those conditions.

Finally, the third group of vulgar socialists advocated an abstract and indiscriminate rejection of capitalism. According to Marx capitalism develops within a contradictory framework. It produces poverty, wretchedness, physical and mental suffering and alienation; however, it also produces technology, the natural sciences, leisure, art, literature, material comforts, and so on. The bourgeois apologists praise its achievements and ignore its evils; the vulgar socialists under consideration stress its evils and reject its achievements. Even as the former justify capitalism on the basis of its achievements alone, the latter condemn and reject it altogether on the basis of its evils alone. As Marx puts it:[33]

In this respect they share the narrow-mindedness of the economists (although from a diametrically opposite position) for they confuse the *contradictory form* of this development with its content. The latter wish to perpetuate the contradiction on account of its results. The former are determined to sacrifice the fruits which have developed within the antagonistic form, in order to get rid of the contradiction.

Further, under capitalism the economic life acquires a naturalistic character. The social relations between men appear as if they were relations between things, and the socially acquired properties of objects appear as if they were inherent in them. The bourgeois apologist, concerned to present capitalism as natural, finds all this to his advantage, and offers a naturalistic and objectivistic account of it. By contrast the vulgar socialist, concerned to highlight the human suffering, leans towards an idealistic and subjectivist account of capitalism. He insists that the 'real wealth is man', the 'living immediate labour' is the sole source of wealth, the accumulated past labour 'has no value in itself', and that the wealth of a society consists solely in the 'skill' and 'knowledge' of its workers.[34] In his account 'the whole objective world . . . vanishes' and is reduced to the human subject. While the vulgar bourgeois apologist overemphasises the objective elements in production, the vulgar socialist overemphasises the subjective elements.[35] While one stresses only the mediating entities, the other is obsessed with immediacy. While one conceals the role of immediacy or the living labour, the other conceals the part played by mediacy or the accumulated past labour. Both alike insist on the abstract 'identity of capital and labour', one from the standpoint of capital, the other from that of labour. Marx argues that, while the vulgar socialist's extremism is 'quite all right' as an antidote to the 'economic fetishism' of his bourgeois counterpart, it is nevertheless one-sided and unsatisfactory. His biased account leads him to falsify facts, ignore counterevidence and 'sin against science'.

Marx's well-known description of 'crude' or 'vulgar communism' in the *Paris Manuscripts* shows what kind of society results from the vulgar socialists' indiscriminate rejection of capitalism. It is a society which rejects the 'entire world of culture and civilisation', degrades human personality, lacks respect for individuality, is hostile to differences, levels down all men to a preconceived minimum, rejects material comforts, and glorifies the 'unnatural simplicity of the poor and undemanding man'. Marx frequently alludes to the evils of such a society in his later writings as well. He argues that vulgar socialism has a constant tendency to reject 'civilisation' and idealise asceticism. Since the vulgar socialist finds that in the capitalist society the luxury of some is produced and enjoyed at the expense of the basic necessities of others, and since the development of technology is accompanied by poverty and unemployment, he tends to condemn luxuries, material abundance and technology. Thus Ravenston, Hodgskin and others idealised simple life, championed asceticism and even classified all those engaged in producing non-basic goods as unproductive workers. In Marx's view the vulgar socialists turn back the clock of history, and fall 'below' the level of civilisation and culture achieved by the capitalist society. What is more, their allegedly socialist society so offends the workers, whose needs and expectations are shaped by capitalism, that they reject it altogether. Unwittingly the vulgar socialism reinforces capitalism. Its fierce and uncompromising rejection of capitalism has the opposite effect of strengthening people's allegiance to it. Being largely an abstract antithesis of and as one-sided as its enemy, it does not represent a higher stage.

4 HEGEL

Marx's discussion of Hegel is of considerable importance for the understanding of his thoery of ideology. First, it highlights what he takes to be the crucial links between idealism and apologia. Second, since Marx takes Hegel's philosophy to be the paradigm of the philosophical form of thought, his criticism of it is designed to show why, in his view, philosophy as a form of thought is inherently uncritical. Third, Marx thinks that Hegel's manner of theorising is not peculiar to him or to the philosophers in general, but shared by other writers as well. His critique of Hegel therefore became a model of his critique of other writers, especially the classical economists.

I

Hegel's followers were puzzled by many aspects of his philosophy. The most important, from our point of view, was the apparent incompatibility between his 'revolutionary' method and 'conservative' conclusions. Hegel's dialectical method implied, among other things, that nothing in the world is permanent, every form of life and thought is ridden with internal contradictions, history is the story of the progressive self-realisation of the *Geist* and that the forms of consciousness and ways of life are periodically superseded by ones less inadequate to the *Geist*'s rational nature. While the basic thrust of Hegel's method was revolutionary, his doctrines were all almost invariably conservative. For example, according to Hegel Christianity was the highest form of religion possible and a higher religion will not emerge in the future; the Reformation represented the highest stage of Christianity and none higher will ever appear; Hegel's own philosophy represented the most satisfactory form of reconciliation between man and the world and will not be superseded; the constitutional monarchy as it was developing in nineteenth-century Prussia represented, after minor institutional modification, the most rational form of the state; and so on.

The contradiction could, of course, be easily resolved by arguing that Hegel genuinely held that the *Geist* had at last discovered the fully rational and adequate forms of self-realisation and that the modern social, political, religious and other institutions were as good as the human institutions can ever be. The Left Hegelians and even some Right Hegelians found it difficult to believe that Hegel could really hold the view that history had somehow come to an end in his epoch, and that his age represented the pinnacle of perfection.

Accordingly they felt that, since Hegel's conclusions were so obviously at odds with the general thrust of his philosophy, the reasons for them must lie outside it. Rosenkranz distinguished between Hegel as a philosopher and a human being, and suggested that his partiality for the contemporary German society was an understandable human failing. The Left Hegelians were less charitable. In their view Hegel had deliberately drawn conservative conclusions in order to placate the established authority, further his professional career, or out of conservative political inclinations. Accordingly they distinguished between the 'esoteric' and 'exoteric' Hegel, and contended that he had deliberately concealed his revolutionary message and left it to his disciples to spell it out under more propitious circumstances.[1]

Marx was not satisfied with these and other explanations. In his view a great philosopher's inconsistencies cannot be adequately explained in terms of such contingent factors as his personal opinions and professional interests, and must be traced to the basic structure of his thought. He observed:[2]

Also in relation to Hegel it is mere ignorance on the part of his pupils, when they explain one or the other determination of his system by his desire for accommodation and the like . . . It is quite thinkable for a philosopher to fall into one or another apparent inconsistency through some sort of accommodation; he himself may be conscious of it. But what he is not conscious of, is the possibility that this apparent accommodation has its deepest roots in an inadequacy or in an inadequate formulation of his principle itself. Suppose therefore that a philosopher has really accommodated himself, then his pupils must explain *from his inner essential consciouness* that which for *him himself* had the form of an *exoteric consciousness*. In this way, that which appears as progress of conscience is at the same time progress of knowledge. No suspicion is cast upon the particular conscience of the philosopher, but his essential form of consciousness is construed, raised to a definite shape and meaning and in this way also transcended.

Marx examined Hegel's system and concluded that the alleged contradiction between his method and conclusions did not, in fact, exist. In his view Hegel's method was not at all revolutionary as the Right and the Left Hegelians had imagined, but profoundly conservative. The dialectic was, in principle, a revolutionary method, but not as Hegel had defined it. He observed that 'despite its thoroughly negative and critical *appearance*', Hegel's dialectic contained 'as a germ, a potentiality a secret the uncritical positivism' of his doctrines.[3] For Marx this was so because Hegel had conceived and defined it within the framework of his idealism. And since his idealism was inherently uncritical and positivist, so was the dialectic. Accordingly Marx undertook a detailed analysis of Hegel's idealism to show how it was inherently positivist, and emasculated the radical character of the dialectical method.

II

As Marx undestands him, Hegel aims to provide a general theory of the world. For Hegel the world is prima facie strange and puzzling in the sense that there is no obvious reason why nature and man should exist at all, and why the human history has occurred the way it has. Hence, argues Hegel, the human mind, which is inherently rational and demands to see the point of everything, feels alienated from the world. In his view philosophy, which represents the highest form of rational thought, can alone meet the fundamental demands of the human reason by developing a general theory capable of demonstrating the necessity of the world and the events occurring in it.

For Marx Hegel is an idealist. He believes that the particular entities within the world of experience are not real, and have 'no veritable being'. When analysed they turn out to be nothing more than the embodiments of universal qualities or what Hegel calls universals. The universals are not sense-objects, but products of thought, 'thought-objects' or 'ideas'. Accordingly Hegel concludes that thought or idea is the ultimate reality. As he puts it, 'The proposition that the *finite is ideal* constitutes idealism.' He goes on, 'Every philosophy is essentially an idealism or at least has idealism for its principle, and the question then is only how far this principle is actually carried out.'[4] Marx observes that, like the other forms of idealism, Hegel's idealism entails what he calls the 'realism of universals', and assigns 'independent existence' to ideas.

Marx argues that, as an idealist, Hegel is concerned to abstract the general features shared in common by the particular entities.[5] He takes a specific class of entities, abstracts and analyses their commonly shared properties, and arrives at what he calls the concept of the class of entities in question. He similarly analyses other classes of entities, and encapsulates their common features in his concepts of them. Having arrived at the vast range of concepts which between them cover the entire range of experience, Hegel analyses them yet further. He abstracts their commonly shared properties, progressively subsumes the narrower under more general concepts, and arrives at the most general concept in which the rest of the concepts are implicitly contained. He calls such a general concept the Absolute Idea, the Idea or simply the Concept.

Unlike most of his predecessors, Marx goes on, Hegel takes the fact of change seriously and aims to explain it. He cannot consistently locate the source of movement outside the Concept, as he would then have a dualistic system with all its attendant difficulties. Hegel therefore locates the movement within the Concept itself, and maintains that the latter is self-moving; that is Hegel interprets the ultimate reality not as substance but as self-moving Subject or Spirit. In Marx's view Hegel's Concept or *Geist* represents a union of Spinoza's Substance and Fichte's Ego. Hegel is dissatisfied with Spinoza's Substance because it is static and lacks inner differentiation; and he is critical of Fichte's Ego or Self-Consciousness because it is entirely spiritual and excludes nature. Hegel's *Geist* incorporates their insights and avoids their limitations.[6]

Having arrived at the concept of the *Geist* and an elaborate framework of logically interrelated categories, Hegel returns to the world of experience with a twofold objective. First, the *Geist* is abstract or entirely ideal in nature, and must be given content or concrete existence. And second, Hegel aims to answer the questions that had inspired his whole enterprise and demonstrate the rationality of the world. In Marx's view Hegel's two objectives coincide and point in the same direction. To give the *Geist* a worldly content *is* to show that the world is rational; that is to show that the *Geist* requires a particular content as a matter of inner necessity *is* to demonstrate that the content in question is rationally necessary. By arguing that the *Geist* creates and realises itself in the world, Hegel both explains the latter and gives the *Geist* a content.

Hegel's explanation of the world consists in tracing the *Geist*'s development. The *Geist* 'externalises' or 'embodies' itself in nature and creates the progressively higher forms of being culminating in man. Hegel's account of nature begins with matter, which is pure exteriority and moved by attraction and repulsion, proceeds to the living organisms which are individuated, self-centred, internally self-differentiated and represent an inseparable unity of form and content, and ends with the emergence of man. Within history Hegel similarly begins with the primitive forms of social life, and shows how the *Geist*, finding them inadequate vehicles of self-realisation, goes on to create the progressively higher forms of social life until it arrives at the modern age which fully embodies its rational nature. Marx seems to think that Hegel's account of the world rests on four basic principles. First, whatever exists, when purged of its accidental features, is a necessary moment in the *Geist*'s progress towards self-realisation. Second, each form of consciousness or way of life represents the highest possible level of rationality possible at the relevant historical stage. Third, everything — forms of being, consciousness and social life — contains an internal contradiction in that it is both finite and a vehicle of the infinite, and must eventually go under. Fourth, the development of the world corresponds to the ontological require-ments of the *Geist*, and follows a logical pattern.

For Marx, then, Hegel's philosophy is constructed in two stages. First, he 'abstracts' the universals and progressively 'ascends' to the Concept. Second, he then progressively 'descends' to the world and both explains it and gives the universals a worldly reality. In Marx's view Hegel's *Logic* shows how he executes the first stage of his inquiry, and his philosophies of nature, state and history show how he executes the second. Marx summarises Hegel's two stages in three remarkable paragraphs. They obviously caricature Hegel, but give a fairly clear idea of what Marx imagined to be the basic structure of his philo-sophical procedure.[7]

If from real apples, pears, strawberries and almonds I form the general idea '*Fruit*', if I go further and *imagine* that my abstract idea 'Fruit', derived from real fruit, is an entity existing outside me, is indeed the *true essence* of the pear, the apple, etc., then in the *language of speculative* philosophy — I am declaring that '*Fruit*' is the '*Substance*' of the pear, the apple, the almond, etc. I am saying, therefore, that to be a pear is not essential to the pear, that to be an apple is not essential to the apple; that what is essential to these things is not their real existence, perceptible to the senses, but the essence that I have abstracted from them and then foisted on them, the essence of my idea — 'Fruit'. I therefore declare apples, pears, almonds, etc., to be mere forms of existence, *modi*, of 'Fruit'.

If apples, pears, almonds and strawberries are really nothing but '*the* Substance', '*the* Fruit', the question arises: Why does 'the Fruit' manifest itself to me sometimes as an apple, sometimes as a pear, sometimes as an almond? Why this *semblance of diversity* which so obviously contradicts my speculative conception of *Unity*, '*the* Substance', '*the* Fruit'?

This, answers the speculative philosopher, is because '*the* Fruit' is not dead, undifferentiated, motionless, but a living, self-differentiating, moving essence. The diversity of the ordinary fruits is significant not only for *my* sensuous understanding, but also for '*the* Fruit' itself and for speculative reason. The different ordinary fruits are different manifestations of the life of the '*one* Fruit'; they are crystallisations of '*the* Fruit' itself. Thus in the apple '*the* Fruit' gives itself an apple-like existence, in the pear a pear-like existence. We must therefore no longer say, as one might from the standpoint of the Substance: a pear is '*the* Fruit', an apple is '*the* Fruit', an almond is '*the* Fruit', but rather '*the* Fruit' presents itself as a pear, '*the* Fruit' presents itself as an apple, '*the* Fruit' presents itself as an almond; and the differences which distinguish apples, pears and almonds from one another are the self-differentiations of '*the* Fruit' and make the particular fruits different members of the life-process of '*the* Fruit'. Thus '*the* Fruit' is no longer an empty undifferentiated unity; it is oneness as *allness*, as '*totality*' of fruits, which constitute an '*organically linked series of members*'. In every member of that series '*the* Fruit' gives itself a more developed, more explicit existence.

III

Marx finds Hegel's philosophy wholly unsatisfactory. His criticisms of it are not easy to follow, nor always clearly stated. Basically they are three. First, Hegel's conceptual realism is an untenable doctrine. Second, Hegel's philosophical procedure is fundamentally mistaken, and unable to deliver the promised results. And third, Hegel's idealism is ideological or apologetic in nature. Since the last criticism is the most relevant to our discussion, we shall concentrate on it.

Marx rejects Hegel's conceptual realism on several grounds, not all of which are clearly stated, defended or persuasive. In his view the universals are nothing but the 'predicates of general description' of particular entities.[8] They do not and cannot exist independently of the latter. We know from experience that all existence is 'determinate', that only the particular entities exist, and that we do not encounter qualities subsisting by themselves or occupying an independent realm of their own. The so-called universals are nothing more than the qualities of determinate entities from which they are abstracted. They are mere abstractions or 'thought-objects', and by definition cannot enjoy an independent and autonomous existence. It is therefore wrong to say that the particular entities 'embody' the universals, as this involves treating the universals as independent subjects. What is more, Hegel's conceptual realism leads to the paradoxical conclusion that the thought is real but the man who thinks is not, or, at any rate, that the thought is more real than the thinker!

Marx argues that, although Hegel treats the universals as subjects in their relation to the particular entities, he cannot consistently maintain the view. He realises that they cannot be independent subjects, and accordingly introduces the *Geist* or Pure Spirit or Consciousness as their bearer. Marx observes:[9]

> Precisely because Hegel starts from the predicates of the general description instead of from the real *ens* (subject), and since nevertheless, there has to be a bearer of these qualities, the mystical idea becomes this bearer.

Hegel, however, has not proved and cannot prove the existence of the *Geist*, whom he is forced to introduce *only* because the universals need a subject. In other words, Hegel simply assumes that the *Geist* exists, and thus his whole system rests on a 'dogma', on a hypothetical subject only introduced to get him out of a difficulty.

Again, since for Hegel only the universals are real, and the particular entities are nothing but the diverse combinations of them, he is unable to explain how one entity differs from another. He lacks the principle of individuation, and cannot make the transition from the universal to the particular. Marx takes Hegel's category of organism. In his view it was a 'great' insight on Hegel's part to have treated the state as an organism whose parts were all closely connected.[10] Now Hegel treats not only the state but also the animals, men and several other entities as organisms. Marx asks to know how the state as an organism differs from the other organisms. As he puts it, 'the same statement can be made with the same truth about the *animal* as about the political organism. By what, then, is the *animal* organism distinguished from the *political*?'[11] In Marx's view Hegel has no answer, for he was only interested in the general idea of the organism and did not develop 'the specific idea of the political constitution'. Hegel abstracted the formal features shared in common by all organisms, and formulated the concept of organism. By its very nature such a concept is too general and abstract to capture the specificity or the distinctive organic features of the state. Thanks to Hegel's method, which is unable to appreciate the 'specific' nature of an entity, 'No bridge has been built *whereby one could pass from the general idea of organism to the specific idea of the organism of the state or the political constitution*, and no such bridge can ever be built.'[12]

Marx argues that, in order to individuate the specific nature of the political organism, Hegel should have analysed the nature of the state, examined the *specific* form of interdependence between its various institutions, and elucidated the distinctive character of its organic unity. By abstracting the minimally common features shared by all organisms and formulating the idea of organism in general, Hegel made it impossible for himself to explain the specificity of different types of organism. In Marx's view, what is true of Hegel's concept of organism is true also of his other concepts. To Hegel 'It is immaterial whether atom or personality is adduced to explain "being-for-itself", or the solar system, magnetism of sexual love as an example of attraction.'[13] Hegel does not see that these are all 'totally different things, and it is just this that constitutes their determinateness'. For Marx Hegel's idealism can only account for instantiation not individuation, and is inherently unequipped to deal with the individuality of an institution, a form of consciousness, a way of life or an historical epoch. As he puts it, in Hegel's philosophy the historical institutions and ways of life remain 'uncomprehended because they are not grasped in their *specific* character'.[14]

In Marx's view Hegel's conceptual realism creates yet further difficulties. As we saw, Hegel first developed an abstract set of logical categories, and then went on to give them content or worldly existence. Marx cannot see why Hegel should want to do this. If the ideal alone is real, as Hegel's idealism maintains, then the universals are already real and cannot need a worldly embodiment. What is more, the finite has 'no veritable being' and cannot, by definition, confer reality upon the universals embodied in it.[15] For Marx Hegel's entire enterprise is self-contradictory. Again, Marx argues that since, as Hegel himself acknowledges, the conceptual forms are in themselves abstract and need content, there is no reason whatever why he should have first broken up the unity of form and content, abstracted the form, and then reunited it with its content. On Hegel's own testimony the form and content are inseparable, and cannot be understood in dissociation from each other. It is therefore wrong to abstract the form, analyse it by itself, impose it on its content and call this an explanation of the latter. Marx observes, 'Hegel separates *content* and *form*, *being in itself* and *being for itself* and brings in the latter externally as a *formal* element . . . The separation of the being *in itself* and the being *for itself* is abstract mysticism.'[16]

In Marx's view the idealist separation of the form and content, the initial abstraction of the form and its subsequent imposition on the relevant content, is the source of most of Hegel's difficulties. Hegel approaches the world with a set of abstract categories. His concern is to show that everything within experience can be subsumed under or, what comes to the same thing, shown to be a worldly realisation of one or more of them. By means of a more or less superficial analysis of the different aspects of the empirical world, he brings them to a point where they neatly fit into his categories. Marx does not say that Hegel does not study empirical reality. On some occasions Hegel studies the world in great detail, on other occasions he does not. However, even when he does, his concern is to analyse his subject matter so that it can be subsumed under the relevant category. His analysis therefore has a predetermined goal, namely to 'find an empirical existent' for one of his categories. Marx observes that Hegel[17]

does not develop his thinking from the object, but expounds the object in accordance with a thinking which is cut and dried — already formed and fixed in the abstract sphere of logic . . . The soul of objects . . . is cut and dried, predestined, prior to its body, which is really mere appearance.

Hegel is primarily interested in somehow subsuming his subject matter under one of his logical categories; that it fits into it only with the greatest of difficulty and only after considerable distortion does not worry him much. Marx observes that 'not the logic of the matter but the matter of logic' is Hegel's overriding concern. As a result his logical categories 'in no way really ripen to true social reality'. They are already fixed, and it is the world that is expected and required to conform to them. The infinitely complex world does not easily fit into his categories. And therefore Hegel dismisses parts of it as contingent or 'accidental', 'quarrels with his subject matter', and often gives a misleading account of it.[18]

Further, since Hegel does not critically examine his subject matter, but more or less accepts it 'just as it is' and subsumes it under appropriate categories, the latter are crammed with crude content.[19] Hegel takes over a familiar experience or institution and invests it with a new philosophical form and significance, but does little to analyse its real nature and structure. As Marx puts it, there is a good deal of 'transubstantiation' in Hegel, but not much analysis. Hegel's analysis is elegant and dazzling in its form, but poor and superficial in its content. For example, in the course of his analysis of the Greek city-states, Hegel observed that the development of the *Geist* required differentiation and that, since the Greek states could not provide it, they had to go under. Marx argues that Hegel did not analyse the Greek social and economic life, nor explain its internal contradictions, nor show who demanded subjective rights and spearheaded the movement for differentiation. Hegel simply imposed on the Greek city-states a philosophical pattern and goal and imagined that this by itself offered an explanation of their historical development. When therefore he claimed to have demonstrated the necessity of the decline of the Greek city-states, he was being disingenuous, for the necessity 'is not derived from their own essence, still less critically established', but only asserted at the abstract philosophical level.[20] In the ultimate analysis, says Marx, Hegel does not *explain* their decline; he only gives it a 'philosophical testimonial'.[21]

In Marx's view, then, Hegel's whole philosophical procedure is fundamentally mistaken and his claim to demonstrate the rationality of the world and the events occurring therein rests on a philosophical 'trick'. As we saw, Hegel starts, and cannot but start, with the empirical world which he studies in more or less detail and with different degrees of rigour. He abstracts its essential features, relates them in ways he considers logically valid and formulates the Concept. He then deduces the empirical world from the Concept. In his writings Hegel suppresses the first step, namely one by which he had arrived at the Concept, and presents only the second step, namely one in which he deduces the world from the Concept. His philosophy therefore *appears* to deduce the world from a higher reality, and creates the 'deep mystical impression' of saying 'something mystical and profound'.[22] In actual fact the world is only deduced from itself, albeit in an indirect and circuitous manner, and is therefore given no foundation at all, let alone a transcendental one. Hegel's so-called explanation of the world is not an explanation at all, but a mere 'paraphrase', a restatement of the *explanandum* in a different and mystifying language.

Instead of explaining the world, Hegel's philosophical method mystifies it. Since he deduces the world from the Concept, the latter becomes the subject of which the world is a mere predicate. Hegel is therefore constantly forced to reverse the relationship between the subject and the predicate, and to mystify reality. For example, he notices that the monarch *has* the last word in a monarchically organised state. He abstracts this empirical fact, turns it into a concept, and asserts that the monarch *is* the last word, the final expression and realisation of the concept of ultimate determination or sovereignty! Similarly, instead of saying that the personality is a characteristic of a person, and the subjectivity of a subject, Hegel is led to say that the person is the mode of existence of personality, and that the subject is the self-realisation of subjectivity. Again, he notices that every independent state possesses sovereignty. He abstracts this property, calls it a universal, and remarks that the state is the embodiment of the concept of sovereignty. By constantly reversing the relationship between the subject and the predicate, Hegel is forced to populate the world with ghostly entities.[23]

Marx's strongest objection to Hegel's philosophical procedure is that it leads to the positivist endorsement of the *status quo*. For Hegel the whole of human history is the story of the *Geist*'s self-realisation. He is therefore required to argue that whatever occurred in history is an 'embodiment of the Idea' and 'a vehicle of *Geist*'. No doubt, it is eventually superseded; however, while it lasts, it represents for Hegel the highest level of rationality possible at the time. Thanks to his idealism, Hegel is forced to accept uncritically the changes as they occur, and assert that they are all rational. He is unable to argue that a particular way of life or social institution might be utterly irrational and without any historical significance. Marx observes:[24]

The inevitable outcome of this is that an *empirical existent* is *uncritically* accepted as the actual truth of the idea; for it is not a question of bringing empirical existence to its truth, but of bringing truth to an empirical existent, and so what lies to hand is expounded as a *real* element of the idea.

According to Marx, then, Hegel's idealism requires him to glorify whatever exists. By definition it requires him to glorify the present. For Hegel the contemporary social, religious, political and other institutions represent a necessary stage in the self-realisation of the *Geist*, and are rational. They may eventually be superseded, but while they last, they are beyond criticism. Hegel is not, however, satisfied with this. As we saw, he goes further and maintains that the contemporary institutions are not only rational, but represent the perfect realisation of the *Geist* and mark the end of history. He not only justifies but deifies the contemporary society.

Marx seems to think that the explanation of Hegel's deification of the present cannot lie in his idealism, since the latter only requires and indeed permits him to say that the present stage in history is higher than its predecessors, and not that it is the highest possible. For Marx the explanation of Hegel's *uncritical* positivism is to be found in his *uncritical* idealism. His idealism suffers not only from the defects characteristic of all idealism, but also from the additional ones arising from his uncritical view of the *Geist*.

For Hegel the *Geist* is rational in nature. In saying that the *Geist* progressively realises itself in history, he intends to say that history represents a progressively higher realisation of Reason. For Hegel Reason is 'divine' in nature. As he says, the divine and human reason are not two different kinds of reason; there is only the divine reason in which the human reason participates. No doubt, Reason becomes conscious of itself in man; however, it is not a human capacity. It works through human passions but is in no way influenced by them; it has its own purposes which are not amenable to and in no way altered by human needs. Marx examines the way Hegel defines the divine Reason. Hegel is obviously not a privy to the divine mind. He must therefore interpret it and give it content on some other basis than a privileged access to God. In the ultimate analysis Hegel could only interpret the divine Reason on the basis of his own. Marx argues that, if we examined the institutions Hegel deified, we would find that they were all part of his own society. Hegel glorified philosophy, and was a philosopher himself; he glorified Christianity and it was his own religion; he glorified Protestantism and was himself a Protestant; he favoured the constitutional monarchy, and one was already developing in Germany. The harmony of views between Hegel and God was too striking to be a mere coincidence.

Marx argues that Hegel had to give some content to the divine Reason, as otherwise it could not provide the required criterion of historical evaluation. Hegel could only derive the content from a specific way of life, and it had to be a way of life of which he approved and whose standards of rationality he could defend. He could not obviously define the divine Reason in terms he disapproved. Not surprisingly he turned to his own society which he liked and approved.

Marx is not clear as to how in his view Hegel derived his standard of Reason. On different occasions he traces it to his historical epoch, society and class. For the most part he seems to think that Hegel derived it from his society. Even as Hegel abstracted the common features of the particular entities and set up a realm of self-subsistent universals, he abstracted and turned the reason of the members of his society into a transcendental principle. Like the rest of us, Hegel was profoundly shaped by his society, whose values and standards of rationality he had imbibed and found persuasive and indeed self-evident. It is true, says Marx, that Hegel did criticise some of the contemporary practices and institutions. However, in his view, Hegel did so on the basis of the standard of rationality immanent in most of them. In short, Hegel's view of Reason was an idealised version of the one dominant in his society. He unwittingly 'inflated' the reason of the members of a specific class of a specific society in a specific historical epoch to the status of the divine Reason. Or, what comes to the same thing, he reduced the divine Reason to the limited proportions of the socially and historically limited reason of a nineteenth-century German bourgeois.

Hegel's view of Reason then was really the idealisation of the contemporary view of reason. He judged the previous historical epochs by such a biased standard and reached the predictable conclusion that the nearer they approached his own, the higher they were. Since Hegel judged his own age by a standard ultimately derived from it, he reached the obvious conclusion that his age represented the highest possible realisation of Reason and constituted the 'absolute rational truth'. Hence for Hegel the modern monogamous family was the only fully rational way to organise the family; the modern bourgeois institution of property was the highest form of property, and poverty was a regrettable but unavoidable fact of life; the modern state represented the 'essential structure' of the state; and so on. Indeed he even presented such unfortunate current dualisms as those between the civil society and the state, and the egoistic private individual and the public-spirited citizen, as wholly rational and inherent in the human condition.[25]

For Hegel history came to an end with his epoch because his epoch was, from the very beginning, assumed to be its ultimate end. Since his standard of rationality was derived from an uncritical acceptance of the present, he was unable either to criticise the present or objectively to understand the past epochs in their own terms. For him the past was merely a stepping stone to the present; the present marked the end of history; and the future was only an infinite continuation of the present. Like all ideologists Hegel degraded the past and the future, and eternalised the present.

Marx argues that since Hegel's view of Reason was grounded in and shaped by his uncritical idealism, it was not and could never be a 'negative', 'critical' and 'revolutionary' principle as the Left Hegelians had maintained; it was inherently positivist, uncritical and conservative. It was designed to reconcile man to the world, and not to arouse in him a sense of indignation at its sorry state.[26] Since Hegel took a conservative and justificatory view of Reason, he took a conservative and uncritical view of criticism. For him the goal of criticism was not to expose unreason and evil, but to uncover the rationality assumed to be inherent in every form of life.[27] Hegel's criticism was therefore directed, not at the prevailing way of life, but the alleged misunderstanding of those who complain against it. Thanks to his idealism, Hegel was concerned not to change the world but only to reinterpret it. In Marx's view Hegel's idealist and positivist conception of Reason simply did not allow him to develop a genuine concept of criticism.[28]

IV

Marx argues that Hegel's uncritical idealism profoundly emasculated his dialectical method. In his view the Left Hegelians were right to stress that the dialectic was *in principle* a revolutionary method in the sense that while acknowledging the rationality of what exists, it also recognises its limitations and eventual supersession. However, they were wrong not to see that *in Hegel's hands* it had become an uncritical and positivist method. Marx goes on to show how Hegel's uncritical idealism informed his views of the nature and scope of the dialectic as well as such crucial structural concepts as opposition, mediation and the negation of the negation.

Marx argues that, despite its apparent fierceness, Hegel's dialectic is essentially timid. Although Hegel stresses the creative role of conflict and even gives it an ontological status, he takes a basically conservative and quietist view of it. He assigns it a limited role, and so defines it that it can *always* be resolved. Hegel's society is 'spoiling for a fight but is too afraid of bruises to engage in a real fight'.[29] In Marx's view Hegel's idealism does not allow him to develop the full dialectic of conflict. Being an idealist, Hegel reduces all entities to the Absolute Idea. The conflict is therefore between the two moments of the Idea, and not between two hostile entities, with the result that the Spirit passes smoothly through its self-generated oppositions without ever being confronted with a truly hostile entity. In Marx's view this is clearly seen in Hegel's analysis of the conflict between man and nature, for Marx the basis of the dialectic in history. Since Hegel reduces nature to consciousness, the conflict occurs only *within* consciousness. It is therefore an extremely tame phenomenon and lacks genuine antagonism. According to Marx this is also the case with nearly all of Hegel's contradictions. One of the conflicting entities is reduced to the other and deprived of its independence and identity. Hence it is unable to come into its own and put up a genuine fight. Hegel's dialectic is emasculated by his idealism and lacks a revolutionary potential. Hence Marx's search for its 'rational kernel' and his adoption not of Hegel's dialectical method as a whole, but only its 'rational' essence.

Marx is uneasy also with the lack of futuristic perspective in Hegel's dialectic. For Hegel philosophy is primarily concerned to demonstrate the necessity of and reconcile the human mind to the world as it exists and has evolved. It is therefore concerned entirely with the past and the present, the latter constituting the absolute horizon of knowledge. Hegel did, no doubt, make several remarks about the future direction of the world's development, as when he said that America might become the future seat of the world spirit. However, these were incidental and not fully integrated into his general perspective. Consequently, his dialectical method remained an exclusively explanatory device unequipped to anticipate the future.

Marx took a very different view of the nature and role of philosophy. Even before he dismissed philosophy as a form of intellectual masturbation, he insisted on the unity of thought and action, and argued that, when confronted with the irrational world, philosophy, the epitome of reason, is compelled by its inner logic not merely to interpret but also to change it. Clearly the world cannot be changed without some conception of the future, conceived not abstractly and ahistorically in the manner of the Utopian writers, but as it organically grows out of the present. For Marx a dialectically orientated study of society must therefore enable us not only to understand the present, but also to anticipate the future by elucidating the trends implicit in the present. In his view the futuristic perspective is inherent in the dialectical method, and Hegel was wrong to ignore it. For a dialectician the present is inherently unstable. It is in the process of ceasing to be itself, and both is and is not what it appears to be. Becoming is not incidental to being, but its necessary dimension. Even as the present contains the past, it also contains the future. Hence no society or historical epoch can be understood without taking into account *both* what it was and is likely to become. Sartre is right to describe Marx's method as a 'progressive-regressive method', seeking to illuminate the present by performing a series of intellectual oscillations backwards into the past and forwards into the future.

The addition of a new temporal dimension to the dialectic meant that unlike Hegel, Marx was able to see the future as holding new prospects and possibilities. While, for Hegel, history effectively comes to an end with the Reformation, the subsequent eras being largely concerned with the realisation of its central principle in different areas of life, for Marx history does not even *begin* until after the overthrow of capitalism, the mother of the Reformation. Again, Marx sees communism as representing 'absolute becoming' and holding unexpected possibilities. And despite his occasional arrogant remarks, he did not view his thought as marking the last word in man's intellectual history, and frequently outlined problems which, he hoped, would be solved by future thinkers. While Hegel's *Phenomenology* closes with a chapter on Absolute Knowledge, Marx doubts the coherence of the concept of absolute truth.

In Marx's view Hegel's uncritical idealism shaped not only his general conception of the nature and scope of the dialectic, but also its basic categories. We shall take Marx's analyses of three of them, namely opposition, mediation and the negation of the negation.

In a couple of highly compressed, complex and confusing paragraphs in the *Critique of Hegel's Philosophy of Right*, Marx observes that things can be opposites in one of the three ways.[30] First, the opposites share a common essence; for example, the North and South Poles, or the male and the female. Both North and South Poles are poles; 'their *essence* is identical'. In the same way both female and male sex are of 'one species, one essence, that is human essence'. In each case the two entities involved are 'opposed aspects of one essence, the differentiation of one *essence* at the height of its *development*'. They are '*distinct* attributes' of a common essence.

Second, the opposites have mutually exclusive essences; for example, the pole and non-pole, or the human and non-human gender. Unlike the first pair of opposites where the difference is one of 'existence', the difference here is one of 'essence'. Marx called these 'real', 'actual' or 'true' extremes or antitheses. His concept of essential opposition is rather confused. Sometimes he has in mind entities which have *nothing* in common, for example, the pole and the non-pole. Since they have nothing in common, they are mutually indifferent. It is therefore difficult to see how they can conflict. On other occasions Marx has in mind entities with *opposed* or *mutually exclusive* essence. Here each entity is so constituted that it can only exist and develop by destroying the other. The opposition between the civil society and the state and, as we shall see, between the bourgeoisie and the proletariat is of this type.

Third, the opposites are inseparable aspects of a common entity, but *appear* as opposites because each abstracts one aspect of it and presents this in a partial and one-sided manner; for example, the opposition between idealism and materialism, the individual and general interest, or egoism and altruism. These are not genuine entitites but 'hypostatised abstractions', and their opposition is not real but a product of misconception.

The opposites of the third type differ from those of the first because they are not genuine differentiations of a common essence, but its one-sided interpretations, and differ from those of the second because they do not have mutually exclusive essences. Take, for example, the opposition between idealism and materialism. Marx takes the view that as man increasingly shapes nature in the light of his needs, the world of nature becomes permeated by human consciousness. It ceases to be merely material and becomes a unity of matter and spirit. Idealism emphasises the role of consciousness and views it as the sole reality; materialism singles out the material aspect for exclusive emphasis; and the two set themselves up as irreconcilable opposites. Each generates and accentuates the other. Since materialism emphasises the material aspect of reality, it provokes its opposite, namely idealism. Once it provokes idealism, the very existence of the latter gives materialism its rationale, and keeps it in being. Their opposition, however, is not genuine, and only arises from the fact that each misunderstands the nature of reality and equates one aspect of it with the whole.

Marx maintains that the three types of opposition require distinct modes of resolution. In the first type of opposition, the entities involved are differentiations of a common essence. Their opposition occurs within a shared framework, and is therefore necessarily moderate. Further, their opposition brings out the inner potentialities of each, and is therefore beneficial to both. Finally, since they share a common essence, the mediation between them is possible; and since they are interdependent and each 'calls for' the other, the mediation is also necessary.

By contrast, the second type of opposition can never be reconciled. The entities involved are mutually exclusive: 'one infringes upon the other but they do not occupy a common position'. Mediation here is not possible because the entities concerned do not share a common ground, and also because no mediating entity can be found which partakes of the nature of both. Nor, however, is it necessary, since the mediating entities do not complete, complement and call for each other. As Marx puts it:[31]

> Real extremes cannot be mediated precisely because they are real extremes. Nor do they require mediation, for they are opposed in essence. They have nothing in common, they do not need each other; they do not supplement each other. The one does not have in its own bosom, the longing for, the need for, the anticipation of the other.

Real extremes can resolve their conflict only by a fight in which one of them is ultimately victorious. Their conflict is necessary for their 'self-knowledge', their clear perceptions of their true nature, and in the interest of progress. Instead of prematurely terminating their conflict, they are best left to 'form into extremes'.

The third type of opposition requires a very different mode of resolution. Unlike the other two, it is not a genuine opposition, and consequently the extremes involved cannot be taken at their face value. We need to probe below the surface, demonstrate that the extremes are one-sided abstractions, and reassert the true nature of the underlying reality. In so doing, we do not *reconcile* but *dissolve* or eliminate the entities involved. The opposition between idealism and materialism is overcome, not by arbitrating between them, nor by determining their respective merits and weaknesses, but by demonstrating that reality is a dialectical unity of matter and spirit. Similarly, when it is realised that the individual is necessarily a social being, and society nothing more than a network of relationships between individuals, the opposition between the individual and society or between individualism and collectivism disappears.

Marx contends that Hegel did not distinguish the three types of opposition. Indeed, being an idealist he *could not*. As an idealist he viewed the whole of reality as a manifestation of the Absolute Idea, and thus sharing a common essence. Hegel therefore stressed the *'identity* of opposites', not the *'unity* of opposites'. He saw differences only as differentiations, as the 'self-distinction' or manifestations of a single essence, regarded them as 'unimportant', as less 'real', than the identity, and constantly 'suspended' their action. For example, he correctly grasped the unity of production and consumption, for what is produced must be consumed, and nothing can be consumed unless it is produced. But he wrongly stressed only their identity and ignored their differences in orientation and objectives. This prevented him from noticing that the two can and do part company and create the crisis of overproduction. Hegel is interested in 'the dialectical balancing of concepts and not the grasping of real relations'.

Hegel's ontology, then, enabled him to notice only the first type of opposition, namely, one in which the opposed entities share a common essence. In particular it prevented him from recognising the second type of opposition, namely, the opposition of essence or what Marx calls 'essential contradiction'. Marx argues that since Hegel reduced the three types of opposition to the first, he ended up committing 'a threefold error'.

First, he confused the second type of opposition with the first. Consequently he failed to notice that the actual extremes can never be reconciled. Unlike Hegel who thought that *all* extremes share a common essence and can be reconciled, Marx maintained that some extremes 'infringe' upon each other but 'do not occupy a common position', and that their struggle is both inevitable and desirable. This seems to be the logical basis of Marx's theory of class struggle. It was not entirely a coincidence that he first developed his view of the proletariat as the total antithesis of the bourgeoisie in the same work in which he also first developed his conception of essential contradiction. Marx recognises that the capitalist and the proletariat are interdependent, and that their opposition shares some features in common with that between the North and the South Pole, but argues that as the capitalist society develops, the character of the relationship between the two classes changes. Their interests become locked in an irreconcilable conflict, and the existence of one entails the non-existence of the other. What is more, the organised proletariat becomes capable of sustaining society without the controlling presence of the capitalist. At this stage, their opposition belongs to the second type; each infringes upon the other, but they do not share a common essence. We cannot pursue this point further and shall only note that Marx's uncompromising attitude to class struggle is better understood when seen against the background of his logical theory, and that in order to attack (or defend) the former effectively, one needs to attack (or defend) his logical theory, particularly his conception of the 'essential' or 'real' opposition.

Second, Hegel confused the third type of opposition with the first, and thought that it could and should be resolved in the same manner as the latter. For example, he treated the opposition between the individual and society, and between idealism and materialism, as if they were of the same logical type as the first, and failed to see that they are pseudo-oppositions which dissolve when the true nature of the underlying reality is grasped.

Hegel's third error was a product of the first two. Since he confused the last two types of opposition with the first, he did not notice the limits of mediation. For example, when he was confronted with the actual extremes of civil society and the state, he tried to mediate them. When the mediating entities did not do the trick, he supplied yet more, and ended up constructing a chaotic and incoherent state. Similarly, when confronted with such abstractions as idealism and materialism, or egoism and altruism, he either opted for one of the two extremes, or sought to mediate them without noticing that the mediation was neither possible nor necessary. To put the point differently, Hegel's idealism denied him the criterion by which to distinguish between genuine and sham opposition, with the result that he ignored or papered over the real opposition, and took the sham opposition much too seriously.

Marx seems to have thought that Hegel's philosophy (and his dialectical method) was successful in those areas of life where the opposition involved belonged to the first, and a failure where it belonged to either of the other two types. In the world of ideas, the opposition is generally of the first type. Hence Hegel was able to make brilliant and fascinating syntheses of moral, religious and other ideas, as well as the past philosophical systems. By contrast, when he dealt with the real world where the opposition is generally of the other two types, his successes were considerably limited. For example, the class conflict represents the second type of opposition. Since Hegel's logical theory is inherently incapable of dealing with it, it comes to grief in social and political life where the class conflict is of utmost importance. The opposition between the individual and general interest is of the third type. And since Hegel's logical theory is, again, too narrow to take account of it, he remains unable to provide a satisfactory solution to it.

Since Marx finds Hegel's analysis of the concept of opposition defective, he finds his analysis of mediation also unsatisfactory. In his view Hegel's use of the concept of mediation is generally non-dialectical. Even as Hegel imposes abstract logical categories on the recalcitrant empirical reality, he introduced a mediating entity not because it is called for by the two opposing entities, but because some third entity or, worse, Hegel's philosophy requires that they should be mediated. Since the mediating entity is not internally related to the entities mediated, it is unable to mediate them, and its whole point is defeated. Further, since the mediating entity is called upon to play a role incompatible with its nature, it comes to be viewed as a mere means, and is deprived of its intrinsic character and significance.

Further, since Hegel is not sensitive to the need of the mediated entities, his mediating entity ends up playing a role opposite to that intended. A mediating entity is introduced in order to reconcile and unite the two opposing entities. It is therefore designed to play a subordinate role. In actual fact, the opposite happens. The mediating entity becomes a higher or superior entity, and those mediated become the vehicles of its self-realisation! In theory, the mediating entity is deemed to have value and importance because it represents the common essence of the mediated entities; in actual fact, the latter have value and importance to the degree to which they embody the mediating entity. Marx observes,[32] the mediating entity

> because it comprises the opposed poles, and ultimately always appears as a one-sidedly higher power vis-à-vis the extremes themselves, the movement, or the relation, which originally appears as mediatory between the extremes necessarily develops dialectically to where it appears as mediation with itself, as the subject (*Subjekt*) for whom the extremes are merely its moments, whose autonomous presupposition it suspends in order to posit itself, through their suspension, as that which alone is autonomous.

Marx had noticed this phenomenon in religion. In Christianity, for example, the figure of Jesus, originally introduced to mediate God and man, becomes more important than either, so that God has no will independently of that of Jesus and is what Jesus says He is, and man has no dignity independently of his allegiance to him. Similarly the priest, initially introduced to mediate Jesus and the 'lay' man, becomes more important than either. Marx contends that the same thing happens in Hegel. The mediator becomes the master. It makes itself indispensable by keeping the mediated entities separate and dependent upon it for integration. The process of mediation is therefore a subtle way of consolidating the hierarchical rule, and the logic of mediation is at bottom the logic of domination. To avoid misunderstanding, Marx is not opposed to mediation as such, but only to a kind of mediation which degrades the mediating entities to a mere means and constitutes a form of domination.

Marx comes down rather hard on Hegel's conception of the negation of the negation, for Althusser and many other Marxists the key to Hegel's political conservatism. Following Feuerbach, Marx argues that although the negation of the negation is a 'necessary' stage, it is not 'the goal' of the dialectic. The entity resulting from the negation of the negation is not 'self-grounded', 'self-originating', and 'valid for itself'. It postulates its existence through what it negates, and is therefore 'burdened with its opposite'. In other words the negation of the negation is a negative and parasitic stage, and does not represent the 'true' or 'the absolute positive'. This is one of Marx's reasons for refusing to call communism 'the goal' of history. Since it is 'mediated to itself by the annulment of private property', communism represents the negation of the negation, and must be eventually superseded by a 'self-originating positive humanism'. Like Feuerbach, Marx believes that Hegel's triadic dialectical pattern does not provide for a truly positive stage, but he does not explain how the dialectic can be made tetradic. As so often happens in history, this long-forgotten notion was recently revived by Eric Weil. J.N. Findlay's response to it is worth citing:[33]

> I also agree with Prof. Weil and am interested in his doctrine that Hegel's triplicity should be made into a quadruplicity. I've never understood this before, that is, that you have a notion and then you have a negation of the notion, then you negate the notion, and then there is a fourth step and you get a new positive notion emerging from it. I mean it is tetradic rather than triadic. This is an interesting and valuable concept, and of course there are passages where Hegel says things of this sort.

Following Feuerbach Marx calls Hegel's negation of the negation phoney and uncritical, 'the root of Hegel's false positivism'. Marx argues that although the dialectical method both acknowledges the rationality of what exists and insists upon the necessity of its eventual supersession, Hegel emphasises only its conservative character. For example, Hegel recognises that religion is a form of human self-alienation and claims to supersede it in philosophy; yet he not only does not abolish it, but even looks upon it as human self-affirmation. Marx finds this extraordinary. If religion is alienated human self-consciousness and is sublated in philosophy, then by definition the human reason must demand its abolition.

In Marx's view the negation of the negation remains a positivist and uncritical principle in Hegel for two reasons, both closely linked with his idealism. First, since Hegel is an idealist, he does not deal with the actual institutions, but only with our ideas of them. The negation of the negation therefore occurs in thought, not in reality.[34] For example, in his philosophy of religion Hegel deals with religion not as a concrete social activity, but as a category of thought, and does not supersede religion but only the prevailing *thought* or *philosophy* of it. Similarly, when he says in his *Philosophy of Right* that private right is superseded in morality, morality in religion, and so on, what he really means is that the *thought* or concept of private right, when superseded, generates the *thought* or concept of morality, and so on. Hegel thus subverts the *'conventional conceptions'* and modes of *'understanding'* private property, family, religion, etc., but not the actual institutions themselves. Consequently, although his philosophy is genuinely revolutionary and subversive, its radicalism has no practical consequences and is 'merely apparent'.

Second, since Hegel is an idealist, he views every existing institution and practice as an expression of the *Geist*, and wishes to conserve it. Hegel's philosophy thus contains a tension. His idealism requires him to preserve whatever exists, while his dialectical method requires him to negate it. The conflict is resolved by means of the concept of negation of negation. The initial negation satisfies the radical demands of the dialectical method; the subsequent negation of the negation restores the original entity and satisfies the conservative demands of his idealist ontology. The negation of negation thus plays the self-contradictory and 'peculiar role' of both abolishing and preserving an entity, of securing both 'denial and preservation, denial and affirmation'. Since Hegel rejects an entity at one level to reinstate it at another, his negation of the negation never involves its 'annulment' of 'abolition', and only sanctifies the *status quo*.

V

Before concluding the chapter it would be useful to highlight some of the important implications of Marx's critique of Hegel. First, Marx's analysis of Hegel led him to conclude that philosophy as a form of inquiry was inherently suspect.[35] For Marx philosophy, by which he meant the metaphysical inquiry of the traditional kind, was no more than a rationalist substitute for religion. The ordinary man is puzzled by the world, and asks such questions as who created it, why man should have been created at all, why the human history has taken the form it has, and so on. And he generally turns to religion for answers. The philosopher finds the ideas of personal God, heaven and hell unacceptable. However, he too takes all, or at least some, of the questions seriously. Having rejected religion, he goes on to provide the 'rational' answers of his own.

Marx argues that the questions the philosopher asks are religious in nature, in the sense that they are predicated upon the existence of a transcendental being. To ask why nature should exist at all is to presuppose that someone created it, and had a purpose in so doing. And to ask why history should have taken a particular 'form' or 'direction' is to assume that a transcendental being pilots human history. Since the questions are religious in nature, philosophy can only answer them by itself becoming religious. It rejects the idea of God, but only to replace it with not too dissimilar entities such as the Absolute, the *Geist*, Substance, Ego and the Transcendental Principle. It rejects the two-world theory of religion, but only to replace it with one of its own. It rejects the religious idea of incarnation, but introduces one of its own when it asserts that the Transcendental principle 'embodies' or 'manifests' itself in the worldly entities. It rejects religious miracles, but is forced to introduce its own when it talks about the Ego creating nature, or the Absolute Idea creating the world, or the Substance assuming or appearing in different modes. In short Marx takes the view that philosophy is ultimately 'nothing but religion conceptualised and rationally developed', a way of acquiring a religion while pretending to reject it.

According to Marx the religious questions presuppose the truth of idealism, that is the priority of consciousness over matter and the possibility of its independent existence. Hence no form of inquiry can answer them without itself becoming idealistic. For Marx this explains why the philosophers, including the so-called materialists, have generally ended up embracing idealism in one form or another.[36] Since Marx rejects idealism, he rejects metaphysics itself as a legitimate form of inquiry. As we saw earlier, he rejects it on other grounds as well. In his view its highly abstract concepts are not legitimate objects of investigation. It necessarily involves the two-stage inquiry he criticised in Hegel. And its standard questions, such as how we know that the world, other men and we ourselves exist, could only be asked by an individual who defines himself as 'pure reason', and pretends that he stands on some extra-worldly Archimedean location, and refuses to trust his sense perceptions unless they are guaranteed by reason.

Second, Marx's critique of Hegel became a model for his subsequent critique of the classical economists. When he later examined their writings, he found that they, too, generally employed the method he had castigated in Hegel. In Marx's view the classical economists did not appreciate the historical specificity of the different modes of production. Instead, they abstracted their shared features, and contended that they were all basically nothing more than diverse combinations of the universally common elements. Since Marx took this view of classical political economy, he sometimes refers to it as metaphysical and abstract.[37] Like Hegel it employed abstract and ahistorical concepts, took an uncritical view of the prevailing social order, and employed the idealistic two-tier mode of analysis.

In Marx's view Hegel and the classical economists were connected not merely at the methodological, but also at the anthropological level. For both alike, labour was man's most creative and distinctive activity. Thanks to it, he was able to raise himself from the animal world, develop his rational powers, create civilisation and shape his historical destiny himself. In Marx's view Hegel's 'standpoint was that of modern political economy'; he had taken over and given a speculative expression to the basic insights of Adam Smith, Fergusson and the Scottish historical school.[38] If they were the economists of the modern age, Hegel was its philosopher. Despite the differences in their idioms of expression, Marx thought that the forms and content of their thought and even their modes of analysis were substantially similar. Given this view, it is hardly surprising that Marx should have read one through the eyes of the other, and offered both fascinating and distorting accounts of each.

Third, although Marx was convinced that Hegel viewed human history from the standpoint of and offered an apologia for the contemporary German society, he did not wish to say that Hegel's philosophy was merely an apologia. Far from it. He called him a 'genius', a 'mighty thinker' and declared himself his 'pupil'. He also paid most handsome tributes to Hegel's brilliant 'discoveries' in the fields of logic, history and philosophical anthropology and his penetrating analyses of the past and, especially, present historical epochs. Nor did Marx think that Hegel consciously set out to be an apologist. He made it abundantly clear that Hegel was a disinterested seeker after truth.

It is not entirely clear how, in Marx's view, Hegel became an apologist. He seems to offer five interrelated explanations. First, Hegel's view of philosophy was partly responsible. Since philosophy, for him, is concerned to reconcile man to the world, it is inherently positivist and uncritical. Second, as an idealist Hegel dealt with the ideas at a highly abstract and formal level. Since these were too general and 'empty', he had to give them content which he could only derive from a specific historical society, principally his own. Third, since Hegel never appreciated how very much man's conciousness is shaped by his society, he never explored the social basis of his own, and remained prone to the illusion that whatever appeared self-evident to him was, in fact, so. Fourth, Hegel did not take a critical attitude to his society and more or less accepted it as it was. He did not intellectually step outside and distance himself from his society. Consequently he had no real appreciation of its historicity, and no standards by which to judge it. He could not therefore help universalising its values and standards of rationality.

Although one cannot be certain, Marx seems to have thought that of the four, the last was crucial. It was largely because Hegel did not examine his society critically that the other three factors held sway. If he had been critical of his society, he would not have taken the view that the philosopher's task was to reconcile man to the world. Nor would he have espoused uncritical idealism. Nor, finally, would he have so easily universalised the values of his society. In Marx's view a radical critic of society wishes to change it. He cannot therefore avoid emphasising its historicity, and developing a rigorously historical attitude in general. Further, he is likely to be intensely suspicious of idealism, especially its justificatory view of the nature of philosophy. He is also likely to notice that since human consciousness is historically bounded, the institutions and ideas of his own society cannot be eternalised. We shall later discuss these and other related points at length.

Fifth, for Marx Hegel's philosophy was an extremely complex body of thought. It was ideological, but also contained profound insights. Further, being a profound thinker who was determined to grasp the innermost nature of human history, Hegel continually examined his assumptions, subjected them to a relentless critique, and developed insights that sometimes undermined his own apologetic bias. His system is therefore characterised by an internal tension. It is structurally biased, but also contains ideas that objectively undermine the bias. As Marx puts it, Hegel constantly overreaches himself in thought, his argument sometimes 'goes far beyond his point of view', and indeed 'all the elements of criticism' of his biased social assumptions are 'contained within' his philosophy.[39] Since, however, Hegel's thought was limited by his bias, he could not fully appreciate the basic thrust of some of his arguments and exploit his profound insights. His thought lacked 'self-clarity'. It was up to his sympathetic critics to liberate his insights from their restrictive ideological framework, and build on them.

We shall later examine this extraordinary view that a system of thought can point beyond itself, and objectively say far more than what its author subjectively intends to say. For the present we need only note that it is a recurrent theme in Marx, and constitutes one of the structural principles of his thought. In the course of his analysis of Eugene Sue's *Mysteries of Paris* he observes that, although imprisoned within the bourgeois ideology, Sue from time to time transcends its limits and says things that imply 'a slap in the face of bourgeois prejudice'. Marx takes similar views of Diderot, Balzac, the classical economists and several other writers.[40]

5 CLASSICAL POLITICAL ECONOMY

Marx summed up his assessment of classical political economy in an extraordinary statement. He said that it 'really and *impartially* investigated [economic life] *within the bounds* of the *bourgeois* horizon'.[1] In his view it was genuinely scientific, but also ideologically biased. Accordingly, he frequently referred to it as a 'scientific bourgeois economy' and a 'bourgeois science of political economy'.[2] For some Marx's juxtaposition of the terms 'bourgeois' and 'science' is an example of intellectual crudity, category confusion or even contradiction in terms. For others it demonstrates the depth of his penetration into the structure of classical political economy. In this chapter we shall examine how Marx substantiates his assessment of classical economy and answers some of the important questions it raises.

I

For Marx classical economy was scientific. By this he meant three things. First, it studied social relations, and not the abstract ideas and concepts as Hegel and other philosophers had one. Second, it was not confined to the surface of society as the vulgar economists were, but aimed to penetrate its innermost essence. And third, it was not 'base' and partisan, but 'honest', 'impartial', 'disinterested' and inspired by the 'love of truth'.[3] The classical economists were not hired prize-fighters, but men of unimpeachable intellectual integrity and committed to the pursuit of truth. We quoted above some of the highest compliments Marx paid to Ricardo. He held Adam Smith and several others in equally high esteem.

Marx thought that, although it was scientific, classical political economy was also bourgeois. As he put it on different occasions, it analysed economic life 'from the bourgeois point of view'; was confined 'completely within the bounds of the bourgeois horizon'; remained a 'prisoner of the capitalist standpoint'; never shed its 'bourgeois skin'; and did not manage to transcend its bourgeois 'assumptions'. By all these Marx meant that classical political economy looked upon the capitalist mode of production 'as the absolutely final form of social production instead of as a passing historical phase of its evolution'.[4]

Even as Hegel had absolutised the contemporary society and regarded it as the highest manifestation of Reason, the classical economists absolutised capitalism and presented it as the most rational method of organising the economy and in complete harmony with human nature. Even as Hegel had thought that his epoch marked the end of history, the classical economists believed that capitalism represented 'the final product, the *non plus ultra* of history', the full secret and the 'final truth' of economic life at last discovered.[5] For them, while some aspects of it might undergo change, its basic form was 'eternal' and 'everlasting'.[6] Capitalism was not, like the others, a historical mode of production that would one day be replaced by another based on a higher and altogether different principle, but the most rational form of material production ever likely to be discovered by man. For them 'there has been history, but there is no longer any.'[7] Even as Hegel had argued, that the present historical epoch summed up all that was best in the previous epochs, the classical economists argued that the capitalist mode of production encapsulated all that was best in its predecessors. It 'freed' labour, property, contract, exchange, man, etc. from the restrictions to which they were subject in the pre-capitalist societies and enabled them at last to come into their own. As Marx put it, the classical economists are 'like a man who believes in a particular religion and sees it as *the* religion, and everything outside of it as *false* religions'.[8] They '*resemble the* theologians who likewise establish two kinds of religion. Every religion which is not theirs is an invention of men, while their own is an emanation from God.'[9] They 'smudge over all historical differences and see bourgeois relations in all forms of society'.[10] In short, like Hegel, the classical economists de-historicised the present and arrested history. They dismissed the past, foreclosed the future and eternalised the present. It is this absolutisation of capitalism and the consequent suppression of its historical and contradictory nature that Marx has in mind when he accuses them of never transcending the bourgeois horizon of thought.

Classical political economy then was profoundly biased towards capitalism. It assumed that capitalism was the most rational mode of production, in harmony with human nature, and neither transient nor contradictory. The bias of its assumptions permeated and distorted its analysis of economic life and, as a result, it noticed some aspects of capitalism but not others, asked certain types of question and overlooked others, adopted biased methods of analysis and concepts, found certain types of answer persuasive but not others, and probed the inner structure of capitalism up to a point but not beyond.

In describing classical political economy as a 'scientific bourgeois economy' and calling it *both* scientific and ideological, Marx intended to say that it was impartial but within a partial framework, disinterested but within a systematically biased framework, rigorous but not rigorous enough to examine its own basic assumptions, and genuinely but not wholly scientific. Unlike the vulgar economy, classical political economy made a determined and disinterested effort to probe the innermost essence of capitalism, and to a large extent succeeded in doing so. It was therefore a scientific and not merely an apologetic body of ideas. At the same time, however, it was profoundly biased towards capitalism. It was therefore not a wholly scientific body of ideas, and had an apologetic dimension. In short the scientific aspirations and achievements of classical political economy were ideologically bounded; it was, as Marx said, a science 'within the bounds of the bourgeois horizon'.

Marx's assessment of classical political economy raises several extremely important and difficult questions. Of these the following five are most relevant from our point of view. First, we need to know how the ideological assumptions of classical economy distorted its scientific investigations, where they misled it, what questions they prevented it from asking or led it to formulate wrongly, how they distorted its methods of investigation, and so on.

Second, we need to know why its ideological bias did not frustrate its scientific ambition altogether or, conversely, why its scientific penetration did not enable it to detect and counter the influence of its ideological assumptions.

Third, as Marx himself acknowledges, classical political economy was not static. The successive economists built on the achievements of their predecessors and penetrated further and further into the nature of capitalism. This raises the question as to how the interaction between its scientific ambition and ideological bias changed over time, and whether classical political economy became more scientific or more ideological or both.

Fourth, we need to know why the classical economists made the ideological assumptions in question or, what comes to the same thing, why they absolutised the capitalist mode of production.

Finally, given that classical political economy was at once both scientific and ideological, we need to know how a critic should respond to it. He obviously cannot accept or reject it *in toto*, and must devise ways of extracting its scientific insights from the ideological framework within which they were acquired.

With the exception of the first and the last, Marx did not explicitly discuss these questions. However, he seems to have been aware of their importance, and from time to time remarked upon them. Whenever necessary we shall therefore have to reconstruct his answers from his isolated remarks, both private and public, and his actual practice.

II

In Marx's view the scientific achievements of classical political economy were considerable. Its greatest achievement was to have created the science of economics itself, a task requiring extraordinary effort and energy. Adam Smith, who laid its foundations, was confronted with a 'double' task.[11] First, during his time the economic activity was just beginning to acquire a distinctive character, and ordinary language lacked the vocabulary to describe it. The economic activity could not be thought about, much less talked about, unless a way of describing it could be evolved. Adam Smith had to create 'a nomenclature and the corresponding abstract ideas for these phenomena, and therefore for the first time to reproduce them in language and in the process of thought'. Second, he had to undertake the specifically scientific task of penetrating the innermost nature of the economic phenomena, and develop an adequate body of scientific concepts and methods of investigation.

Adam Smith, then, had to develop both the ordinary and the scientific language. This was an extremely difficult task, and although he had had some success, he could not always clearly separate the two languages. Consequently he kept 'passing over from one kind of explanation to another', and moved 'with great *naiveté* in a continuous contradiction', switching from the scientific to the ordinary mode of discussion, and then back again. Marx thought that Ricardo acheived the 'categorical break', and 'completely' separated the 'esoteric' or the scientific and the 'exoteric' or the common-sensical levels of discussion. 'This is therefore the great historical significance of Ricardo for science.' In his *Theories of Surplus Value* Marx devoted a good deal of space to tracing the complex process of evolving a distinct scientific vocabulary. He argued, among other things, that the scientific concepts have humble and 'profane' origins in the ordinary language, are at first used in several senses and confused with their ordinary meanings, the conceptual gains of one writer are sometimes lost upon his successors, the concepts take a long time to acquire even a moderate degree of precision, and that the development of the discipline of economics was a slow and painful process requiring the concerted efforts of many a powerful mind.

Classical political economy not only developed the science of economics, but also offered many important insights into the inner nature of capitalism. Thanks to Adam Smith whom, following Engels, Marx called the Luther of political economy, classical economy grasped, right from the beginning, the human basis of wealth.[12] Even as Luther placed man at the centre of religion, Smith placed man at the centre of economic life and made human labour the sole source of wealth.[13] Other economists built on his insight, developed the labour theory of value and used it to explain prices. Further, classical economy destroyed the 'illusion of the holy trinity' and offered a scientific explanation of how capital earns interest, land rent and labour wages. It broke through the apparent independence of the three major forms of revenue, elucidated the nature and mechanism of their inner connections and demonstrated that interest and rent were parts of profit and that profit was a form of surplus value. Marx observes:[14]

> It is the great merit of classical economy to have destroyed this false appearance and illusion, this mutual independence and ossification of the various social elements of wealth, this personification of things and conversion of production relations into entities, this religion of everyday life. It did so by reducing interest to a portion of profit, and rent to the surplus above average profit, so that both of them converge in surplus-value; and by representing the process of circulation as a mere metamorphosis of forms, and finally reducing value and surplus-value of commodities to labour in the direct production process.

Marx argues that, despite these and other considerable achievements and its scientific determination to get to the truth of the capitalist mode of production, classical political economy remained severely handicapped by its basic ideological assumptions.

Since the classical economist absolutised the capitalist mode of production and assumed that it alone was in harmony with human nature, he took the view that its basic features were to be found, albeit in less developed forms, in all modes of production. As Ricardo put it, capitalism has no 'definite specific characteristics' and 'its distinctive traits are merely formal'. Accordingly the classical economist so defined its distinctive features that they could be shown to be common to all modes of production. In Marx's view his methodological strategy was the same as Hegel's: he de-historicised the historically specific social relations, turned them into abstract and universally valid logical categories and, after a more or less superficial analysis, subsumed the vastly different modes of production under them.[15]

Capital is a distinct social relation which, like its correlative wage labour, is unique to capitalism. In order to universalise it, the classical economist had to define it so that it could be found in all societies. He generally defined it as 'accumulated labour serving as the means for new labour'.[16] On this 'banal' definition even the most primitive implements could be called capital. As Marx puts it, capital was presented as 'a new name for a thing as old as the human race', and a 'necessary condition' of all forms of production.

Even as the classical economist de-historicised capital, he abstracted away the historical specificity of wage labour.[17] Wage labour is a distinctively modern social relation, and presupposes such things as capital, money as a universal equivalent and an exchange-based economy. In order to show that it existed under all modes of production, the classical economist had to define it in extremely general terms. For the most part, he defined it as rendering services to another in return for a reward. Since this form of social relationship obtains in all societies except perhaps the most primitive, the classical economist argued that wage labour was to be found in all human societies. Like capital and wage labour, he de-historicised commodity production. He defined the concept of commodity very widely to mean any kind of product, and argued that all production was commodity production. And again, he so defined the highly complex modern phenomenon of money-based exchange that it was seen to be basically the same as primitive barter. Without the slightest hesitation he talked of the propensity to 'barter and exchange', as if there was no qualitative difference between the primitive barter and the modern exchange.

On the basis of the ahistorical and abstract definitions of such crucial relations of the capitalist economy as capital, wage labour and commodity production, the classical economist contended that they were common to all societies, and that no form of production could be imagined without them. He argued that the capitalist had existed in all societies. For Marx this amounted to saying that 'the Kirghis tribesman who cuts reeds with a knife stolen from the Russians and weaves his skiff out of this reeds is just as much a capitalist as Baron Von Rothschild'. Such an assertion is as valid as saying that the 'Greeks and Romans took communion because they drank wine and ate bread'.[18]

As Marx puts it, the classical economists 'smudge over all historical differences', display 'crude inability to grasp the real distinctions', and see 'bourgeois relations in all forms of society'.[19] They presented the capitalist and the wage labourer as universal figures, the basic features of capitalism as part of the human predicament, and capitalism as the fullest realisation and the most rational development of man's 'basic propensities'. On the basis of their ahistorical and biased definitions, they had no difficulty showing that the proposal to abolish commodity production, wage labour or capitalism itself flouted the human condition, and was Utopian and irresponsible.

While such ahistorical definitions served the classical economist's ideological purposes well, they frustrated his scientific ambition. Since he analysed the pre-capitalist societies in terms of the categories abstracted from the modern capitalist society, he could not say anything meaningful about them. Unable and unwilling to study them in their own terms, he viewed them as immature anticipations of capitalism. As Marx puts it, 'His very lack of a historical sense of the past meant that he regarded everything from the historical standpoint of his time.'[20] He did not appreciate the historically unique manners of organising production in the pre-capitalist societies, and gave highly distorted and misleading accounts of them.

His ahistorical categories did not enable the classical economist to understand capitalism either. Since he had de-historicised the basic categories of capitalist economy in order to make them universally applicable, they were too abstract to capture 'the specific form of bourgeois production'.[21] They prevented him from asking questions and using methods of analysis capable of illuminating the historically unique character of capitalism. For Marx capitalism is characterised by such unique features as commodity production, the pursuit of value, the use of money as a universal equivalent, wage labour, capital and the appropriation of surplus value. It cannot be understood unless these and other features of it are systematically analysed. Therefore the really significant questions to ask about capitalism are those designed to illuminate them. In Marx's view the classical economists, operating with blunt conceptual instruments, did not and could not explicitly and systematically ask such questions. No doubt, the questions were basic and unavoidable, and therefore at least the 'more talented' economists could not help asking them. However, since they did not always ask them 'expressly and with full consciousness', they could not generally formulate them very clearly, nor grasp the full theoretical significance of either their questions or their answers.[22]

Hence they could not capitalise on their insights, and from time to time came close to, but could not quite succeed in comprehending the essence of capitalism. What was more, the discoveries made by an economist were lost upon his successors, and sometimes a whole generation of economists was found grappling with the questions implicitly answered by its predecessors. As Marx puts it, thanks to its ideological bias, classical economy 'never arrived at a consciousness of the results of its own analysis'.[23]

In Marx's view nearly all the classical economists assumed that the commodity form, characteristic of the capitalist mode of production, made no difference to the product, and that commodity circulation did not qualitatively differ from primitive barter.[24] Consequently they never seriously investigated the nature of commodity and commodity production. Since they did not examine the commodity form, they did not carefully examine the nature of value and exchange value either. They did, no doubt, analyse value and its magnitude and made many perceptive observations. However, they analysed them 'incompletely' and 'never once asked the question why labour is represented by the value of its product and labour-time by the magnitude of that value'.[25] Further, since they did not fully analyse the nature of value, they never understood why labour undergoes a qualitative change when its products are exchanged. Exchange presupposes that the qualitatively different products of labour are commensurable and capable of mutual conversion, and that the qualitatively different types of labour are not really so, but part of an abstract and homogeneous social labour. The classical economists did not even notice, let alone explain, how labour undergoes such a radical transformation in the course of exchange, and what it entails.

Unable to appreciate the specificity of commodity production, the classical economists were unable also to understand the nature of money. In Marx's view they naively assumed that money was only a 'medium of circulation', a mere intermediary designed to facilitate exchange, and that its importance was confined to the realm of circulation. As a result they failed to appreciate that money constitutes the driving force of the capitalist production. It does not merely float on the surface, but penetrates 'deeply into the very essence of capitalist production', as seen in the powerful influence exercised by the banks and other forms of finance capital.[26] Marx puts the point well:[27]

It is one of the chief failings of classical economy that it has never succeeded, by means of its analysis of commodities, and, in particular, of their value, in discovering that form under which value becomes exchange-value. Even Adam Smith and Ricardo, the best representatives of the school, treat the form of value as a thing of no importance, as having no connexion with the inherent nature of commodities. The reason for this is not solely because their attention is entirely absorbed in the analysis of the magnitude of value. It lies deeper. The value-form of the product of labour is not only the most abstract, but is also the most universal form, taken by the product in bourgeois production, and stamps that production as a particular species of social production, and thereby gives it its special historical character. If then we treat this mode of production as one eternally fixed by Nature for every state of society, we necessarily overlook that which is the *differentia specifica* of the value form, and consequently of the commodity-form and of its further developments, money-form, etc. We consequently find that economists, who are thoroughly agreed as to labour-time being the measure of the magnitude of value, have the most strange and contradictory ideas of money, the perfected form of the general equivalent. This is seen in a striking manner when they treat of banking, where the commonplace definitions of money will no longer hold water.

Further, since the classical economists did not comprehend the distinctive nature of commodity production, they assumed that the acts of exchange in the capitalist society were essentially like a 'direct barter', and failed to grasp the way money mediates and alters the character of exchange.[28] For basically the same reasons, they talked of demand and supply in the abstract without examining the social origin and economic effectiveness of the demands. As a result they could not explain, or even acknowledge, the fact of overproduction. They admitted the possibility of overproduction in some particular spheres of production, but not the simultaneous overproduction in all areas and the general glut of the market. Marx puts the point as follows:[29]

All the objections which Ricardo and others raise against overproduction etc., rest on the fact that they regard bourgeois production either as a mode of production in which no distinction exists between purchase and sale — direct barter — or as *social* production, implying that society, as if according to a plan, distributes its means of production and productive forces in the degree and measure which is required for the fulfilment of the various social needs, so that each sphere of production receives the *quota* of social capital required to satisfy the corresponding need. This fiction arises entirely from the inability to grasp the specific form of bourgeois production and this inability in turn arises from the obsession that bourgeois production is production as such, just like a man who believes in a particular religion and sees it as *the* religion, and everything outside of it only as *false* religions.

Marx argues that its abstract and ahistorical approach misled classical economy into defining its subject matter in extremely narrow terms.[30] Since it only concerned itself with the elementary and universally common features of production, it was unable to grasp the total pattern of social relationship within which each mode of production takes place. It therefore concentrated only on the *process* of production, and ignored the *relations* of production altogether. In so doing it was forced to treat the economic activity as if it were merely concerned with *things*, and not as an activity going on among socially related *men*. Marx thought it significant that no classical economist recognised the significance of the division of society into the owners of the means of production and the wage labourers. This fact was either ignored or regarded as irrelevant to the understanding of the capitalist society. As a result classical economy not only did not place the social structure at the *centre* of its analysis, but even viewed it as falling *outside* the province of economics. The narrowing of the subject matter limited its explanatory power. Since it excluded any reference to social relations, it was left with no alternative but to explain economic life almost entirely in terms of the relations between things, and to see human relations as their incidental products. It ascribed magical properties and powers of action to inanimate objects, and aimed to discover their patterns of interaction. For example, several classical economists explained exchange value as if it were the natural property of an object, profit as if it inhered in a thing called capital, and thought that a pearl was valuable 'because' it was a pearl. In Marx's view this is simply absurd, for exchange value is a social relationship and cannot by definition be the natural property of an object, and capital is not a thing but a social relation between the owners of the means of production and wage labourers.

Marx argues that the bourgeois bias of classical political economy is evident also in the questions it asked or failed to ask. Just as theology explains the origin of evil by the fall of man and thus 'assumes as a fact ... what has to be explained', classical economy explained economic life in terms of private property without first explaining how the latter came into being and how it was justified. Likewise, it took exchange relations as given, and never asked why exchange should be the basis of economic life. Further, it analysed the division of labour entirely from the standpoint of the manufacturer and saw it as nothing more than a means of increasing productivity and accumulating capital. At no point did it examine it from the standpoint of the worker, and notice its disastrous effects upon him. Again, it regarded the bourgeois relations of production as natural, and not in need of explanation. Even J.S. Mill, who was a 'more advanced, more critical mind' than most and able to see that some aspects of the bourgeois society, such as its relations of *distribution*, were unique to it, clung to the view that the relations of *production* were more or less the same in all societies and 'independent of all historical development'.[31]

The justification of the capitalist society was also built into the conceptual structure of classical economy. The classical economists described wages as the price of labour. Marx argues that in so doing they concealed the reality of the capitalist exploitation. The labourer works for an employer and produces an object which embodies his labour. If he were paid for his labour, his wages would equal the total value of his product, thereby leaving the employer no profit. What he is, in fact, paid for is the use of his *labour power*. The expression 'price of labour' conveniently hides the element of surplus of labour and makes 'the actual relation invisible'. Again, the classical economists talked of overproduction rather than underconsumption, and diverted attention from the poverty of the masses. As Marx puts it,[32]

So long as the most urgent needs of a large part of society are not satisfied, or *only* the most immediate needs are satisfied, there can of course be absolutely no talk of an overproduction of products ... On the contrary it must be said that ... there is constant under-production in this sense.

The term overproduction makes sense only when production is viewed from the standpoint of 'the profit of the capitalist and not ... the needs of the producers'.

For Marx the bourgeois bias is also evident in the classical economists' definition of productive and unproductive labour. For example, Adam Smith divided all labour into productive and unproductive, and defined the former as one 'which adds to the value of the subject upon which it is bestowed'.[33] By value he meant the difference between the price and the cost of production of an object; that is profit. Thus Smith said, in effect, that the productive labour was one that produced profit, and the unproductive labour was one that did not. Like others before him, Smith defined productive labour only 'from the standpoint of the capitalist, not from that of the workman'. On the basis of such a biased definition Smith reached the predictable conclusion that servants, intellectuals, teachers and others were unproductive labourers who impoverished the community, and that only the manufacturers were its useful members. Marx argues that, despite all its limitations, Smith's definition had a critical import in that it did not uncritically accept all sections of society as engaged in equally valuable forms of labour. As the bourgeoisie came to need the services of the parasitic 'ideological professions', they realised that it was not in their interest to be too restrictive in their definition of productive labour. Their usage was taken up by such economists as Malthus, Storch, Garnier and Nassau Senior, who defined productive labour so widely that it included almost everyone promoting the bourgeois interests. The groups which classical economy had, at one stage, vehemently dismissed as unproductive were later presented by it as integral to the productive structure of society.[34]

Marx argues that even as the classical economists asked questions and employed concepts that 'obliterated' the historicity of capitalism, they asked questions and used concepts that 'dimmed' and 'obscured' the reality of class contradictions.[35] They did so in several ways and at several levels. They presented the relation between the capitalist and the labourer as if it were a voluntary relationship between two equal and independent individuals. As we saw, Marx questions this. In his view their relationship is class-mediated, and one between the two classes rather than two individuals. The worker is tied to capital, and his limited ability to change his employer makes no difference to the fact that he cannot live without selling himself to one of them.

Further, Marx goes on, the classical economist assimilates the relationship between the capitalist and the worker to that between the buyer and seller of a commodity. For the classical economist labour is a commodity like any other, and the relation between a worker and his employer is no different from that between a buyer and a seller of any other commodity.[36] Marx argues that this is a wholly biased account for, although the two relationships are similar in form, they differ in several significant respects. Unlike the sellers of other commodities, the worker sells his services, and therefore himself. What is more, labour is totally different from all other commodities in that it alone is capable of producing surplus value, the source of the capitalist's profit. The worker pays back the capitalist far more than the equivalent of his wages and, indeed, keeps him in existence. This has no analogue in the ordinary exchanges occurring at the level of circulation. The classical economist's account suppresses this crucial difference and obscures the reality of exploitation.[37]

In Marx's view the classical economist obscures the profound differences between the worker and the capitalist in yet other ways as well. He uses such abstract and ambiguous terms as labour and payment for services, which obscure the qualitative differences between their respective activities and forms of revenue. The classical economist argues that, even as the worker is engaged in labour, the capitalist is engaged in the 'labour' of superintendence and organisation, and that therefore both alike are labourers and equally necessary for production.[38] He argues, further, that there is no real difference between the wages and profit, for both alike are payments for the different types of service rendered by one individual to another.[39] In Marx's view this is a totally misleading account of the capitalist's role in the process of production. The capitalist does not engage in the labour of superintendence and organisation, but generally hires others to do so.[40] Besides, he is not 'paid' anything for his 'services', but left free to appropriate his entire profit. Further, the ownership of capital and the activity of superintendence are two separate and separable activities. While no form of production can entirely dispense with the latter, it can dispense with the private ownership of capital.[41] The classical economist conflates the two, and attributes to the ownership of capital the role and importance that can only be ascribed to the 'labour' of superintendence. This means that the equation between the wages and profit is false. The wages are only a tiny portion of the surplus value produced by the worker, whereas profit represents a payment not for work but the simple ownership of the means of production.[42]

Marx argues that, since the classical economist could only realise his ideological objective of absolutising capitalism by obliterating its historical specificity, he was constantly led to employ the familiar ideological manoeuvre of emphasising the content and ignoring the form. As we saw, he defined capital not as a social relation but as a thing, that is not in terms of its form but content. And similarly he defined wage labour as a service, which is its content, and not as a specific social relation between the worker and the capitalist, which is its historical form. The emphasis on the content rather than the form has a distinct ideological bias. The form is necessarily specific to a particular mode of production and represents its identity, whereas the content, or 'matter' as Marx calls it, is universally common. For example, the use of implements is common to all societies, whereas their purposes, modes of utilisation and relations to their users vary from society to society. Further, a form is social in nature and refers to a specific type of social relation, whereas the content does not. The form therefore necessarily draws attention to the character of the society in question, especially its class structure, and is understandably avoided or underemphasised by those concerned to absolutise a specific social structure. Again, the forms are necessarily determinate and varied and, as Marx remarks quoting Spinoza, *determinatio est negatio*. A form cannot be discussed without distinguishing it from others. It therefore necessarily draws attention to other forms and raises the inconvenient questions of comparative assessment.

In Marx's view the classical economist's profound ideological unease with the form, as opposed to the content, was the source of many of his difficulties, of which two deserve mention. First, he tended to confuse a thing with one of its forms.[43] Marx takes the example of Adam Smith. In the course of analysing profit, Smith argued that 'the whole produce of labour does not always belong to the labourer. He must in most cases share it with the owner of the stock which employs him.'[44] The worker produces an 'additional quantity' which is the source of profit, rent and interest. Marx argues that Adam Smith had come very close to discovering the fact of surplus value. However, he did not identify it as such, nor did he examine how it was divided between profit, rent and interest. Not surprisingly he called and equated it with profit. As Marx puts it, since Smith 'does not present it [surplus value] explicitly in the form of a definite category, distinct from its special forms, he subsequently mixes it up directly with the further developed form, profit . . . Hence arise a series of inconsistencies, unresolved contradictions and fatuities.'[45] He was unable, for example, to see that the different forms of surplus value were governed by different laws, and that these in turn were different from the law regulating the surplus value itself. Consequently he went on to explain profit and rent in terms of the law regulating the surplus value. Since this created difficulties, he was forced to resort to verbal subterfuges or to deny the obvious facts of economic life. Marx argues that the confusion of a thing with one of its forms remains 'the rule' with 'all later bourgeois economists' and is one of the important sources of their difficulties.[46] Since they absolutised capitalism and lacked a 'historical sense' of the 'specific nature' of the different modes of production, they never acquired a conceptual and methodological sensitivity to their forms. Their whole approach was assimilationist in orientation. They constantly tended to equate an entity with one of its several forms, and conflate rather than distinguish the latter.

In Marx's view the inability to deal with the form is also reflected in the classical economist's preference for the analytical over the genetic method. When confronted with the different types of phenomena, he abstracted their shared features and argued that the phenomena in question were nothing but the diverse combinations of the latter. He did not examine how and why the same elements gave rise to different forms, whether they underwent a change of character when differently combined, and what specific principles of combination underlay the different forms.[47] As Marx puts it, 'Classical economy is not interested in elaborating how the various forms come into being, but seeks to reduce them to their unity by means of analysis.'[48] It was concerned with the analytical reduction, and not the examination of the origin and development of the historically specific forms of social relation, with the immediate identity rather than the mediated unity.[49] As a result it never, for example, asked how the capitalist mode of production came into being, what its distinctive conditions of existence were, how these emerged and coalesced, and so on. Such questions either did not occur or seem important to it. For it the different modes of production were diverse combinations of the same basic 'factors of production'. And their emergence was either ascribed to accidents or left unexplained.

III

We outlined above some of the ways in which, according to Marx, the ideological bias of the classical economists distorted their investigation. Marx does not wish to suggest at all that the relation between the scientific aspiration and the ideological bias was entirely one-sided. As classical political economy developed, it probed deeper into the nature of economic life, and began to break through and even subvert many of its ideological assumptions. In Marx's view it was able to do so for two reasons, its scientific integrity and the changing nature of capitalism.

The classical economists were genuinely interested in discovering the true nature of capitalism. Many of them were highly talented, and some were even 'men of genius'. They were not satisfied with the traditional answers, and kept pressing their inquiries as far as they could. In the course of their investigations, they were sometimes misled by their ideological biases, asked wrong questions, used biased concepts, failed to make crucial distinctions, drew wrong conclusions, and so on. Their successors, especially the more talented among them, detected their mistakes, although not the fundamental bias responsible for them, and sharpened or reformulated their questions, modified their concepts, distinguished the concepts they had confused, improved their methods of analysis, and so on. Their limitations, in turn, were probed and overcome by their successors. Over the decades the classical economists began to get closer to the inner nature of capitalism. As they did so, they found themselves 'pushing' against the 'boundaries' set by their ideological assumptions.[50] As Marx puts it, the 'more economic theory is perfected, that is, the deeper it penetrates its subject matter', the more it comes up against its basic assumptions.[51] The classical economists began to become dimly aware of the assumptions underlying their inquiry and preventing them from making further progress. However, since they were not fully aware of their assumptions, they could not explicitly question them, let alone undertake their radical reappraisal. Not surprisingly they could not exploit their scientific insights whose full theoretical potential remained inaccessible to them. Marx's meaning would become clearer if we took a couple of examples.

The classical economists investigated the 'holy trinity', and attempted to explain the origins of and the inner connections between profit, rent and interest. The earlier economists thought that the three were totally independent. Their successors probed further and saw that they were related, although they did not succeed in specifying the nature of the relationship. Their successors, in turn, probed yet further, and concluded that the three allegedly independent sources of revenue had a common source. Marx argues that they had hit upon, albeit vaguely, the idea of surplus value. If they had investigated the matter further, they would have found themselves inquiring into the source of surplus value, and opening up the whole question of the wealth-creating role of labour and the appropriation of surplus labour. Thanks to their ideological assumptions, the classical economists were *already* convinced that capital was the sole creator of wealth, that capital was a product of the capitalist's hard work, ingenuity and thrift, and so on. Consequently they did not look *beyond capital* for their explanations of the sources of profit, rent and interest. Having got as far as the concept of surplus value, they therefore dropped the subject, went round in circles, drew inconsistent conclusions or gave their investigation a curious twist. As Marx says of Ramsay, he got 'very close to the origin of surplus value', but was 'too bound up' in the ideologically biased assumptions of his discipline 'not to begin immediately straying again along false paths'.[52]

Let us take another related example. As we saw, Marx argues that, to their great credit, the classical economists grasped the fundamental economic truth that human activity was the source of all wealth. The more talented among them wondered which specific human activity created wealth, and concluded that it was labour. Some, not satisified with this, probed yet further, and discovered that the productive or material labour was the source of all wealth. In Marx's view this was a profound insight that penetrated the very essence of capitalism. If followed to its logical conclusion, it implied that capital was nothing more than the materialised and stored up past labour, that it was not an independent source of wealth nor an equal partner with labour in the process of production, that the private ownership of capital was historically, but not permanently, necessary, and so on. In short the insight that the productive labour was the source of all wealth sub-verted some of the basic assumptions of the classical economists. Thanks to their ideological assumptions they were, however, *already* convinced that capital was the sole source of wealth. Accordingly they did not pursue the insight further. Some simply did not grasp its theoretical significance, and continued to argue that capital was the sole source of wealth. Some others, who dimly appreciated both its importance and its incompatibility with their assumptions, redefined labour to include the capitalist's 'labour' of superintendence, equated labour and capital, or covered up the problem by means of conceptual ambiguities and linguistic subterfuges. Marx observes:[53]

> To the same extent as political economy developed it presented labour as the sole element of value and the only creator of use-values . . .
>
> But in the same measure as it is understood that labour is the *sole* source of exchange-value and the active source of use-value, *'capital'* is likewise conceived by the same economists, in particular by Ricardo (and even more by Torrens, Malthus, Bailey, and others after him) . . . the source of wealth and the aim of production, whereas labour is regarded as wage-labour, whose representative and real instrument is inevitably a pauper . . . a mere production cost and instrument of production dependent on a minimum wage and forced to drop even below this minimum as soon as the existing quantity of labour is 'superfluous' for capital . . . in the self-same

breath they proclaim on the one hand, *labour* as such (for them, labour is synonymous with wage-labour) and on the other, *capital* as such — that is the poverty of the workers and the wealth of the idlers — to be the sole source of wealth, they are perpetually involved in absolute contradiction without being in the slightest degree aware of them. (Sismondi was epoch-making in political economy because he had an inkling of this contradiction.) Ricardo's phrase 'labour or capital' reveals in a most striking fashion both the contradiction inherent in the terms and the naivety with which they are stated to be identical.

Marx thinks that in addition to their scientific integrity and penetration, the development of capitalism, their object of investigation, was another factor responsible for the classical economists' increasing awareness of their ideological assumptions. The classical economists did not conduct their investigations in a historical vacuum. The capitalist mode of production was constantly undergoing changes. As its productive potential developed, it began to run into acute economic crises. It created unemployment, suffering, the paradox of poverty amidst plenty, etc., and could not easily present itself as the most rational method of organising the economy. Further, the proletariat was increasingly becoming an organised class, asking disturbing questions and fighting for the overthrow of capitalism. The historical and contradictory nature of capitalism was therefore becoming increasingly evident, and it was no longer easy to assume that it was 'natural', 'everlasting' and did not contain fundamental conflicts of interest. Being 'men of science' the classical economists increasingly began to take account of these changes and come to terms with their basic assumptions.[54]

Some, especially Ricardo, admitted the existence of classes and class conflicts, and argued that the conflicts between rent and profit and between the latter and wages were endemic in modern society.[55] However, it was not easy for them to make a clean break with their ideological assumptions. Ricardo, for example, treated the class conflict as a marginal phenomenon and did not appreciate its implications. Similarly, although he acknowledged the historicity of capitalism, it remained only a passing thought in no way integrated into his theoretical structure.[56] In Marx's view Richard Jones went a step further. He openly and explicitly acknowledged the transience of capitalism, and attempted to construct his economic theory on that basis. However, this required a radical reappraisal of the entire conceptual structure of his discipline, and that was beyond him. As Marx puts it:[57]

> Thus we have arrived at the point where political economy itself —
> on the basis of its analysis — declares the *capitalist form* of produc-
> tion, and consequently *capital*, to be not an asbolute but merely an
> 'accidental' historical condition of production.

Classical economy was, however, too deeply conditioned by its ideological assumptions to take full advantage of its insights.

For Marx, then, classical political economy was a complex structure
of thought. It was rigorously scientific, but within an ideologically
biased framework. Although Marx himself does not put it this way,
he seems to suggest a dialectical account of the nature and development
of classical political economy. For him classical economy contained an
internal contradiction between its *telos* or 'ideal nature' and its assumptions or 'actual presuppositions'. Its *telos* was scientific, its assumptions
were ideological. In Marx's view the history of classical economy is the
history of the dialectic generated by its contradictory character. It
constantly strove to discover the truth about capitalism; however, its
ideological assumptions constantly prevented it from fully realising its
objective. Throughout its history it was involved in the self-contradictory
position of pursuing the truth within an ideological framework, seeking
objective knowledge on a biased basis, securing scientific content within
an ideological form. It is a measure of its scientific integrity and penetration that it constantly kept pushing against the boundaries set by its
ideological assumptions; it is a measure of its scientific inadequacy that
it never wholly succeeded in detecting and overcoming them. As Marx
puts it, classical economy 'nearly touches the true relation of things
without however, consciously *formulating* it. This it cannot do as long
as it sticks in its bourgeois skin.'[58]

As we saw, classical political economy in the course of its development acquired insights that contradicted its basic assumptions. It came
to see, albeit dimly, that capitalism was a historical mode of production,
that it contained fundamental conflicts of interest that the economic
relations were class-mediated, that the surplus value was the source of
profit, rent and interest, and so on, and implicitly 'undermined and
impaired its own premises'.[59] However, since it was not fully conscious
of its assumptions or too deeply committed to them to develop the
courage to reject them, it continued to think within the ideological
framework. As Marx puts it, 'Even the best spokesmen of classical
economy remain more or less in the grip of the world of illusion which

their criticism had dissolved, as cannot be otherwise from a bourgeois standpoint, and thus they all fall more or less into inconsistencies, half-truths and unsolved contradictions.'[60]

Classical political economy, then, contained insights which 'rise above', transcend and 'point beyond' its ideological assumptions. Although it could not take full advantage of them it had nevertheless 'prepared its own criticism' and 'paved the way' for its own eventual 'refutation' and supersession.[61] What was needed was a new perspective, a new orientation of thought, a new point of view, which was free from the ideological assumptions of classical economy and capable of consolidating and building on its insights. The socialist economists provided such a point of view. They took up their inquiry from where their great bourgeois predecessors had left off. They found 'the theoretical ground already prepared' by classical political economy, especially Ricardo, 'who must be regarded its complete and final expression',[62] and attempted to construct a new theoretical structure. This is how Marx thought of his own work. He set himself the task of rejecting the ideological 'shell' of classical economics, abstracting what he judged to be its 'rational kernel', and rehabilitating and building upon it within a more satisfactory framework. No wonder he handsomely complimented a Russian commentator for appreciating that *Capital* was 'in its fundamentals *a necessary* sequel to the teaching of Smith and Ricardo'.[63]

IV

As we saw, Marx criticised classical political economy for being systematically biased. It absolutised capitalism and assumed that it was natural to man, the most rational way imaginable to organise material production, non-contradictory, non-exploitative, and so on. Marx's analysis raises several questions, such as why classical economy made these assumptions, why it did not become fully aware of them, and what happened to it when it did.

According to Marx, a form of inquiry comes into being when its subject matter has a clear and identifiable character, and is generally deemed important enough to merit systematic investigation. Unless it has a firm and independent identity, it is not distinct enough to raise novel questions, or to require an independent body of concepts, or even to allow the theoretical consciousness to take a firm grip on it. Unless it is deemed important, it cannot command the continued attention of a large body of men. Marx observes:[64]

> Man's reflections on the forms of social life and consequently, also,
> his scientific analysis of those forms, take a course directly opposite
> to that of their actual historical development. He begins, *post
> festum*, with the results of the process of development ready to hand
> before him. The characters that stamp products as commodities,
> and whose establishment is a necessary preliminary to the circulation
> of commodities, have already acquired the stability of natural,
> self-understood forms of social life, before man seeks to decipher,
> not their historical character, for in his eyes they are immutable,
> but their meaning.

Marx argues that, for these reasons, the discipline of political
economy could only come into existence when the economic activity
had set itself free from the other human activities, acquired a firm and
independent identity, assumed practical importance, and begun to raise
theoretical perplexities about its nature and mode of operation. These
conditions were first met in the eighteenth-century bourgeois society,
and hence the science of political economy made its historical appearance. Since capitalism was more fully developed in Britain than any
other country, the discipline of political economy was first developed
there. The developing capitalism in Britain threw up interesting problems, suggested new concepts, offered a testing ground for economic
theories and provided a historical continuity necessary to sustain a
tradition of inquiry.

The attempts to develop the discipline in countries where capitalism had not developed led to ludicrous results. Marx took the
example of Germany. For a variety of reasons the capitalist mode of
production did not develop in Germany for a long time, and the economic life did not attain the autonomy and independence it enjoyed in
England and later in France. Hence 'the soil whence political economy
springs was wanting'. When the German economists tried to study
economic life, they found that their subject matter was confused,
lacked a firm identity, could not be easily classified and conceptualised,
and did not raise interesting theoretical problems. Consequently they
could do little more than borrow and comment on the economic
theories developed in England and France. However, this was not easy.
Since they lacked the detailed knowledge of the economic reality that
their theories were designed to describe and explain, the German economists could not help interpreting them wrongly, explaining them by

inappropriate examples, compensating for their limited knowledge by speculation and generously borrowing ideas from incompatible sources. Predictably, despite all their 'parade of literary and historical erudition', their economic writings remained abstract, lacked focus and direction and displayed a 'feeling of scientific impotence and the uneasy consciousness of having to touch a subject in reality foreign to them'. Marx thought that, compared to the British and the French, even the best German economists 'remained schoolboys'.

When the science of economics appeared on the scene, the bourgeois society had already been in existence for some time, the pre-capitalist modes of production had more or less ceased to exist, and the self-confident and energetic capitalism was increasingly consolidating itself. Its various parts were all harmoniously integrated, and behaved with remarkable regularity. Besides, the basic institutions of capitalism — such as the atomic individual, the exchange-based economy, the elimination of the customary restraints on the right to property, the commodity production and the pursuit of value — were all well developed and had 'already acquired the stability of natural' features. Further, the economically dominant capitalism had, to a considerable degree, moulded the other areas of life in its own image. The legal institutions recognised the individual as the subject of rights and obligations, and not the estates and classes as the pre-bourgeois law had done. The law defined property in more or less absolute and exclusive terms. The social institutions recognised only the individual as the bearer of claims and duties, imposed no obligations other than those voluntarily incurred, and made exchange and reciprocity the bases of interpersonal relations. In short the bourgeois mode of production was not confined to the economic realm; it had brought almost the entire society in harmony with its needs and had become a way of life. Like the ordinary men the political economists, whose forms of thought and values were shaped by their society, assumed that the bourgeois society, which harmonised with their own socially shaped nature, was natural, permanent and in the interest of all its members.

According to Marx there was also another important factor that encouraged this belief. Like any other revolutionary group, the bourgeoisie in their early years spoke and acted in the name and interest of the whole society. They were the vanguard of the rest of society in its struggle against the landed aristocracy. Since their interests and aspirations coincided with those of the non-aristocratic sections of society, they were a genuinely 'universal class'. They were also a progressive class, in the sense that they stood for the liberation of man.

They aimed to master nature and liberate man from its 'tyranny'. They aimed also to liberate him from the feudal, social and political restraints.

The bourgeoisie placed a convenient ideological gloss on these historical facts. They claimed that they represented the real interests of all men, and were the vanguard of a new and truly human civilisation. They claimed that the society they had created was in the universal interest of all its members, had replaced the 'archaic' classes with the free, independent and self-determining individuals, had substituted universal harmony for the feudal class-slavery, and so on. Further, they claimed that the bourgeois society was not only more progressive than its predecessors, but had made a historical breakthrough to an entirely new and truly human form of social organisation.

In Marx's view each of these claims had a measure of historical truth.[65] The bourgeois society *was* more progressive; it *did* achieve greater human liberation than ever before, and the bourgeoisie *were* a universal class. However, in each case their claims vastly exaggerated the measure of truth. Although more progressive, the bourgeois society did not represent the end of history; although it represented a new civilisation, it also represented a new 'barbarism' and its civilisation was not the highest man is capable of; although it achieved greater liberation, it also brought new slavery; and although they were *once* a universal class, the bourgeoisie ceased to be so when they consolidated their rule, became a narrow class and could only pursue their interests at the expense of those of the working class. In short the bourgeois claims amounted to turning the historical into a natural truth, a contingent fact into an eternal verity. As we saw, for Marx such a gross distortion and biased exaggeration constitutes the essence of ideology.

Classical political economy was born within this ideological milieu. Like the ordinary men — and the classical economists were ordinary men in matters falling outside their expertise — they accepted the dominant ideological beliefs 'without thinking, naively and unconsciously', especially as these confirmed their experiences of the ideologically constructed social world. Further, although they were grossly exaggerated, the bourgeois claims were not lies or completely false. They had some historical truth and some social 'validity', especially in the early years of capitalism. As such they enabled the classical economists to offer reasonably plausible explanations of economic life. If the claims had been totally false and inapplicable to the contemporary society, they would have led the economists to offer bizarre explanations. Such explanations would have immediately alerted them to the limitations of their assumptions. Again, there was no obvious reason why the classical economists should have wished to question the bourgeois claims. They were not generally at the receiving end of capitalism, did not suffer from its evils, and were therefore not provoked by their interests or needs to examine its ideological claims too closely.

For these and other reasons, they uncritically accepted the ideological claims of the bourgeoisie, which thus found their way into classical political economy and formed its unarticulated and unexamined assumptions. The classical economists investigated economic life within the framework of these assumptions. As we saw, they asked questions, devised methods of analysis and employed concepts that presupposed the truth of these assumptions. Over the years they built up the discipline of political economy on an ideologically biased basis.

While it is understandable that the early economists should have been taken in by the ideological claims of the bourgeoisie, the question arises as to why the later economists were, especially when the ideological claims had begun to wear thin. Marx seems to suggest three interrelated explanations.

First, in learning their discipline the generations of economists learnt not only what questions to ask and how to go about answering them, but also a systematically biased way of understanding their subject matter.[66] They accepted the traditionally handed-down questions, concepts, conceptual distinctions and methods of analysis as 'orthodox articles of faith'.[67] For Marx, to be initiated into a discipline is to be initiated, at first, into a specific way of defining and conceptualising one's subject matter, and ultimately into a specific social bias lying at the basis of the discipline. As we shall see later, Marx does not take the naive phenomenological view that we should dispense with the intellectual traditions altogether, and seems to hint at a more complex and dialectical conception of the nature and role of the tradition.

Second, Marx argues that theoretical investigation does not occur in an existential vacuum. A scientist is not a disembodied spirit, but a human being who has his interests, fears, and anxieties by which his theoretical reflection is deeply affected. His interests, etc., make him sensitive to certain aspects of social life and prompt him to ask appropriate theoretical questions. When he is materially affected in unsuspected ways, the relevant aspects of social life which he had hitherto accepted as unproblematic or not even noticed suddenly become visible and problematic. For Marx those who materially suffer in the capitalist society have a material and an intellectual interest, even a need to ask disturbing questions about it, and to wonder why

the economic life should be organised in this way. The classical economists generally belonged to a relatively privileged group. They did not
suffer under capitalism, and therefore were not 'compelled' by their
'conditions of existence' to examine critically its ideological claims.
There was no obvious reason why they should *want* to challenge them,
or even *suspect* that they might not be correct. The 'will' to challenge
a social institution or a social order is not the result of a mere intellectual desire to be critical, but has social roots to which it owes its
origin, tenacity, urgency and energy. Some economists were, no doubt,
moved by the human suffering, but most 'shut their eyes' to it. They
did not *wish* to see it, and were convinced by their basic assumptions
that it could not be widespread and last for ever. Accordingly they
ignored human suffering, underplayed its intensity and extent, or
accepted easy and shallow explanations of it. Marx observes:[68]

> The *desire* to convince oneself of the non-existence of contradic-
> tions is at the same time the expression of a pious *wish* that the
> contradictions which are really present should not exist.

Third, although the economists were not provoked by their own
existential conditions to re-examine their ideological bias, they might
have been led to do so if there had been recurrent social crises and an
organised class asking searching questions about and even challenging
capitalism. For a long time the crises faced by capitalism were sporadic
and manageable, and there was no organised class systematically mount-
ing a radical critique of it. In their absence the economists were not
alerted to the historical and contradictory nature of capitalism and to
the ideological bias of their assumptions. This seems to be the import of
Marx's otherwise baffling remark that consciousness can come into
conflict with the prevailing pattern of relationships *only when* the
latter itself comes into conflict with the forces of production. For Marx
it is only when a society is in a state of crisis, created by the incompatibility between the forces and the relations of production, and an
organised class capable of creating a new social order is in sight, that
its members are able to take a critical and historical attitude to it.
Its transience and historicity then 'become a truth demonstrable to
every unprejudiced mind and only denied by those whose interest
it is to hedge other people in a fool's paradise'. The occurrence of a
social crisis breaks the naturalistic illusion, and makes it possible to
study both the present and the past objectively. The social scientist
is able to view his own society as a distinctive historical formation

which will one day disappear. His historical consciousness enables him to see past societies also as distinctive historical units. Marx puts the point well:[69] 'Bourgeois economics arrived at an understanding of feudal, ancient oriental economics only after the self-criticism of bourgeois society had begun'

For Marx classical economy rested on several ideological assumptions of which two were most important, namely that capitalism is natural and non-contradictory. When, thanks to the inner dynamics of capitalism itself and the proletarian praxis, the falsity of the assumptions was demonstrated beyond a shadow of doubt, the classical economist was confronted with a crisis. He could no longer continue to think within the traditional framework. His 'more or less' conscious assumptions had now been brought into the open and exposed; the moment of truth had at last arrived; and the classical economist was forced to choose between science and ideology. He could either jettison his ideological assumptions and construct a radically critical political economy on a new basis, or retain them and abandon his scientific ambition. It became the very precondition of his remaining a scientist that he must radically reappraise the conceptual and methodological tools of his discipline. As Marx put it,[70]

In so far as Political Economy remains within that horizon, in so far, i.e., as the capitalist regime is looked upon as the absolutely final form of social production, instead of as a passing historical phase of its evolution, Political Economy can remain a science only so long as the class-struggle is latent or manifests itself only in isolated and sporadic phenomena.

In Marx's view this was the fateful choice before the economists after 1830 when the bourgeoisie, having subdued their feudal rivals, gained power and turned on their former allies. The classical economists responded to the challenge in one of four ways.[71]

First, some continued to study society in their wonted ways, and reiterated old theories as if nothing had changed. However, this became an increasingly difficult intellectual option to adopt. The more the established social order is exposed as transient, 'the fictitious, of course, becomes the consciousness which originally corresponded to this form of intercourse', and 'the less they [its categories] satisfy the understanding'.[72] A point was eventually reached when even the most orthodox economists began to notice that their methods of study were patently partisan. Denied the cosy comfort of unexposed prejudices, they were forced either to resort to 'conscious illusion, deliberate hypocrisy', or to abandon their traditional manner of thinking.

Second, some others, the 'vulgarians' or 'sophists' as Marx called them, gave up all scientific pretensions and became the 'hired prize-fighters' for the established social order. They distorted unpalatable truths, employed pseudo-scientific arguments to support their thinly disguised prejudices, talked the unpleasant facts 'out of existence', and conveniently spent their time attacking the exaggerated claims of their opponents rather than defending their own. For them it was 'no longer a question of whether a theorem was true, but whether it was useful to capital or harmful, expedient or inexpedient, politically dangerous or not'.[73]

Third, some economists saw the force of the challenge. However, rather than undertake a radical reappraisal of their assumptions and methods, they tried to combine the new ideas with the old in a spirit of 'compromise', and ended up producing a 'mediocre pap', an 'insipid' system of thought distinguished only by a 'shallow syncretism'.[74] Marx took J.S. Mill to be an example of such an 'academic' approach.

Finally, some economists abandoned the study of social reality altogether and either retreated to the history of economic thought, or devoted themselves to formalising the available knowledge.[75] Their theories lacked a 'living foundation', their 'raw material was no longer reality' but empty concepts, and they had nothing to offer save 'formal, logical consistency'.

In Marx's view no economist accepted the intellectual challenge posed by the exposure of his discipline's ideological bias, and undertook a profound and radically 'self-critical' appraisal of his discipline. For Marx this explains why the discipline of economics after Ricardo was in its 'twilight . . . indeed on its very death-bed', and unable to make 'decisive leaps'.[76] It had 'reached the limits beyond which it could not pass'.[77] Marx observes:[78]

The history of modern political economy ends with Ricardo and Sismondi . . . just as it begins at the end of the seventeenth century with Petty and Boisguillebert. Subsequent political-economic litera-ture loses its way, moving either towards eclectic, syncretistic compendia . . . or into deeper elaboration of individual branches . . . It is altogether a literature of epigones; reproduction, greater elaboration of form, wider appropriation of material, exaggeration, popularisation, synopsis, elaboration of details; lack of decisive leaps in the phases of development, incorporation of the inventory on one side, new growth at individual points on the other.

When a discipline reaches such a pathetic stage, it has clearly 'reached the end of its scope as a science'.[79] The works produced by its practitioners both symbolise and expedite its decline.

V

We outlined above some of Marx's basic criticisms of classical political economy. It is sometimes argued that, for Marx, *all* the limitations of classical economy sprang from its ideological bias, and that the influence of the bias, like that of a virus, was direct and easily identifiable. Both these are mistaken readings of Marx. For Marx not all the limitations of the classical economists could be explained in terms of the ideological bias, and the bias operated in a highly complex, mediated and uneven manner. Since the point is of considerable importance, it would be useful to list most of the limitations and briefly explore how each is related to the ideological bias. Needless to say, our analysis is extremely sketchy and tentative, and only designed to show how complex the whole question is, and how much work still needs to be done by Marx's commentators if they are to give an adequate account of his theory of ideology.

Marx made the following criticisms of the classical economists. First, they committed factual errors and were not always rigorous in their investigations. Second, they sometimes made mistakes in logic, drew wrong conclusions and failed to notice the inconsistencies and contradictions in their arguments. Third, they were not always able to liberate themselves from the ordinary ways of thinking about economic life. They sometimes borrowed the ordinary man's vocabulary, and asked questions which made sense at the common-sensical but not the scientific level. Fourth, they were guilty of indiscriminate abstraction, or what one might call overabstraction. They abstracted and concentrated on the general features shared in common by all modes of production. As a result they more or less completely ignored the historical specificity of each mode, especially capitalism, and used ahistorical concepts and methods of analysis. Fifth, they were guilty of inadequate abstraction or what one might call underabstraction. They did not sufficiently abstract an entity from its different forms, and tended to confuse it with one of them. Sixth, they asked questions, used concepts and drew distinctions, etc. which were biased, and made sense only on the assumption that the capitalist mode of production was natural, non-contradictory and the most rational way to organise the economy. Seventh, which is but a converse of the sixth criticism, the classical economists did not ask questions and use methods of analysis capable of illuminating the innermost nature and historical specificity of capitalism, and took an extremely narrow view of their subject matter.

Marx nowhere says that *all* the limitations of classical political economy listed above are traceable to its ideological bias. Although he is not entirely clear, his view seems to be that its ideological bias was the *sole* source of *some* of its limitations, and an important *contributory* factor in the case of the others. Let us briefly examine how this is so.

For Marx the ideological bias was obviously responsible for the last two limitations. In his view it explains, and can alone explain, why the classical economists asked biased questions, used biased concepts, and so on, and, conversely, why they did not ask certain questions, stopped short of pursuing certain lines of investigation and narrowly defined their subject matter. It is, of course, possible to explain some of these limitations in terms of such common human failings as intellectual carelessness, inadequate analysis, an uncertain grasp of their subject matter and a limited imagination. However, when the limitations reveal a *structural* pattern and a *systematic* trend, and are shared by a host of writers over generations, such subjective explanations are totally inadequate. Further, as we saw Marx argue in connection with Hegel, the great writers' limitations cannot all be fully explained in terms of contingent factors. In his view their roots lie deep in their 'principles' or 'essential form of consciousness'. Accordingly he seeks to identify the *theoretical* sources of the limitations of the classical economists. He argues that their unquestioned basic assumptions about the nature of the capitalist mode of production delimited their intellectual horizon, and imposed objective and structural barriers on their thought. As a result their ideas moved within a certain range, pointed in a certain direction, and had certain inherent tendencies, of which their theoretical limitations were necessary products.

The first five limitations are not so easily accounted for. Although not directly and sometimes not even indirectly traceable to the ideological bias, Marx seems to think that they were all affected by it in varying degrees. It is true that even the most unbiased economists could have committed factual errors. However, Marx takes the view that when a writer *tends* to overlook specific *kinds* of fact, and his empirical errors form a *pattern*, something more than simple inadvertence is at play. As we saw, the classical economists systematically ignored, underplayed or misinterpreted the facts relating to such subjects as the working class conditions, the nature and social origin of demand, general overproduction, the effects of the detailed division of labour and the working class habits and character.[80] These errors fall within a recognisable area, reveal a clearly identifiable tendency and can only be explained in terms of their ideological bias. It is because their investigations were based on certain biased assumptions that they tended to look out for certain types of fact, and overlooked those that did not conform to their ideologically shaped expectations.[81]

Like the factual, the logical mistakes could have been made by even the most objective economist. However, when these mistakes tend to occur in convenient contexts and generally help the writer avoid unpalatable conclusions or cover up glaring inconsistencies, the role of the ideological bias cannot be entirely ruled out. Marx gives several examples, some of which were cited earlier, to show how the classical economists committed logical errors, resorted to linguistic ambiguities and subterfuges, and employed 'cunning argument' at suspiciously convenient stages in their discussions of a subject.[82] He shows also how, from time to time, they started with one question but 'unconsciously' replaced it with another, covered up awkward conclusions by vague and evasive expressions, freely used such conjunctions as 'therefore', 'so' and 'hence' to help them effect illegitimate logical transitions, and on occasion became 'very cautious' and reticent as if prompted by a 'bad conscience'.[83]

Again, even the most objective scientists can fail to liberate themselves from and occasionally lapse into the vulgar and unscientific ways of thinking about their subject matter. However, Marx seems to think that when their lapses are recurrent, follow a pattern, occur in some contexts and not others, and when no stringent steps are taken to prevent them, one may wonder if they are entirely accidental. As we saw, Marx argues that the ordinary ways of thinking about society are derived from the ideologically constructed social world, and therefore necessarily apologetic.[84] This means that a social scientist who is already biased towards the dominant ideology would tend to lapse into them far more easily, be less conscious of such lapses and less anxious to guard himself against them than one who is critical of it. Indeed, some of the questions asked by the ordinary men are precisely the ones he is himself likely to ask, and some of the concepts employed by them are likely to be his own. As we saw, this was the case with the classical economists. Since their ideological bias coincided with that underlying the ordinary modes of thought, from time to time they took over the ordinary concepts and questions without noticing their scientific impropriety. What is more, they tended to invoke the authority of common sense and use such expressions as 'self-evident', 'obvious' and 'normal' precisely when they found themselves confronted with the ideologically awkward questions and conclusions.

As we saw, the method of overabstraction is, in Marx's view, a perennial feature of the Western thought and not peculiar to the classical economists. Although they did not invent it, it fitted in well with their ideological assumptions, and hence they adopted and refined it. Since they absolutised the capitalist mode of production, they had to universalise such distinctive categories of it as capital, wage labour, commodity, commodity production and greed; the traditional idealist method of overabstraction served the purpose well. For more or less similar reasons they adopted the method of underabstraction, and preferred the analytical over the genetic method of presentation. They did so not as a direct but as an indirect result of their ideological bias. As we saw, the bias led them to overlook the specificity, at first of social forms and then, of all forms, and thus prepared the grounds for their methodological tendencies towards underabstraction and reductionism. Marx seems to think that overabstraction and underabstraction are complementary polarities and have a common root, namely the neglect of the specific and distinctive nature of social institutions and structures. When the specificity of their forms is no longer kept at the centre of one's attention, one tends to swing between the interdependent extremes of overabstraction and underabstraction. Indeed one cannot overabstract without, at the same time, underabstracting. To universalise a specific form of an institution *is* also to equate the latter with one of its forms. As we saw, the classical economist could not universalise the historically specific capitalist mode of production without, at the same time, presenting it as the *only* rational method of organising material production.

For Marx, then, the ideological bias of classical political economy exerted its influence in ways that were varied, and sometimes extremely subtle and complex. In some cases its influence was easily detectable; on other occasions it was so elusive that a rigorous analysis was needed to uncover it. Besides, sometimes it directly affected the economists' questions, selections of evidence and modes of reasoning; more often it shaped their ideas indirectly by first influencing their definitions of their subject matter, choices of concepts and methods of investigation.

Further, in some cases the ideological bias was the sole course of their limitations; on most occasions, however, it intensified the understandable human tendency to overlook uncomfortable facts, exaggerate the value of the familiar, misinterpret the unfamiliar, or make do with the intellectually unsatisfactory but cosy conventional explanations. Finally, the ideological bias is not like the original sin, corrupting the innermost essence of a theory and rendering it useless, but rather like a distorting lens that circumscribes its range and distorts its view. As we saw, the ideological bias hindered and distorted the classical economist's scientific investigations, but did not altogether prevent him from making significant discoveries, getting 'close' to the inner nature of his subject matter, and even implicitly subverting the bias itself.

VI

Before ending the chapter it would be useful to highlight a few general implications of Marx's critique of classical political economy.

First, for Marx a body of thought can be both scientific and ideological. As we saw, classical political economy was both. Although science and ideology are mutually exclusive concepts it is possible for a body of thought to contain the elements of both. Marx has no name for such a body of thought. Since it has both the scientific and ideological dimension, it cannot be called an ideological or a scientific theory *sans phrase*. Nor can it be called a scientific ideology, for that implies that an ideology can be scientific, and Marx rules out such a possibility. Perhaps it could be called an ideological science. The expression implies that a body of thought is *primarily*, that is in its intentions and achievements scientific, and for various reasons fails to achieve its ambition. Marx not only admits the possibility, but believes that it is the most common characteristic of almost all scientific thought. What is more, Marx's own description of classical political economy as the 'bourgeois science' or 'bourgeois political economy' would seem to support such an expression. In any case the point worth noting is that, for Marx, classical political economy, Hegel's philosophy and such other systems of thought were not simply or primarily *ideologies*. They were primarily scientific, although they had an *ideological orientation* or dimension. Marx's analysis seems to point towards a distinction between ideology as a noun and an adjective. Only the small class of purely justificatory bodies of thought can be called an ideology. Most theories are not ideologies, but have an ideological orientation.

Some of the intellectual confusion and hostility surrounding Marx's theory of ideology could be avoided if the adjectival expression were as a rule to be preferred over the substantive.

Second, there is no evidence to support the view advanced by some commentators that, for Marx, classical political economy was a science until 1830 and only became ideological thereafter. For Marx it was, from the very beginning, a 'bourgeois science' and a 'prisoner of the capitalist standpoint'. After 1830, when its ideological assumptions were brought into the open and exposed, it was required either to abandon its scientific aspirations and become a vulgar economy, or to reconstitute itself on a new foundation. As long as it was unaware of its bourgeois bias, it impartially investigated the capitalist mode of production, albeit within an ideological framework. Once its bias was exposed, it had no choice except either to overcome it or resort to lies. Marx's commentators who believe that classical economy only became ideological after 1830 do so because, in their view, a discipline is either a science or an ideology, but not *both*. As we saw, this is not at all Marx's view.

Third, for Marx the fate of a social science is inextricably tied up with that of a particular historical epoch. A social science comes into being at a certain time, reaches its zenith, and then declines.[85] It comes into being when its subject matter acquires an autonomous and independent character. For Marx its autonomy is not its inherent and natural property, but socially derived. Every social order is structured in a certain manner, and separates, classifies and organises human activities appropriately. When a differently constituted social order comes into being, it restructures, redefines and differently relates the human activities. An activity which was once autonomous may lose its autonomy. And then the discipline concerned to study it no longer has an independent subject matter. It either ceases to exist altogether, or becomes an integral part of another discipline. For example, the science of economics cannot retain its present theoretical independence in the communist society in which the economic activity no longer enjoys material and social independence, is collectively regulated and subordinated to non-economic purposes.

Further, for Marx when a discipline comes into being, it rests on a specific body of social assumptions derived from the contemporary cultural milieu. It defines its subject matter in a certain way, evolves a specific body of concepts, methods of investigation, and so on, and builds up a tradition. Since the traditional mode of practising it rests on certain social assumptions, it flourishes as long as the latter have at least some validity, and faces a crisis when they have none. For Marx the crisis of a tradition is not the crisis of the discipline itself, although for obvious ideological reasons it may be presented as such by those with a vested professional interest in preserving the tradition and discouraging new intellectual experiments. A tradition is in crisis when its social assumptions forfeit their validity; a discipline is in crisis when its subject matter loses its autonomy or importance.[86] Although the two may sometimes coincide, it is not necessary that they must. As we saw, Marx argues that when classical political economy faced a crisis after 1830, it was not the discipline of economics itself but the traditional manner of practising it that was in difficulty.

Although Marx does not put it this way, his analysis suggests that the relation between a discipline and its tradition is dialectical in nature. A tradition provides the intellectual framework indispensable for the growth of a discipline. It provides a body of concepts, the methods of investigation and a way of defining a subject matter without which a form of inquiry lacks coherence and character. It also provides the standards of judgement and evaluation which indicate to the scientist the level below which his investigation may not fall, and guard him against the seductive appeal of the vulgar modes of thought. It provides also a common world of discourse and the historical continuity necessary for the consolidation of its theoretical insights. In these and other ways a tradition preserves the 'scientific soul' of a discipline, and allows it to grow and flourish at its own pace.

Marx takes the view that while a tradition is intellectually indispensable, it is also inherently restrictive, in the sense that the assumptions upon which it rests limit its horizon and distort its perception of its subject matter.[87] A discipline cannot grow outside a tradition; at the same, however, a tradition only allows it to grow in a specific direction and up to a certain point. When that point is reached, the tradition becomes a hindrance and requires a radical reappraisal. For Marx a tradition is to a discipline what the relations of production are to the productive forces. It constitutes the form within which a discipline grows and acquires intellectual content. A form can only permit a certain type of content, and deserves to be replaced when its theoretical potentialities are fully and exhaustively exploited. A discipline necessarily needs *a* tradition, but not a *particular* tradition. It grows within a particular tradition and then grows out of it. Even as the relations of production stimulate, and are then discarded in the long-term interest of the productive forces, a tradition, once it has generated a certain body of theoretical content, becomes a hindrance to the growth of knowledge and needs to be replaced by a more hospitable tradition.

Fourth, Marx's account of the nature, origin and development of classical political economy is both dialectical and materialist. As we saw, he argued that, from the very beginning, political economy contained two contradictory tendencies, namely the ideological and the scientific. Its history is a story of the constant tension between its scientific *telos* and ideological bias. The scientific *telos* was often frustrated by, but it continually pushed against and eventually subverted the underlying bias. Like a good rationalist Marx was convinced that the truth must eventually prevail.

Marx's account raises the obvious question as to how the two were related and whether classical economy could have developed on a non-ideological foundation. He does not discuss the question, and makes ambiguous and even contradictory remarks. Sometimes he suggests, following Hegel, that the *telos* and the conditions of existence of a form of inquiry are organically related, that historically speaking classical economy could only become a science by viewing the capitalist society from the bourgeois point of view, that it needed the ideological framework to develop as a science, and that, in general, a science initially grows up within and then out of an ideology. On other occasions Marx takes a different view. He suggests that classical economy need not have made the ideological assumptions in question, and that its doing so was historically understandable but not necessary.[88] It is difficult to say which is his well-considered view. In any case there is little doubt that Marx's general account of classical economy is dialectical in nature.

Marx's account is also materialist in the sense that he explains the origin and development of classical economy in terms of the relations of production. As we saw, he argues that classical political economy came into being when the economic life acquired autonomy, independence and importance, and explains the latter phenomenon in terms of the atomistic and egoistic nature of the capitalist mode of production. Further, for Marx, classical economy derived its basic assumptions from the current ideological construal of the capitalist mode of production. As Marx puts it, it took over the material conditions of existence of capitalism, and 'reproduced them in thought' as its 'basic presuppositions'. When, in the course of its development, the capitalist society turned out to be historical and contradictory, the basic assumptions of classical economy lost their validity, throwing the discipline into an acute crisis. For Marx, again, the development of classical economy 'keeps pace with the real development of the social contradictions and class-conflicts inherent in capitalist production'.[89] As the class contradictions became acute, the contradictions between the scientific *telos* and the ideological presuppositions of classical economy also become acute.[90] And when the class contradictions became explosive, so did the internal contradictions of classical economy. For Marx the dialectic of classical economy is integrally tied up with, and owes it origin and pattern of development to, the dialectic of the capitalist society.

To avoid misunderstanding three general points need to be made. First, we are not concerned here to assess the historical accuracy of Marx's account of classical political economy, but only to elucidate its underlying logical structure. Second, in saying that Marx's account of classical economy was materialist *and* dialectical, we are not saying that he was a dialectical materialist. Marx himself called his approach 'materialist dialectics', and never used the ambiguous term 'dialectical materialism'.[91] Third, our interpretation only relates to Marx's analysis of classical political economy, and not to his theory of history, let alone his philosophy of nature. We are not committed to saying that *because* Marx gave a materialist-dialectical account of the origin and development of classical political economy, and perhaps of capitalism itself, he *must* be presumed to have offered a similar account of the pre-capitalist societies and man's relation to nature as well. Whether or not Marx intended to extend the dialectic outside the narrow confines of capitalism is too complex a question to discuss here.[92] We may also note that, as Lukács and Schmidt have ably argued, there is no inconsistency involved in offering a dialectical account of capitalism and a non-dialectical account of the other modes of production. For Marx the dialectic is not an 'ontological law' as it was for Hegel, but a mode of development presupposing a specific set of material conditions. As such it comes into being when the relevant material conditions obtain, and occurs in a form and degree dictated by the latter.[93]

6 THE FORMS OF IDEOLOGICAL AND CRITICAL THOUGHT

In the previous chapters we outlined Marx's analysis of the various ways in which social theorists unwittingly develop apologetic bodies of thought. His analysis raises several large questions of which it would be useful to pursue two in further detail. First, what, in his view, are the forms of reasoning characteristic of the ideological thought? Or, which is really the same question from a different angle, what are the logical manoeuvres and fallacies involved in the construction of an apologetic body of thought? Second, how can a writer become genuinely critical? That is what forms of reasoning and modes of analysis must he adopt or eschew in order to eliminate the possibility of a systematic bias?

I

For Marx the ideologist is an apologist. He 'canonises the existing world' by explaining away its disagreeable features, especially its fundamental conflicts of interest and historicity. In the course of developing such a systematically biased body of thought, he is led to resort to what Marx calls 'logical tricks' or 'lapses' and which might perhaps better be called logical fallacies.[1] Marx was deeply interested in identifying and exposing the characteristic fallacies of ideological reasoning. Although he nowhere lists them, he seems to think that the following are the most common.

First, the ideologist de-historicises and universalises the ideas and forms of thought of his society. For Marx every social order is characterised by a specific set of social relations which are best conceptualised by a specific set of concepts. The ideologist generalises these concepts and, in so doing, confers universal validity on the underlying social relations and experiences. For example, as we saw, the classical economists so defined the concepts of capital, wage labour and commodity production that the capitalist and the wage labourer were presented as universal figures who were in no way unique to the capitalist society. Their universalisation of the capitalist relations of production had two crucial consequences. First, they presented capitalism not as a historical and transient mode of production, but as a universal feature of the human condition. Second, they presented it as marking the end of history, as the most rational method of organising production ever likely to be discovered by man. Since the classical economists judged all human societies by a single set of criteria, they were able to grade them hierarchically. And since the criteria were derived from the capitalist society, they had no difficulty showing it to be the best of them all. As we saw they argued that capital and labour, subjected to all kinds of 'restraints' in the pre-capitalist societies, at last emerged in their fully 'rational' and 'free' form under capitalism. In Marx's view the ideologist constantly blurs the historical specificity of his society and commits the fallacy of de-historicising history.

Second, the ideologist has a persistent tendency to reduce history to nature, and present the prevailing practice, institution or social order as if it were part of the natural order.[2] He may actually refer to them as natural, or use such equally elusive terms as normal, rational, reasonable and necessary, or employ circumlocutions whose import and impact are basically the same. Whatever his mode of expression, the ideologist obliterates the historicity of a given institution, makes it appear unalterable and places it outside the pale of discussion. In so doing he forestalls all criticism, and presents the critic as Utopian, mad, irresponsible, or naive.

The obliteration of the distinction between history and nature is, in Marx's view, the most common and effective device employed by the ideologist. For example, the ideologist 'justifies' the capitalist society on the ground that it alone is in harmony with human nature. He justifies hard work and attacks the demand for a relaxed social existence on the ground that scarcity is a natural human predicament. He explains overpopulation as an 'inherent' tendency in man, and turns 'a social law into a law of nature'.[3] He presents conflicts between individuals and groups as inherent in human nature and indeed in nature itself. He presents the socially created differences between men and women as natural, and argues that it is natural for women to be confined to homes or to less demanding jobs. He presents the historically created intellectual, moral and other inequalities between men as part of their 'natural endowment', and turns 'the consequences of society into the consequences of nature'.[4] He argues that it is natural for social institutions to be hierarchically organised, for the intellectual skills to be better rewarded than the manual, and so on. As Marx frequently puts it, the ideologist 'eternalises' or 'deifies' a given social practice or order, and eliminates history.

Since the ideologist presents the historical as the natural, Marx is intensely suspicious of any reference to nature in human affairs. In his view it is almost always a cloak for legitimising a social practice by concealing its historicity and alterability. Marx frequently comes close to saying, especially in his early writings, that man is entirely a product of history, and that nothing distinctively human is natural. In his later writings he is more cautious, and admits that certain things are part of human nature or, rather, the human condition; for example, the necessity to labour and the need for self-objectification. However, he remains averse to describing human relations, experiences and qualities as natural. He insists that nothing should be considered natural without the strongest possible evidence and that, since the 'boundaries of nature' are constantly 'receding', it must be appreciated that what is deemed natural today may later turn out to be historical.

The first and second fallacy are not necessarily connected, for one can universalise a relation or an experience without implying that it is natural. However, the two generally tend to go together. If an experience or a relation is assumed to be universal, there is a presumption in favour of its being natural. If it is natural, it is bound in one form or another to be universal. Although Marx's usage is not consistent, he sometimes says that when a relation or experience is presented as natural, it is eternalised, 'deified' or 'absolutised'.[5]

Third, the ideologist constantly conflates the distinction between form and content, and attributes to one the properties of the other as his ideological purpose dictates. For Marx a social structure is characterised by a specific set of production relations and a particular level of productive forces, the former constituting its form and the latter its content. He argues that, since the ideologist's primary concern is to legitimise the social form and present it in the most favourable light, he attributes its evils to, and gives it credit for the benefits of technology. The social relations of capitalism create alienation, unemployment and acute division of labour, dehumanise the worker, cripple his personality, etc. The ideologist explains all these in terms of the machines, and deflects the attack on the capitalist social structure to its technology. While producing the social evils, technology also eliminates poverty and disease, conquers nature, creates material abundance, and so on. The ideologist ascribes these benefits to the capitalist social relations. Marx admits that the productive forces would not have developed to the historically unprecedented degree without the bourgeoisie, but insists that a point has now arrived when the latter have become a hindrance to their further development. Although once valid, the 'technological justification' of capitalism is no longer so.[6]

Fourth, the ideologist has a constant tendency to reduce a relation to a quality and prefer a quality-signifying to a relation-signifying vocabulary. To say that a glass broke because a stone hit it is to describe the relation between the two; to say that it broke because it was brittle is to describe a quality of the glass. Similarly to say that a group of men died of starvation is to highlight the non-availability or even denial of food, which is a social relation; to say that they died of hunger is to focus on the natural quality of the dead.[7]

According to Marx a good deal of justification of the established social order is of this kind. Men are said to compete or fight because they are competitive or aggressive; the rich are said to be rich because they are thrifty, hard-working, enterprising, clever, etc.; the poor are said to be poor because they are extravagant, imprudent, lazy and stupid, and so on. For Marx the explanations offered are patently 'childish'.[8] Men are not aggressive by nature, because no such behaviour is to be found in many past and present societies, and in some men even in the modern capitalist society. Aggressiveness is a socially acquired quality. Since society is a system of relationship, a socially acquired quality can only be a product of the preventing pattern of relationship. Men learn to behave aggressively in a society which is so structured that they cannot otherwise survive or attain socially prized goods. It is a social relation that has generated the quality, not the other way round.

Again, a man is often poor because he has nothing to sell but his manual labour; and this, in turn, is the case because he was born into a family which could only equip him with limited skills. At the opposite end of the economic scale, a man is rich because he owns the means of production with which his hired workers produce surplus value for him. Capital is self-reproducing. The capitalist's moral qualities are almost totally irrelevant; and so are his intellectual qualities, for he can always compensate for his modest gifts by hiring competent managers. Marx admits that in the early years of capitalism, the moral and intellectual qualities did matter, and that they do matter today in the occasional cases when by luck, self-debasement or superhuman acts of will, an individual rises from poverty to affluence. However, he is convinced that in general the rich remain rich and the poor remain poor because of their specific social conditions, not their personal qualities.[9]

The attribution of the effects of the social relations to personal qualities has an additional ideological consequence. When the rich become richer, the ideologist praises their personal qualities, although it is their inherited wealth and the attendant educational, social, and other advantages that are really responsible. When the poor get poorer because of unemployment, poor skills, restricted opportunities, etc. the ideologist, again, blames their personal qualities, although it is their initial social conditions and the consequent educational, economic and other handicaps that are really responsible.[10] The reduction of the social relations to personal qualities makes the rich *appear* intellectually and morally far better, and the poor far worse than they really are. The ideologist uses their apparently vast inequality of talents to justify the existing vast inequality of wealth and status. In other words, the ideologist is guilty of a double fallacy. First, he conveniently reduces the social relations to personal qualities, and then uses the latter to justify the former. Second, he mistakes the appearance for reality. He so analyses the social relations that the rich and poor *appear* vastly unequal in their 'endowments', and on this flimsy basis he asserts that they *are* unequal.

Fifth, the ideologist conflates the different stages in the development of a society, and invokes the arguments relevant at one stage to justify the conditions prevailing at another. For example, as we saw, capitalism was initially responsible for the development of the productive forces. The ideologist uses the argument to justify the modern capitalism which has, in fact, become a hindrance to their development. Again, he justifies modern capitalism on the ground that every man has a right to the fruits of his labour. Apparently he does not notice that the concept of the reward for one's labour made sense in the early days of small-scale property, but not in the advanced capitalist society in which the capitalists do not labour but appropriate others' labour, and the contributions of the labour of different individuals are no longer separable. Marx puts the point well:[11]

Political economy confuses on principle two very different kinds of private property, of which one rests on the producers' own labour, the other on the employment of the labour of others. It forgets that the latter not only is the direct antithesis of the former, but absolutely grows on its tomb only . . . To this ready-made world of capital, the political economist applies the notions of law and of property inherited from a pre-capitalistic world with all the more anxious zeal and all the greater unction, the more loudly the facts cry out in the face of his ideology.

For Marx the confusion between two different types of property, or between property and capital, runs right through the history of political and economic thought from the seventeenth century onwards. The writers involved began by justifying one kind of property — which is easy to justify — and illegitimately extended the justification to a very different kind of property. He observes:[12]

> The universal *juridical* conception from Locke to Ricardo is consequently that of *petty bourgeois property*, while the relationships of production which are portrayed by them belong to the *capitalist mode of production* . . . the *ideology* of that *private property* which rests upon labour is simply transferred to that property which rests upon the *expropriation of the immediate producers*.

Sixth, Marx argues that the ideologist generally employs inherently 'indeterminate' concepts. For example, he talks about preserving 'freedom', but does not say whose freedom to do what he wishes to preserve and what consequences this has in practice. Similarly he talks about maintaining the law and order, or upholding the dignity of man, without indicating the types of law and order he wishes to maintain, or specifying what he means by dignity, why he so defines it and how his theory upholds the dignity of 'real, living concrete individuals'. For Marx the language of indeterminate abstractions serves the ideological purpose in several different ways. It allows the discussion to be 'torn away from the facts'. It enables the ideologist to present himself as a champion of not just a particular class or social order, but a whole civilisation and even 'basic human values'. It absolves him from the obligation to attend to specific social evils, since he is only interested in preserving perennial values and his concepts are such that they never connect with or are embarrassed by social reality. Further, as we saw, the debates about abstractions are necessarily irresoluble, and hence the ideologist can never be cornered. Since the abstractions lack empirical content, the ideologist remains free to define them as he pleases. His critic is therefore forced to do battle with him on his terms, and obviously cannot win.

Seventh, the ideologist has a constant tendency to stress the virtues of a 'realistic' and 'responsible' attitude and invoke the authority of experience, facts, common sense and conventional wisdom to discredit his critic.[13] In Marx's view his reasons are obvious. As we saw, the world of social experience is ideologically constituted, and the so-called facts embody the dominant ideology. As such they serve the ideologist's purpose well, especially as he can so easily present them as a neutral authority. Again, common sense and conventional wisdom are built up from the experiences within the ideologically constituted world, and therefore profoundly shaped by the dominant ideology. They are not neutral, but partisan. According to Marx the ideologist's view of realism rests on an ideologically biased definition of reality. The social reality is a product of human praxis, and therefore can be altered to suit human needs. The ideologist defines it in extremely narrow terms. For him the prevailing pattern of social relations constitutes the reality; not to acknowledge it as inviolable is to be unrealistic.

For Marx, then, the ideological reasoning involves a number of logical fallacies. (In addition to the ones listed above, Marx also mentions several others.[14]) The ideologist's apologia for his class and/or society rests on specious arguments, some of which can be easily seen through whereas others are subtle and difficult to detect. Marx does not say that the ideologist deliberately uses fallacious arguments. Although sometimes he may deliberately deploy them, more often his use is inadvertent. He is primarily concerned to understand, not to defend the established social order or promote the interests of his class, and advances arguments which seem valid to him, although a careful analysis might show otherwise. Marx seems to think that one of the reasons why the ideologist does not notice the fallacies is that he is sympathetic to the conclusions entailed by his arguments; indeed, he finds them self-evident and obvious. Hence he is not prompted to examine critically his arguments and forms of reasoning. If he had taken a critical attitude to his society, he would have strongly disapproved of the conclusions of his arguments. This, in turn, would have led him to examine the arguments themselves, and perhaps he could have seen through them.

II

Marx's critical examination of the logical structures of the apologetic writings shows that, in his view, the social theorists end up producing the apologetic bodies of thought for different reasons and in different ways. The base writers developed apologetic theories because this is what they wished to do. They were patently partisan, and not at all interested in the pursuit of truth. The vulgar writers became the apologists of their society because they remained confined to the ideologically constituted world of appearances, and could do little more than reproduce the underlying ideology. Despite his great theoretical achievements, Hegel's thought remained systematically biased because he was an idealist, adopted ahistorical concepts and methods of analysis, did not appreciate the social bases of ideas, took an uncritical attitude to his society, and so on. Finally, in spite of their scientific integrity, the classical economists remained systematically biased because, among other things, they uncritically accepted the ideological claims of the bourgeois society, made no attempt to transcend its horizon of thought, adopted an ahistorical method of analysis, and did not elucidate and examine their basic assumptions. For analytical convenience we may sum up Marx's general conclusions in the form of somewhat simplified and programmatic theses. Needless to say, our list is by no means exhaustive, and only intended to highlight those conclusions that are important and relevant from our point of view.

For Marx a student of society becomes an ideologist if, among other things, he lacks impartiality, is confined to the surface of society, unaware of the social mediation of knowledge, has an uncritical attitude to his society, and uses abstract and ahistorical concepts and methods of analysis. This means that if he is to avoid becoming an apologist, he must, among other things,

(A) be honest and impartial, and investigate the inner structure of society rather than its phenomenal forms;

(B) be critically aware of his position in society and the way it mediates his relations to his subject matter;

(C) take a rigorously critical attitude to his society;

(D) fully grasp the historical specificity of the prevailing social order and eschew ahistorical concepts and methods of investigation.

We shall take each in turn. Some of Marx's theses are unproblematic, whereas others raise large questions. Accordingly we shall concentrate on the latter.

Marx's first thesis is relatively unproblematic. A writer who lacks the elementary virtues of scientific honesty and impartiality cannot obviously offer a disinterested account of his subject matter. Marx's discussion is noteworthy because of his emphasis on the social nature of impartiality.

Unlike most of the traditional epistemology, which tends to isolate the knowing subject from the social world, Marx locates him firmly within it and analyses the concept of impartiality within the wider context. Accordingly he sees impartiality not as a natural or socially acquired *property* of the knowing subject which he carries around with him and exercises as he pleases, but as a social *relation*. For Marx the pursuit of knowledge involves both the subject and the object, and must be discussed not in terms of the subject alone but the relation subsisting between the two. Since the relation between the subject and the object is socially mediated, so is impartiality. Human beings are not gods, but socially and historically situated beings characterised by specific interests, values and ways of looking at the world. As such we cannot inquire whether and how *men in general* can be impartial, but rather how men who are socially and historically situated in a certain manner can be impartial, in what areas, and within what limits. Likewise we cannot inquire how men can be *impartial in general*, but rather whether and how they can be impartial in their investigation of specific areas. A man may be impartial in his investigation of one area, but not another; he may be able impartially to investigate the former under one condition, but not under another.

For Marx it is far more difficult to be impartial in the social than the natural sciences. In the former the knowing subject is intimately connected with his subject matter, which only consists of other human subjects. While he can distance himself from them at the theoretical level, he is deeply involved with them at the practical level. At the theoretical level he is the subject and they are his objects; at the practical level they are his fellow-subjects and, in some cases, he is their object. At the practical level which is both pre- and para-theoretical, he struggles with or against them in his day-to-day pursuits, forms alliances with or against them, and finds that his own interests as well as those with whom he is closely connected are deeply affected by their actions and interests.[15] For Marx it is naive to imagine that a social theorist can altogether purge his mind of the tensions, anxieties and fears of the practical level simply because he has decided to put on a theoretical hat. As Marx observes:[16]

In the domain of Political Economy, free scientific inquiry meets not merely the same enemies as in all other domains. The peculiar nature of the material it deals with, summons as foes into the field of battle the most violent, mean and malignant passions of the human breast, the Furies of private interest.

Marx argues that the relation between theory and practice acquires a new intensity and urgency when the established social order is torn by acute conflicts. The social theorist, then, is involved in passionate conflicts at the practical level, and cannot easily regain his theoretical calm. Further, the ideas tend to travel faster than usual from one level to the other. The practical struggles reappear at the theoretical level in an open or disguised form. The theoretical ideas are freely chartered by the combatants in the service of their respective causes, evaluated not by the theoretical but practical criteria, and their originators are no longer allowed or able to remain aloof. In Marx's view this is what happened to classical political economy. Once the class struggles broke out, they[17]

> sounded the knell of scientific bourgeois economy. It was thence-forth no longer a question, whether this theorem or that was true, but whether it was useful to capital or harmful, expedient or inex-pedient, politically dangerous or not. In place of disinterested inquirers, there were hired prize-fighters; in place of genuine scien-tific research, the bad conscience and the evil intent of apologetic.

As we saw, Marx argues that the knowing subject's relation to his subject matter is socially mediated. He approaches the world with specific social assumptions which delimit his horizon of thought and circumscribe the extent of his impartiality. For Marx this means two things. First, since a social theorist is impartial within the limits of his assumptions, his impartiality is put to a severe test when his assump-tions are exploded. As long as his assumptions are valid or he is not fully aware of them he can remain impartial in his investigations. Once they are shown to be mistaken, the very foundations of his thought are shaken and his entire framework of thought is disorientated. He must now completely reappraise his conceptual framework. However, since he is generally reluctant to do so and insists on continuing with his accustomed mode of investigation, he becomes its fierce and parti-san supporter and forfeits his impartiality. In Marx's view this happened to the classical political economists after 1830. Once their basic assumptions about the non-historical and non-contradictory nature of capitalism were exploded, they found it exceedingly difficult to remain impartial. As Marx put it, once the social conditions exposed their basic assumptions 'they no longer allowed of their being really and impartially investigated within the bounds' of the old assumptions.[18]

Second, since the social theorist is impartial within the limits of his social assumptions, he is deeply partial, even though his mode of investigation may be rigorously impartial. As we saw, some of the classical economists were rigorously impartial in their investigations. However, their impartiality was grounded in the socially partial and ideologically orientated absolutisation of the capitalist mode of production and was deeply partial. Similarly some of the vulgar economists were impartial in their investigations of the ideologically constituted surface of society; however, since their subject matter was partially or ideologically constituted, their impartial investigations faithfully reproduced its partiality and transmitted it to their conclusion.

For Marx an otherwise impartial investigation may contain deep and unsuspected sources of partiality. Its method of investigation, manner of conceptual analysis, concepts, questions, etc. may at first sight appear impartial, but on closer examination turn out to be profoundly biased. For example, the empiricist appeal to experience appears unproblematic, and yet is not. The social experiences in an ideologically constituted world are not neutral, but inherently ideological. Besides, as we saw, the world of appearances to which the human experiences are confined is in the capitalist society highly deceptive. It not only conceals the real world, but also presents it in an opposite manner. Further, the social experiences of the same object vary and hence there is always the danger of selecting some of them as genuine and dismissing others as less authentic. Again, experience has to be interpreted, and this requires a point of view which could be narrow and biased.

Like the empiricist appeal to experience, the positivist appeal to facts seems objective and unbiased, but is not. The facts of an ideologically constituted social world are inherently ideological. Besides, as we saw, the facts may be illusory or merely apparent as, for Marx, they generally are in the capitalist society. No natural scientist accepts the 'facts' of experience without critical examination; he does not accept the 'fact' that the sun seems to go round the earth or that the air seems simple in constitution. For Marx the social facts are not very different, as they too can deceive and mislead. Further, the facts are constantly made by men. As we shall see, the social facts are products of human acts. By *treating* some men as inferior and confining them to the soul-destroying jobs, we end up *making* them inferior. The social facts cannot therefore enjoy the same epistemological status as the natural, and since they are constantly made and unmade by men, they cannot be dissociated from the human praxis, and accepted as authoritative in the abstract. For Marx positivism and empiricism are both 'vulgar' theories; they are confined to the surface, and profoundly ideological.

III

For Marx a student of society is in danger of becoming an apologist if he lacks a critical awareness of his position in society, and the way in which it mediates his relations with his subject matter. He is not a disembodied soul, but a member of a specific group in a specific society in a specific historical epoch. He grows up within it, imbibes its values, traditions and ways of understanding man and society, occupies a specific position in it, is structurally related to others and experiences the world in a certain way. By the time he learns to theorise, he is already shaped by his society; and while he is engaged in the theoretical pursuits, he does not cease being involved in non-theoretical activities. The individual who theorises is also a father, a husband, a teacher, an Englishman, a Protestant, and so on. The theorising self is not super-added to the rest of his personality. Theorising is one among the count-less other activities in which an individual engages, and cannot be dissociated from them. In short a social theorist brings to his study of society a specific social point of view, a body of pre- and para-theoretical attitudes, assumptions and interests which mediates his approach to and shapes the selection, organisation and interpretation of his subject matter.

In Marx's view much of traditional epistemology did not fully appreciate the social mediation of knowledge. While it recognised the importance of the conceptual, methodological and other assumptions, it more or less completely overlooked the influence of the social, largely because it viewed the knowing subject as a transcendental being in no way shaped by his society. Since it is the social presup-positions that play a crucial role in the study of society, the traditional epistemology overlooked the most powerful source of bias. It never encouraged the social theorists to ask *who* they were, where in history and society they were situated, how they were affected by the practical struggles going on in their society, how their society was constituted and what its dominant ideology was, how they were structurally related to others and how this shaped their experiences and modes of thought, what assumptions they were likely to bring to their study of man and society, and so on. Since they never asked these questions, they never became fully aware of the social biases they had unwittingly acquired from the dominant ideology, their own social groups, or both. And since they never became aware of these, they took no steps to counter their influence. Not surprisingly they unwittingly universalised the values, modes of thought, criteria of rationality, etc. of their social group and/or society, and ended up producing apologetic bodies of thought. In Marx's view a social theorist cannot hope to avoid producing an apologia for his society or class if he pretends that he is in no way shaped by his social experiences, closes his eyes to the non-theoretical sources of social bias, and takes no steps to combat their influence.

For Marx, then, social self-consciousness or a critical awareness of his social presuppositions is crucial if a social theorist is to provide an objective account of his subject matter. He must recognise that he is not a pure and disembodied intellect, but a social being who is socially constituted in a certain manner and has a certain range of experiences, values, forms of thought, interests and preferences. Since they socially constitute and define him, he takes them for granted and does not even notice their influence. As we saw, Proudhon, the Left Hegelians and others never examined their basic assumptions; as a result they ended up generalising the experiences and ideas of the petty bourgeoisie. Hegel, the classical economists and others never explored the nature and structure of the dominant ideology of their society; as a result they ended up adopting and universalising it. Marx imagines, rather optimistically, that complete social self-consciousness can be attained, and that it is possible to rise above not only one's class but also society. Although one cannot expect him to provide a neat formula or write 'receipts . . . for [the social scientists] of the future', one is entitled to expect a detailed exploration of the ways of becoming socially self-conscious.[19] Unfortunately Marx's discussion of the subject is tentative and somewhat unclear. He seems to suggest the following ways of combating the influence of the socially derived biases.

First, a social theorist must carefully and critically examine his questions, concepts, methods of investigation, form of reasoning and modes of thought with a view to uncovering and evaluating their underlying social presuppositions. Second, since others are more likely to spot his assumptions than the social theorist concerned, interpersonal criticism is of utmost importance. Marx does not say anything novel about this familiar point, except that the criticism or, rather, a critique of a social theory should be directed not merely at its mistakes of fact and logic, but primarily at its social assumptions. Since the social presuppositions are, for Marx, the most important sources of ideological bias, they are the principal object of criticism. Marx's criticism of classical political economy outlined earlier well illustrates how he would like such a socio-critique to be executed. In his view the scientific objectivity is a product of, among other things, a continuous and relentless critique, for it is only by constantly criticising each other's social presuppositions that the social theorists can become socially self-conscious. A critique of an ideology is therefore not a destructive and debunking exercise, but a process of clarification and a necessary moment in the growth of knowledge.

Third, Marx argues that, although every social point of view has its characteristic limitations, some are less limited and limiting than others. A social theorist must therefore examine the structural limitations and epistemological potentialities of the social points of view available in his society. Since no social point of view is free from limitations, he must anchor himself in the one least biased, take advantage of the insights offered by the other points of view and arrive at as full, self-critical and objective an account of society as he can. We shall see later what all this involves.

Marx's proposal implies that, in his view, the study of society presupposes a wider epistemological investigation with a twofold objective. As observed earlier, it elucidates the points of view and social assumptions characteristic of different social groups; and second, it evaluates the epistemological potentialities of these points of view, and decides which of them offers the most satisfactory vantage point for studying society. Such an epistemological charting of the social terrain spares each social theorist the task of undertaking it himself. Although Marx frequently made passing remarks, he never undertook such an investigation, nor did he even identify it as a distinct form of inquiry. However, a good deal of what he says about ideology does not make sense without such an investigation. When he says that from the bourgeois, petty-bourgeois or feudal standpoint, society cannot but appear in a certain manner, that certain forms of thought are characteristically bourgeois or petty-bourgeois, or that the social reality is more clearly visible from the proletarian than any other point of view, his remarks presuppose that he has, at least for himself, investigated the epistemological structures and potentials of the different social points of view.

Finally, as we saw, ideology is for Marx a characteristic phenomenon of the class-divided and, more generally, a rigidly stratified society. A class-divided society requires not only a shared body of beliefs as every society does, but also that they be systematically biased towards the dominant class. For Marx therefore, the abolition of the classes is a necessary social precondition of the disappearance of ideology. It is not, however, a sufficient condition. As we saw, Marx argues that when men are confined all or most of their lives to particular social positions, they experience and perceive the world in a uniform manner. Not knowing any other forms of experience or modes of thought, they are unable to imagine alternatives, and consider them natural. A rigidly stratified society is a breeding ground of ideology; men of limited and one-dimensional experiences cannot easily resist generalising their conditions of existence and modes of thought. This is one of the reasons why Marx is so strongly opposed to the division of labour. It 'fixes' men, casts their personalities in a particular mould, 'cripples' their thoughts and renders them unimaginative.[20] Perhaps somewhat naïvely, he suggests that in the communist society men should be encouraged to become versatile, engage in very different kinds of activity, experience their society from diverse standpoints, and acquire as wide a range of experiences and modes of thought as possible within the limits of the available level of technological development. Marx is opposed not only to the classes, but also to all forms of social stratification and immobility.

IV

For Marx even as a social theorist must be self-critical, he must also be critical of his subject matter. If he did not approach his subject matter in a critical spirit, he would unwittingly reproduce and endorse the values embodied in it. As we saw, the social world is ideologically constituted and structured. It is not merely a world of facts but also of values; indeed it is a world in which values masquerade or are presented as facts.

A social theorist who imagines that he is only describing facts is, in fact, describing values. For example, in the bourgeois society the worker, a human subject, is treated as an object. He is described in a language befitting an object, and his wages are viewed as the payments necessary to keep the human machine in good repair. The classical economists, interested only in describing and explaining the social reality, unwittingly accepted the view of the worker embedded in the bourgeois practices and language, and asked how the 'price' of labour and, ultimately, of the labourer was determined and what his 'cost of production' was. In so doing, they not only reproduced and endorsed the bourgeois values, but also invested them with a scientific dignity and made it seem normal to refer to men in such degrading terms. As Marx puts it, the 'cynicism is in the facts'.[21] By uncritically accepting them, the classical economists made the implicit 'cynical contempt' for man theoretically respectable.

Again, Proudhon attempted to give a neutral and uncritical account of the rise of Louis Bonaparte. Not surprisingly, he ended up showing that the latter's rise was 'natural' under the circumstances, and became his apologist. The historical school of Savigny and Hugo insisted that the historian should refrain from passing judgements on the historical actors and societies, and ended up taking a 'very respectable' attitude to whatever was done or happened to exist.[22] It censored historians for projecting their values onto their subject matter. Yet, by asking them to 'respect' their subject matter, it urged them to respect the values embodied in it; its moral positivism was a logical corollary of its moral relativism or scepticism. As Marx puts it, the historical school 'legitimates the baseness of today by the baseness of yesterday, a school that declares rebellious every cry of the serf against the knout once that knout is a time-honoured, ancestral historical one'.[23] Again, as we saw, Hegel aimed to do no more than analyse the past; in fact, he ended up showing that whatever had occurred in history was rational. Similarly he only aimed to demonstrate the rationality of his society; in fact, he ended up absolutising it and presenting it as the end of history.

For Marx then a positivist or value-free social theory is inherently apologetic. It treats facts as sacred, and therefore the values embodied in them. Objectivism or letting the facts speak for themselves is a form of social subjectivism, and the enemy of objectivity; it reproduces and endorses the dominant values of one's society or class.[24] However impartial and scrupulous he might be in his investigation, a fact-worshipping social theorist cannot avoid becoming the spokesman of his society or class. Indeed, the more impartial his investigation, the more faithful is his reproduction of the values embodied in the facts, and the more apologetic and ideological is his thought.

For Marx the truth about society is only revealed to the critical eye. The facts cannot be allowed to speak for themselves, because they can only speak an ideological language. They must be interrogated and confronted with an alternative set of values. The scientific objectivity is attained not by adopting a non-interventionist approach to facts, but by subjecting them to a rigorous and systematic critique. Unless the subject is equipped with a carefully worked out critical perspective, he has no defence against the morality dictated by the object. He is overwhelmed by the object, has no means of countering its claims to be natural, everlasting, the epitome of reason, and so on, and cannot avoid becoming its spokesman. The critical dimension that the subject brings to his object cannot be added after he has completed his investigation. Once the object has already dictated its morality to the subject in the course of his investigation, he is forced to reach biased conclusions. It is no longer open to him to add a different critical gloss on them without becoming inconsistent or appearing to 'quarrel with his subject matter'. For Marx the social theorist must approach his subject matter with a body of critically constituted concepts that do not merely interpret but also evaluate.

For Marx, then, a social theorist must take a rigorously critical attitude to his society. He rules out three types of critical approach which, in his view, are insufficiently critical and even perform an apologetic function. First, he rules out 'superficial' criticisms, such as those made by the vulgar socialists. Since they do not transcend the established framework of thought, they obviously cannot effectively criticise it. Second, Marx also rules out 'sentimental' criticism 'which knows how to judge and condemn the present, but not how to comprehend it'.[25] Such a criticism, not being grounded in the detailed knowledge of the manner in which the established society works, lacks relevance and makes no impact. Since it does not permeate the actual analysis of the social order, it remains external and ineffective. Finally, Marx rules out external or abstract criticism based on a general moral principle. Such a criticism, again, is sociologically naïve, does not connect with the established order, is not grounded in the frustrated needs of the masses and is ultimately ineffective. For Marx a rigorously critical attitude to society must be based on a systematic *critique* designed to uncover its inner nature, expose its limitations and confront it with an image of its own historically developed potentialities. We shall see later how Marx constructs such a critique.

V

For Marx overabstraction and the consequent obliteration of the specificity of the subject matter is the most common, yet the least appreciated, source of ideology. Since in his view overabstraction is encouraged by idealism, Marx says that idealism is one of the commonest sources of ideology. Marx's thesis has received very little attention from his commentators, and deserves careful consideration.

For Marx every scientific inquiry aims to explain its subject matter. In his view explanation is qualitatively different from 'paraphrase' with which it has often been confused. Paraphrase is basically a descriptive activity. It consists in ordering, classifying and making inductive generalisations about one's subject matter. It does not leave the phenomenal level, and does little more than restate the *explanandum* in a different language. Explanation is very different. In explaining the behaviour of an entity, a scientist is concerned to show *why* it behaves in this way. Ideally he aims to show that its behaviour is not accidental, but a necessary expression of its inner tendencies, and that these, in turn, arise out of the way it is constituted. For example, copper has a certain atomic structure, hence an innate tendency to behave, combine and interact with other entities in a specific manner, and therefore it displays specific properties and forms of behaviour under specific conditions. Similarly for Marx the capitalist mode of production is constituted in a certain manner, hence it has a specific set of inherent tendencies, and hence it generates such phenomena as overproduction, trade crisis and the declining rate of profit. As Marx says, 'it is a work of science to resolve the visible external movement into the internal actual movement'. We shall later outline Marx's theory of science at length.

A scientist, then, is concerned to explain the behaviour of an entity, and hence to elucidate its inner nature. In order to elucidate the inner nature, he must abstract away its contingent features, as well as the contingent relations in which it stands with respect to other entities. The phenomenal world is infinitely complex. Unless the scientist temporarily abstracted away its contingent features, he would get lost in his subject matter and not be able to articulate its inner nature. Abstraction is integral to science. It is not, however, important in itself, but only as a means to articulating the inner structure of his subject matter.

In Marx's view abstraction is a highly complex activity, and must steer clear of two extremes. If a scientist did not abstract adequately, he would remain lost in the phenomenal world, not be able to study the inner nature in its purity, and in constant danger of confusing some of the contingent features with the inner structure. On the other hand, if he abstracted at too general a level, he would have abstracted away the inner nature of the entity concerned, and lost sight of his subject matter altogether. For Marx the scientific level of abstraction must be abstract enough to eliminate all the contingent features, and yet concrete enough to retain a firm grasp of the distinctive nature of his subject matter. The balance between the two demands is not easy to strike. However, unless a scientist determined the appropriate level of abstraction and developed concepts which were, at once, both abstract and concrete, he would either over- or underabstract and commit some of the mistakes mentioned earlier.

Marx gives several examples of what he calls 'rational' or legitimate abstractions, some of which were noticed earlier.[26] The concept of wage labour is a rational abstraction, since it abstracts the characteristics shared in common by, and only by, all forms of industrial labour under the capitalist mode of production. It is abstract enough to conceptualise them all, but also concrete enough not to obliterate their historical specificity. It is, as Marx says, a 'rational' and 'historical abstraction'. A more abstract concept, such as labour or service, would have missed the historical specificity, whereas a more concrete concept would have excluded several forms of industrial labour.

Marx argues that 'value', 'capital', etc. are also rational historical abstractions. As he puts it, value is 'the most *abstract* form of *bourgeois* wealth', and the most *general* social relation historically *specific* to capitalism. It encapsulates all forms of wealth, such as interest, profit and rent that are to be found, and only to be found, under the capitalist mode of production. Marx observes: 'Although an abstraction this is an historical abstraction which could only be evolved on the basis of a particular economic development of society.'[27]

For Marx the concept of capital, too, is both appropriately abstract and concrete, or general and historical. Within the capitalist mode of production there is a class of men who own the means of production, hire the wage labourers to produce commodities, pursue value, and so on. *Qua* capitalists they are all concerned to maximise value. They are objectively related to each other and to their workers in a manner dictated by their pursuit of value. *Qua* capitalists their behaviour, freely chosen at one level, is dictated by their objective relations. Although capital exists 'through' the capitalists, it is 'distinct from' any one of them. It is an objective social relation which constrains and compels those involved in it. They are free not to be capitalists; but once they decide to be one, they enter into certain objective relations. In reality, of course, we see only the capitalists, not capital. However, the concept of capital is a 'rational' abstraction, since it abstracts what is common to the capitalist *qua* capitalist and does not lose sight of the specificity of capital as a social relation.[28] As Marx puts it, it is 'an abstraction which grasps the specific differences which distinguish capital from other forms of wealth. These are the features common to each capital as such or which make every specific sum of value into capital'.[29] Capital is therefore the most basic concept necessary to conceptualise the bourgeois mode of production. Such concepts as money and wealth are too general to illuminate its specificity.

In Marx's view, although the philosophers have appreciated the importance of abstraction, they have rarely explored its nature, limits and appropriate level. Under the influence of idealism they have treated the historically specific characteristics as contingent, and abstracted them away in their search for the universally valid concepts. The following quotation is obviously a caricature of the traditional method of abstraction; however, like all caricatures it highlights rather well what Marx took to be its central weakness.[30]

Is it surprising that everything, in the final abstraction — for we have here an abstraction, and not an analysis — presents itself as a logical category? Is it surprising that, if you let drop little by little all that constitutes the individuality of a house, leaving out first of all the materials of which it is composed, then the form that distinguishes it, you end up with nothing but a body; that, if you leave out of account the limits of this body, you soon have nothing but a space — that if, finally, you leave out of account the dimensions of this space, there is absolutely nothing left but pure quantity, the logical category? If we abstract thus from every subject all the alleged accidents, animate or inanimate, men or things, we are right in saying that in the final abstraction, the only substance left is the logical categories. Thus the metaphysicians, who in making these abstractions, think they are making analyses, and who the more they detach themselves from things, imagine themselves to be getting all the nearer to the point of penetrating to their core.

Marx argues that, although they did not all carry it to this absurd degree, the metaphysicians, the classical economists and others subscribed in one form or another to such a method of abstraction. As we saw, they abstracted away the historically specific features of their subject matter and formulated ahistorical and abstract concepts. They defined the concepts as they thought proper, related them in a manner dictated by the logic of their definitions, and developed conceptual systems, which they then used to explain their subject matter. Thus Hegel explained the world in terms of the realisation of his abstract logical categories and their abstract subject. The classical economists explained the different economic systems as different combinations of such universally common features as production, material instruments, labour, exchange, self-interest and money. Proudhon explained history in terms of the struggle between the principles of liberty and equality.

Marx questions the whole enterprise on several grounds, some of which were mentioned earlier. It leads to a two-stage procedure whose weaknesses he had commented upon in his discussion of Hegel. Further, since such a method of abstraction destroys the specificity of its subject matter, it does not take us closer to the inner structure of the *explicandum*, but further and further away from it, and is 'useless' for explanatory purpose. Again, the concepts arrived at by means of abstraction have no empirical content, do not apply to any specific subject matter and 'have no value whatsoever'.[31] What is more, at the highly abstract level at which one operates, the real world is so far left behind that it can neither exercise restraint nor offer any guidance.[32] The theorist therefore is at liberty to define and relate his concepts as he pleases subject only to the restraints of formal logic. For example, one philosopher may define liberty and equality one way and demonstrate that they are 'necessarily' compatible. Another may define them differently and demonstrate the opposite. In Marx's view the whole exercise and the controversy it generates are entirely pointless. The arbitrarily defined abstract concepts cannot illuminate the concrete world of social relations in which men are not concerned with liberty and equality in the abstract, but as these relate to and conceptualise their specific social relations. Men demand liberties to do specific things and, finding that the prevailing inequalities prevent them from doing so, ask whether they should be reduced and how this will affect the liberties they seek. The logically elegant theories constructed on the basis of the abstract and arbitrary definitions of liberty and equality can throw no light whatever on their historically specific situation. How equality effects liberty cannot be determined *a priori*, but only on the basis of the types of equality and liberty men seek, the way they define them, the prevailing distribution of power and wealth, the level of technological development, and so on.

Marx takes another example. The philosophers have asked how man is related to nature. For Marx the question is meaningless. Men are differently related to nature in different historical epochs. In some they are wholly dominated by it; in some others they enjoy a small measure of independence; and in a highly industrialised society they exercise a considerable degree of domination over it. It makes sense to ask how men are related to nature in a specific society, type of society or historical epoch, but not how man in general is related to nature in general, for man in general and nature in general are mere abstractions and correspond to no historical reality. Marx agrees that it is possible to abstract the formal features shared in common by men's relations with nature in different historical epochs, but makes two points. First, such a general statement cannot be used to *explain* specific historical epochs, as it is not an explanatory principle, but merely 'a summary of the results' of historical inquiries. It 'fixes the common element and thus saves us repetition'; it has no other value.[33] As Marx puts it, the universally common features are 'nothing more than . . . abstract moments with which no real historical stage . . . can be grasped'.[34] A universal statement can be abstracted from historical generalisations, but the latter cannot be derived from it.

Second, the preoccupation with such universal statements encourages the view that only the general truths are of theoretical value and constitute the principal goal of the social scientist. For Marx the opposite is the case. The universal statements of the trans-historical kind have little empirical content, do not illuminate any specific historical epoch, and are ultimately trivial.[35] One may wonder how he intended his own materialist conception of history to be understood. As he himself says, it was suggested to him by his critique of Hegel.[36] It was not based on historical researches into different modes of production, and therefore not a generalisation. Marx seems to have thought of it as what he called 'a guiding principle', a necessarily tentative theoretical hypothesis whose truth must be established by historical research. It is not a 'general historico-philosophical theory', a historical 'master-key' that can be 'applied' to all historical epochs.[37] Taking it as such amounts to 'slandering me too much'. Engels also described historical materialism as little more than a 'guide to history', and thought that its 'dangerous friends' had turned it into a mere 'phrase'.[38] Needless to say, both men from time to time made claims on its behalf that went far beyond its tentative nature, and were wrong to do so.

For Marx man as such, man in general, liberty as such, liberty in general, equality as such, equality in general, etc. are not 'rational' abstractions or legitimate concepts, but 'mere words', 'fantastic notions' and 'infantile abstractions'.[39] The questions about man as such are not about men in specific historical epochs, nor about the common human features of different epochs, but about an abstraction 'man' who nowhere exists and to whom nothing corresponds. We can develop a *general theory of man*, which is a statement of the common features men display in all historical epochs, but not a theory of *man in general*, for man in general is a meaningless expression.[40] Any attempt to theorise about the latter is inherently illegitimate.[41] Marx observes that when the concepts lose 'the last vestige of connection with reality', they lose 'the last vestige of meaning' and become 'mere' words.[42] Such phrases cannot form objects of investigation. When a philosopher establishes logically satisfactory relations between them, there is absolutely no reason to believe that the relations in the actual world even remotely correspond to them. In Marx's view it is 'infantile' to construct an *a priori* definition, distinction or logical relationship 'which things must be made to fit'.[43] One must begin with the social world as it is, articulate the distinctions and relations embodied in it, and 'express [these] in definite categories'.[44] For Marx, so long as one takes 'empty' abstractions as one's objects of investigation, one's whole approach, including methods and concepts, cannot but remain empty and abstract. As he puts it, 'The point of view cannot be concrete when the object of the point of view is abstract.'

Although Marx himself does not put the point this way, he seems to distinguish three types of concept representing three different levels of abstraction. First, some concepts are socially or historically specific or concrete. They abstract away the contingent features and articulate the inner structure of their subject matter. Such concepts as rent, wage labour, capital and the state belong to this category. Second, some concepts are 'abstract' in the sense that they pick out the general features shared in common by the conceptualised entities in all historical epochs, and are arrived at by abstracting away their historically specific properties. Such concepts as property, wealth, labour, service and power belong to this category. They are second-order concepts, and basically classificatory in nature. They are abstracted from the first type of concepts, and depend upon them for their meaning and significance. Finally, there are concepts which conceptualise nothing, for nothing corresponds to them. They are not 'rational' but 'infantile abstractions'. Man as such and nature as such are such 'concepts'. For Marx we can abstract features men share in all historical epochs, but cannot abstract away all human societies and form a conception of man in himself, man as such or man in general.

According to Marx, philosophers and social theorists have generally made two types of mistake. First, they have sometimes thought that the third type of concept is a legitimate object of investigation. As a result a good deal of their work consists of little more than arbitrary definitions. Second, they have sometimes confused the first two types of concept, and treated the second as if it were the first. They have treated abstract concepts as explanatory rather than classificatory in nature, used them to understand a historically specific social order or relation, deduced historically specific conclusions from them, and in general employed them to do the job they are inherently unequipped to do.

VI

For Marx the idealist method of ahistorical abstraction or overabstraction is the vehicle *par excellence* of the ideological bias. It not only allows the bias to operate undetected by the author and his audience, but also creates a theoretical space which the bias is encouraged to fill. Marx seems to think that this happens in the following three inter-related ways.

First, the ahistorical and abstract concepts are by definition 'empty', and cannot be discussed unless they are given some content. Since all content is historically specific, the social theorist cannot define general concepts in other than historical terms. As Marx puts it, 'The most abstract definitions, when more carefully examined, always point to a further definite concrete historical basis. (Of course — since they have been abstracted from it in this particular form.)'[45] A social theorist intimately knows his own society and, especially, his own group within it. Not surprisingly he draws upon it to define and interpret general concepts, and in so doing generalises its characteristic forms of thought. As Marx observes, a social theorist 'abstracts from historical epochs, nationalities, classes, etc., or which is *the same thing*, he inflates the *consciousness* predominant in the class nearest to him in his immediate environment into the normal consciousness'.[46]

Second, which is but a converse of the first, a social theorist who does not grasp the fundamental fact that all concepts are conceptual-isations of historically specific relations and experiences, and limited in their applicability is prone to the illusion that whatever appears natural and self-evident to him is, in fact, so. For him the contem-porary man or form of liberty is man or liberty 'as such'. As we saw, this is how, in Marx's view, Hegel ended up universalising the con-temporary view of reason, and the classical economists ended up universalising the basic features of capitalism. According to Marx, if they had first explored what views of man, reason, etc. prevailed in different historical epochs, they would have seen how very differ-ent and historically rooted they all were. Since they did not under-take such an inquiry, they were never alerted to the danger of universalising what appeared self-evident to them personally, or to the members of their class, or their society. Thanks to their idealist method of abstraction, it never occurred to them that they might conceivably universalise the contingent and the historical. As Marx says, the separa-tion between town and country 'must become an eternal law for Mr Proudhon *since* he knows neither its origin nor its development.

All through his book, he *therefore* speaks as if this creation of a particular mode of production would endure until the end of time.'[47]

Third, the abstract categories 'cover up' and make 'invisible' the
historical differences and class conflicts. The idealistically inclined
social theorist is concerned to bring the widest possible class of phenomena under a single universally applicable category, and cannot
avoid obliterating the historical specificity of social relations and
experiences. As we saw, the classical economists did not appreciate
the historical specificity of capital and wage labour, and turned them
into the integral features of human existence. Further, they reduced
labour to the abstract category of service and, since even the capitalist
renders some service to production, they obliterated the qualitative
difference between the capitalist and the labourer. In short the preoccupation with ahistorical abstractions serves the diversionary
function of distracting attention from the 'real differences', and 'cloak',
'disguise' or 'veil' the ugly reality. What one cannot see, one obviously
cannot protest against or wish to change.

We have so far seen how idealism as Marx has defined it leads to
ideology. He goes further, and suggests that ideology, too, needs
idealism as its necessary epistemological basis. By its very nature
ideology de-historicises and universalises a historically specific social
relation, and turns it into a universally valid concept. It therefore needs
an epistemology which sanctions its characteristic preoccupation with
ahistorical concepts. Idealism meets the need well. It regards ahistorical
concepts as valid objects of investigation, equates abstraction with
analysis, encourages the subsumption of the largest possible class of
phenomena under a common concept, glorifies an ahistorical form of
reasoning, makes the construction of eternally valid concepts the
supreme goal of theory, and so on. Because of all this it provides a
philosophical framework within which ideology can strike roots and
flourish. Unless the basic theses of idealism were accepted, the ideologist's deployment of ahistorical concepts and methods would appear
illegitimate. In other words idealism both makes ideology possible
and veils it. It is itself an ideology, the ideological basis of ideology.

Since ideology derives its legitimacy from idealism, Marx maintains that the best way to expose it is to demonstrate the historical
roots and limits of all general ideas.[48] A *specific* ideology is seriously
impugned when its basic ideas are shown to conceptualise a historically specific set of social relations to which their validity is limited.[49]
And the entire ideological mode of reasoning, *the whole realm of
ideology* as Marx calls it, is subverted when it is shown that *all* general

ideas have historical roots, and have no validity beyond the limits of
the historically specific relations conceptualised by them. Hence Marx
argues that historical materialism, which insists upon the historicity of
ideas, undermines ideology. By challenging idealism, the epistemological basis of ideology, it challenges the ideological mode of reasoning
itself, and undercuts the ground upon which the *realm* of apologetic
thought rests. Being rigorously historical, it leaves no conceptual space
for the absolutisation of a social order or practice; and being material-
istic it insists on relating ideas to relevant social relations, and discredits
the idealist preoccupation with ahistorical concepts and methods.

Since it undercuts the very basis of the apologetic thought, Marx
argues that historical materialism is an inherently *critical* method. It
undermines the epistemological basis of apologetic thought, and cannot
itself be used for the apologetic purposes. It is because he holds this
view that Marx invariably refers to it as the *only* genuinely critical
method, and even equates it with critique. As he puts it, historical
materialism insists upon the historical basis of all thought, and *'for
that reason* is, for the first time, actually a critical view of the world'.[50]
Again, 'Every history of religion that fails to take account of this
material basis is uncritical.'[51] The *German Ideology* is replete with such
remarks. Marx's claim that historical materialism puts an end to
ideology is, no doubt, questionable, and one may even wonder if it is
not itself infected with the virus it claims to eliminate. For the present,
however, our concern is to explore the grounds upon which his case for
it rests.

For Marx, then, the most effective way to expose the ideological
character of a body of thought is to demonstrate its historicity, that is,
to trace its origin and show what social relations or experiences it
conceptualises and illegitimately universalises. An ideology extends
an idea beyond its warranted limits, and hence the first crucial step
towards refuting it is to trace the social context of the idea involved.
To be sure, this is not enough, for one needs to show not only that the
ideologist *extends* an idea far beyond its historical basis, but also that
he does so illegitimately, that is, that he uses it to conceptualise relations to which it does not apply. However, one cannot show that an
idea is illegitimately extended unless one first traces its historical basis
and limits.

In the light of our discussion, it is obvious that Marx is interested
in tracing the historical bases of ideas for two reasons. First, since
ideas derive their content and meaning from the specific social relations
and experiences conceptualised by them, their full meaning cannot be

grasped unless the underlying relations and experiences are uncovered and understood.[52] Second, as we saw, a genetic inquiry into the historical bases of ideas determines their limits, and is the first crucial step towards identifying and exposing their ideological use.

For Marx a genetic inquiry into the social context of an idea and its substantive criticism are closely connected. Contrary to the general impression, he does not think that a genetic inquiry can ever replace substantive criticism. In his view a genetic inquiry is a necessary *precondition* of substantive criticism. By uncovering the underlying relations, it explicates the content and meaning of an idea, without the full knowledge of which the latter cannot be criticised. Further, a genetic inquiry is a necessary *component* of substantive criticism. One important and highly damaging way to criticise a body of thought is to de-absolutise it, deflate its universalist claims, by demonstrating that its universal form harbours a limited content. Such a criticism can only be mounted on the basis of, among other things, a genetic inquiry into its historical basis. For Marx the genetic inquiry is important, but only as *part* of a larger intellectual strategy of dealing with the ideological form of reasoning.

Marx sometimes says that a body of thought is bourgeois, petty-bourgeois, feudal, etc. and *therefore* ideological. This suggests that *since* a body of thought conceptualises specific social relations, it is ideological. Not surprisingly, quite a number of Marx's commentators have taken the view that, for him, every socially based or conditioned body of thought is ideological. Such an interpretation is untenable. For Marx *all* general ideas conceptualise social relations, and in that sense have social bases. If, therefore, he had equated ideology with the socially grounded thought, he would have had to say that *all* ideas are ideological, and he never says this. What is more, he would then have to reject the concepts of truth and objectivity, which he not only does not but cannot do if his theory of ideology is to make sense.

Despite some of his misleading utterances, Marx's remark that a body of thought is bourgeois, etc. and therefore ideological is an elliptical way of summing up a complex piece of reasoning involving the following steps:

(1)   A body of thought becomes an ideology when it is, among other things, illegitimately universalised.

(2)   This particular body of thought has a specifiable social basis in the sense that it conceptualises specific social relations.

(3)   It is, however, illegitimately extended beyond its limited basis.

(4)   It is therefore an ideology.

Marx sometimes suppresses (1) and (3), and conveys the *impression* that (2) entails (4). As we saw, this is not his view. For him a bourgeois body of thought is not ideological simply because it is bourgeois. Rather it is ideological because it generalises the conditions of existence of the bourgeoisie. Marx is therefore *not* saying that to trace the social context of a body of ideas *is* to show that it is ideological. On the very contrary, to trace its social context is to show that it is not a speculative fantasy, but conceptualises a set of 'real' social relations or experiences and has an empirical content. To trace the social context of a body of thought is to show both its strength and limits; to show that it is not a collection of 'empty phrases', but has an empirical or 'real' content; and also that its empirical content has a limited 'validity' and becomes ideological if a universal or absolute validity were to be claimed for it.

7 THE PROLETARIAN POINT OF VIEW

As we saw earlier, Marx argues that every social theorist studies society from a particular social point of view. The points of view differ greatly in their ability to illuminate society. Some are extremely narrow; they illuminate only a small segment of social life and conceal or distort the rest. Some illuminate larger areas of social life, and some others enable one to perceive the whole of society in all its complexity. It is therefore of utmost importance what point of view a social theorist adopts. As we saw, for Marx the ideas of Hegel, Proudhon and the classical economists had a large apologetic content because, among other things, they looked at society from the narrow bourgeois point of view and failed to transcend its horizon of thought. Thanks to his point of view, Marx thought that he was himself not an ideologist and had discovered the inner structure of both capitalism and human history. What, then, was the point of view from which Marx studied society and which enabled him to succeed where all others had failed?

The question has exercised the Marxists for nearly a century, and the answer they have almost unanimously given is that Marx looked at the capitalist society from the proletarian point of view. According to them Marx's examination of Hegel, the classical economists and others led him to conclude that they became apologists of the capitalist society because they looked at it, and indeed at the whole of human history, from the bourgeois point of view, and that a truly critical perspective on capitalism and on human history could only be attained from the proletarian point of view. This interpretation has been advanced in different forms, on different grounds and with varying degrees of sophistication by such eminent Marxists as Lenin, Lukács, Gramsci, Althusser, Ernst Bloch, Colletti and Adam Schaff.[1] In this chapter we shall outline and criticise the interpretation, and offer a more satisfactory way of reading Marx.

I

The basic thesis of the advocates of the proletarian point of view is relatively simple. Briefly it is as follows:

164

The capitalist society is divided into two major classes. Each class occupies a distinct position, has distinct interests and experiences, and represents a distinct perspective or point of view. Accordingly there are two points of view from which the capitalist society can be examined. For Marx an individual can rise above his class, but not above the classes altogether. He can therefore study the capitalist society only from one of the two points of view available to him. He must adopt one that in his view allows him fully to comprehend the inner nature of capitalism. For a variety of reasons, to be discussed presently, Marx concluded that only the proletarian point of view satisfied the condition. Accordingly he adopted it himself and recommended it to others.

Before discussing this interpretation of Marx, three general points need to be made. First, its advocates maintain that Marx consciously adopted, and not that he ended up taking, the proletarian point of view. It could be plausibly argued that, like the classical economists who aimed to study the capitalist society objectively, but ended up looking at it from the bourgeois point of view, Marx, too, aimed to study it objectively, but ended up looking at it from the proletarian point of view. The advocates of the proletarian point of view do not advance such a thesis. For them Marx's investigation led him to conclude that the capitalist society could be best analysed from the proletarian standpoint, and accordingly he decided to adopt it. Second, the advocates of the proletarian point of view do not say that only the proletariat can grasp the truth about capitalism, but rather that the truth about it can only be grasped from the *standpoint* of the proletariat. The distinction is crucial, for the former rules out all but the proletariat from understanding capitalism, and disqualifies not only Marx and Engels but also his commentators, many of whom come from the ranks of the petty bourgeoisie. Third, to their credit the advocates of the proletarian point of view do not say that, for Marx, truth is relative to the class, or that there are bourgeois and proletarians truths about capitalism. They insist that Marx was concerned to attain the objective truth about capitalism, and adopted the proletarian point of view because it alone enabled him to attain his objective. For them there are no proletarian truths; rather the objective truth can only be attained from the standpoint of the proletariat. The proletarian point of view is *more likely* to attain the truth, not that it yields *more* or *higher* truth.

II

Although the interpretation under consideration was advanced by others before him, Lenin's forceful advocacy and characteristically neat formulation gave it considerable authority and a wide circulation. For Lenin the class is the fundamental social reality, and also the basic epistemological subject. One cannot perceive society except 'from the view point of a definite class'. He dismisses as theoretically naïve and practically impossible the attempt 'so beloved of the liberal professors' to rise 'above all definite classes'. Of the three class points of view he notices, Lenin thinks that the bourgeois and the petty-bourgeois points of view lead to distortions. Since they have a vested interest in preserving the bourgeois society, the two classes 'fear contradictions', and are willing and afraid 'to look straight at the economic basis of the system'. The proletariat have no such fears; indeed their material interests *require* them to understand the true nature of capitalism. They are therefore uniquely equipped to discover the truth about it. Accordingly, argues Lenin, Marx analysed the capitalist society from the proletarian point of view.

Lukács, one of the ablest advocates of the proletarian point of view, gives it the philosophical depth it lacks in Lenin. Briefly he argues as follows.[2] The capitalist society has several basic characteristics. It is a 'structured totality' all of whose parts are integrally connected and mediated by the whole; its essence is radically different from what appears on the reified surface; it is contradictory in nature and consists of two implacably hostile classes; and it is in constant flux and seethes with tendencies whose 'higher reality' is concealed by the 'apparent' solidity of 'immediate' facts. Given these characteristics of the capitalist society, Lukács asks which class point of view is best equipped to comprehend its innermost essence.

He rules out the bourgeois standpoint on several grounds. The bourgeois class is fragmented by competition and cannot view society as a whole; it 'feels at home' in the reified world of appearances and has no need to probe its inner structure; it has a vested interest in preserving the capitalist society and can have no interest in probing its foundations; it is stuck 'in the mire of immediacy' and has no appreciation of the structural mediation; and so on. By contrast, the proletariat has both an 'interest' and a 'need to break through' the reified surface; indeed, this is a 'matter of life and death' for it. Besides, being an organised and self-conscious class, it has the perspective required to grasp society as a totality. Further, it has not only nothing to fear, but also everything to gain from comprehending the full truth about capitalism. Again, like Hegel's *Geist*, the proletariat is not merely the substance, but also the subject of capitalism. As its subject-object, its labour forms the basis of and sustains capitalism. Its concern to know capitalism is therefore at bottom nothing more than its attempt to know itself. Its self-knowledge is 'the self-revelation of the capitalist society'. For these and other reasons, says Lukács, the proletariat 'always aspires towards the truth, and even in its "false" consciousness and in its substantive errors'. Hence the truth about capitalism 'can be seen only from the standpoint of the proletariat'.

For Gramsci the capitalist society is characterised by an acute overt or covert class struggle. Each class uses ideas as a means to promote its interests. The pursuit of truth, therefore, comes to be replaced by the battle of ideologies. It is only when the classes disappear and mankind is unified that truth and objectivity are possible. As he puts it, 'the struggle for objectivity . . . is the same as the struggle for the cultural unification of the human race'. This raises the question as to how we are to choose between the competing class ideologies. Gramsci is vague on this crucial question. He seems to think that an ideology which meets the needs of the masses, accelerates the movement towards a classless society, and provides the basis of a 'more homogeneous, more coherent, more efficient' practice is more 'rational'. As he puts it, 'Mass adhesion or non-adhesion of an ideology is the real critical test of the rationality or historicity of modes of thinking.' The proletarian ideology satisfies these criteria better than the bourgeois, and is therefore superior. In Gramsci's view, Marx's thought is basically a definition and articulation of the ways of satisfying the fundamental interests of the masses.[3] It is not entirely clear whether he sees Marx's ideas merely as a progressive ideology, or as offering a true scientific account of the capitalist society.

For Althusser, as for Lenin, capitalism can only be grasped from the 'position' of a particular class. The 'whole of capitalism' consists in 'the reality of exploitation of wage labour power'. The bourgeois point of view covers up the reality, whereas the proletarian point of view faces up to it. As he puts it, it is 'the only view point that renders visible the reality of exploitation . . . which constitutes the whole of capitalism'. Marx knew this, and adopted the proletarian point of view. Althusser observes, 'It was by moving over to absolutely unprecedented proletarian theoretical class positions that Marx achieved the effectivity of the theoretical conjunction from which emerged the science of history.' Marxism is the theoretical exploration of the social reality 'visible from the standpoint of the proletariat'. Since this is so, argues Althusser, Marx's work cannot be understood unless one 'takes up proletarian class positions'. He observes:[4] historical materialism

> cannot be a science, like any other, a science for 'everyone' . . . This science which brings the social classes face to face with their truth, is unbearable for the bourgeoisie and its allies, who reject it and take refuge in their so-called 'social sciences': it is only accept-able to proletariat who it represents. That is why the proletariat has recognized it as its own property and set it to work in its practice.

Adam Schaff reaches the same conclusion by a slightly different route. In his view the class is the most basic unit in a class-divided society. One may transcend one's class, but not the classes altogether, and hence it is impossible to study society from a non-class point of view. In the modern capitalist society, as in the other class-divided societies, there are two major classes, the 'rising' revolutionary class and the 'falling' conservative class. Since the objective trends in society act against the latter, it has a vested interest in misrepresenting them. It consciously or unconsciously denies their existence, misinterprets them, covers up unpleasant facts, etc. and, as a result, the knowledge it offers is corrupted by 'conservative deformations'. The revolutionary class has nothing to fear from the social changes, and is therefore free from these limitations. Indeed its material and other interests are promoted by social progress, and hence it has every reason to under-take an objective and rigorous study of society. This means that the proletarian point of view offers the 'fullest and richest' perspective on the captialist society and represents the 'cognitively optimum position'. As Schaff puts it,[5] 'If you wish to attain objective truth . . . then consciously adopt class and party positions which are in accord with the interests of the proletariat.' Karl Mannheim, whom he generally follows, had argued that since, like the classical economists, Marx looked at the capitalist society from the standpoint of a class, he too was an ideologist. Schaff rejoins that while Mannheim was right to observe that Marx looked at capitalism from the proletarian point of view, he was wrong to conclude that he was *therefore* an ideologist. The bourgeoisie and the proletariat are epistemologically unequal. For reasons mentioned earlier, the latter is epistemologically privileged and 'higher', and hence, unlike the bourgeoisie, its standpoint is capable of yielding the truth.

For Colletti there are 'two realities' in the capitalist society, namely one that appears on the surface and one that lies deeper.[6] From the capitalist's or 'the "bosses" point of view', only the former is visible. The capitalist buys labour just as he buys raw material, and does not notice the profound difference between the two. Further, since he does not force the worker to sell his labour, his relations with the worker appear to him to be fair and mutually beneficial. For these and other reasons the reality of exploitation is never perceived from the capitalist point of view. The proletarian point of view is different. The worker knows that his sale of labour is not a matter of free choice, that he produces far more than he is paid for, that he sustains capitalism, and so on. The exploitative and contradictory character of capitalism is therefore starkly visible from his point of view. Hence, argues Colletti, Marx 'adopted' the proletarian point of view. As he puts it, Marxism 'is the analysis of reality from the view point of the working class'.

We outlined above the views of some of the eminent advocates of the thesis that Marx examined the capitalist society from the proletarian point of view. Obviously such brief and bland summaries cannot do justice at all to the complexity of their arguments and would be inexcusable if we were interested in examining their ideas. Our concern, however, was much more limited, namely to distil a general line of interpretation and the grounds upon which it is based.

III

According to the standard Marxist interpretation, then, Marx examined the capitalist society from the proletarian point of view. He knew that he could not avoid analysing it from a class point of view and, for various reasons, concluded that only the proletarian point of view offered him an adequate vantage point from which to study capitalism.

This intepretation of Marx is open to several objections. First, the evidence for it is limited and ambiguous. Some of Marx's remarks do, no doubt, lend credence to it. He said in the *German Ideology* that the 'true socialism' in Germany was incoherent and confused because it 'has come into being without any real party interests'.[7] He remarked in the *Poverty of Philosophy* that, just as the economists are the scientific representatives of the bourgeois class, 'so the *Socialists* and the *Communists* are the theoreticians of the proletarian class'.[8] He observed that *Capital* was the most powerful missile ever 'hurled at the heads of the bourgeoisie'. Again, the 'appreciation which *Das Kapital* rapidly gained in wide circles of the German working class is the best reward of my labours', and the fact *Capital* will be read by the working class is 'a consideration which to me outweighs everything else'.[9] After sending off the manuscript of *Capital* to the publishers Marx wrote to Engels, 'I hope to win a victory for our party in the field of science.'

Except a couple, the rest of these remarks are either ambiguous or imply that Marx intended to further the proletarian cause, but not that he studied capitalism from the proletarian point of view. The first remark from the *German Ideology* may not have been authored by Marx, but either Engels or Moses Hess.[10] The second and the last remarks are ambiguous, and could mean not that Marx set out on his scientific journey to defend the interests of the proletariat, but rather that his scientific investigation, not itself conducted from the proletarian point of view, led him to support the proletariat. The rest of the remarks signify that Marx was pleased to have been of service to the proletariat and was deeply concerned about their suffering, but not that he developed his *scientific* analysis from the proletarian point of view.

Even if it were conceded that at least some of these and other remarks not quoted here lend credence to the interpretation under consideration, there are many others, far greater in number and weightier in their significance, where he takes a very different view.[11] He insisted that 'men of science' should remain 'free agents of thought' and not become 'panderers to class prejudice'. He observed that the scientist must take an 'objective, non-partisan view' of his subject matter, investigate it 'impartially' and remain 'disinterested' and 'unprejudiced'.[12] He praised the British factory inspectors for being 'free from partisanship and respect for persons', and admired those 'disinterested inquirers' whose investigations displayed an 'unprejudiced character'. He said in the Foreword to *Capital*, 'Every opinion based on scientific criticism I welcome', implying that a scientific work can only be judged by the scientific criteria. Although he says that the bourgeois society should be criticised from a radical proletarian perspective, he adds the significant qualification that this is so only 'so far as such criticism represents a class'.[13] Again, we quoted earlier Marx's remarks on Ricardo and Malthus, and saw why for him the former was 'scientifically honest' whereas the latter was patently 'partisan'. In contrast to Malthus, Ricardo was only interested in the development of the productive forces, and not the promotion of the interests of a class. He supported the industrial bourgeoisie 'only because and in so far as' its interests coincided with those of production. When the two conflicted, he was 'just as ruthless towards it as he is at other times towards the proletariat and the aristocracy'.[14]

For Marx Ricardo does not 'sin against his science' and his work is 'stoic, objective, scientific' *because* he is concerned not with a particular class, but the well-being of the species as represented by the fullest development of the productive forces. He attempts to rise above the class biases and, although he does not always succeed, he at least tries and sometimes succeeds.

The second objection to the interpretation under consideration cuts much deeper. As we saw, it consists of two basic theses; first, a social theorist cannot avoid studying society from a class point of view, and second, the proletarian point of view is higher. The first thesis is untenable and undercuts the second. The second thesis is tenable, but not on the grounds offered.

As for the first thesis, it is incoherent. From what class point of view is the thesis advanced that society must be studied from a class point of view? If from the standpoint of a particular class, it obviously cannot claim universal validity. And if it is to claim universal validity, it cannot be advanced from a specific class point of view. Further, if the thesis that society must be viewed from a class point of view is not an arbitrary assertion, it must be supported by reasons which cannot themselves be grounded in a class point of view. One cannot say that the class is the basic social reality, or the only coherent epistemological subject, or that a particular class point of view is higher, without stepping outside the classes altogether and appealing to the class-independent standards of evidence and evaluation.

As for the second thesis, its advocates argue that Marx adopted the proletarian point of view because the latter is 'higher', 'cognitively optimum', 'objective', 'free of illusion', 'epistemologically adequate' to the social whole, and so on. The obvious question that all these claims raise is how Marx knew that the proletarian point of view had these features. There can only be two answers. First, Marx knew what capitalism was really like and concluded that, of the various class points of view available to him, only the proletarian point of view was capable of illuminating it. Second, Marx had worked out a general theory of how truth about human societies could be known, applied it to capitalism and concluded that the latter could only be known from the proletarian point of view. Each answer raises fatal difficulties.

The first answer is open to an obvious objection. Since Marx must already know what capitalism is like in order to conclude that it can only be known from the proletarian point of view, he did not need to adopt the proletarian point of view to know the truth about capitalism! To say that only the proletarian point of view enables one to grasp the

truth about capitalism or makes the social reality visible is to imply
that one already knows the truth about capitalism independently of
the proletarian point of view.

The second answer is equally unsatisfactory. First, we need to know
from what point of view Marx worked out a general theory concerning
the best way to obtain the truth about human societies. Since a social
theorist allegedly cannot rise above a class point of view, Marx must
have worked out such a theory from the standpoint of a particular
class, and such a class can only be the proletariat. This means that the
proletarian point of view is its own judge and that it alone can offer
the truth about capitalism because it says so! Further, a general theory
cannot be worked out from the proletarian point of view because the
proletariat is specific to capitalism, and its point of view cannot, on
Marx's own testimony, possess a universal validity. Again, Marx cannot
work out a general theory of how societies can be known and then
apply it to capitalism, unless he already knows independently of the
proletarian point of view what the capitalist society is really like
and whether or not his general theory applies to it.

We may put our objection differently. Marx adopted the proletarian
point of view either as an act of faith or commitment, or because he
had reasons for doing· so. If the former, then his adoption of it is
arbitrary, and does not preclude others from committing themselves to
other points of view. If the latter, then his reasons for adopting the
proletarian point of view lie outside it. He must have a wider and higher
point of view from which to determine both the general reasons relevant to choosing a point of view and the epistemological potential of
the proletarian point of view. The proletarian point of view cannot be
self-sufficient. It must be grounded in a higher point of view that can
specify the reasons why it must be preferred to all others. The higher
point of view cannot itself be a class point of view, for if it were, it
cannot then judge the class points of view without incurring the charge
of circularity. This is not to say that the proletarian point of view may
not be preferable to the others, only that such a claim requires a non-
proletarian point of view to substantiate it. A social theorist cannot
adopt the proletarian point of view unless he is able to rise above the
classes and weigh up the epistemological strengths and weaknesses of
all available points of view. The second thesis can be maintained only
if the first is rejected.

The thesis that Marx viewed the capitalist society from the proletarian point of view is open to other objections as well. Marx's thought is
at two levels. He developed a general theory of history embodied in his

historical materialism, and a specific theory of capitalism. It is not clear which of these two is supposed to have been developed from the proletarian point of view. Lenin, Lukács, Gramsci, Althusser, *et al.* do not distinguish the two, and seem to say that both are so developed.

Now historical materialism cannot be an articulation of the proletarian point of view, for this leads to historical anachronism. The proletariat is the specific product of the capitalist society, and hence its point of view has no relevance to the pre- and post-capitalist societies. If historical materialism were an articulation of the proletarian point of view, we would have to say that its validity is limited to capitalism. Lukács does not hesitate to take this view and says that historical materialism represents the fullest self-consciousness of the bourgeois society. However, he buys consistency at the cost of both drastically curtailing its explanatory claims and distorting Marx. Marx *never* said that historical materialism was only designed to explain capitalism. For him it explains *every* human society. He may be wrong; the point, however, is that this is what he thought. Therefore historical materialism cannot be a theoretical articulation of such a historically specific class as the proletariat. Even if Marx's theory of capitalism were shown to represent the proletarian point of view, his general theory of history could not be so construed.

If Marx were analysing capitalism from the proletarian point of view, it would follow that his writings are only intelligible from this point of view, and only to those who have already chosen to adopt it. As we saw, Althusser does not hesitate to draw this conclusion, and maintains that a worker is better able to understand Marx than a 'bourgeois professor'. Althusser presents Marx almost as an Augustinian for whom only he who believes will ever know. There is no evidence whatever that Marx held such a crude and dangerous view. As he said in his Preface to *Capital*, he welcomed 'scientific' and impartial criticisms from 'every' quarter and not just those made from the proletarian point of view as Lenin and Althusser insist. Like any other writer Marx cannot be fully understood without some measure of intellectual sympathy, or at least without temporarily suspending one's prejudices. However, to say that only those committed to the proletarian cause can understand him is an altogether different matter.

One could also offer other criticisms of the thesis that Marx examined capitalism from the proletarian point of view. Marx could not look at capitalism from the proletarian point of view for the simple reason that the proletariat is itself at least partly a product of Marx's own analysis. The proletariat has no clear conception of its interests, let alone its distinctive historical role. Indeed it becomes a proletariat only when it acquires a clear conception of its economic and historical identity. Otherwise it is not a class-for-itself, and at best only a class-in-itself. The proletariat *qua* proletariat is therefore partly constituted by a scientific theory such as Marx's, which gives it its appropriate self-consciousness. Inasmuch as Marx's theory of capitalism at least partly constitutes the proletariat, it cannot be merely an articulation of the latter's point of view. Lukács and Althusser argue that social reality is not fully visible unless one adopts the proletarian point of view. One could equally say the opposite, namely that the proletariat, as Marx defines it, is not visible unless one adopts his analysis of capitalism. To avoid misunderstanding, it is not being suggested that the proletariat is merely a theoretical construct. That would be idealism, which Marx rejects. Rather it exists only as a class-in-itself, a relatively passive group united by the social conditions of its material existence and lacking the active self-consciousness and social unity of a class-for-itself. As Marx's own theory of the unity of theory and practice, to be discussed later, implies, praxis is incomplete without the crucial element of critique. Marx supplies the proletariat its point of view, and obviously cannot articulate a pre-existing proletarian point of view.

Further, it is not clear what is meant by saying that Marx viewed the capitalist society from the proletarian point of view. Many commentators opt for the reflectionist view and argue that Marx accepted the proletariat's opinions, views, feelings, or interests, and built a theory around them. This view contradicts much of what Marx says.

Marx could not simply take over and theoretically justify the *opinions* of the proletariat, for these are all derived from the ideologically constituted social world, and necessarily 'vulgar'. Marx could not simply accept and theorise their *experiences* either, because they, too, are by definition confined to the surface of society. Nor could he accept and articulate what are called the '*instincts*', 'yearnings' or 'unconscious aspirations' of the proletariat. These are all vague metaphors, and could hardly be the basis of a scientific theory. Besides, as Marx himself says, many of the proletarian 'yearnings' are really bourgeois in nature. One must therefore criticise them and *decide* which of them are socialist. This presupposes a standard which cannot itself be derived from them. Nor, finally, could Marx's thought be an articulation and a defence of the proletarian *interests*. As we shall see, for Marx the proletarian interests are important in so far as they are identical with and promote the interests of the species. Further, the crucial question is who defines the proletarian interests. They can be defined in many different ways, such as those offered by the vulgar socialists, the reactionary Utopians and others, most of which Marx rejects. Marx therefore must have an independent standard by which to define the true interests of the proletariat. Further, Marx cannot accept the proletariat's own definition of them for, as he himself acknowledges, the proletariat is shaped by the dominant bourgeois ideology and lacks a clear conception of its long-term historical interests. Marx defines its interests for it on the basis of an independent analysis of its conditions of existence.

The upshot of our criticisms of the interpretation under consideration, then, is this. Marx cannot be seen as a proletarian social theorist so far as his historical materialism is concerned. And nor can he be so seen as far as his theory of capitalism is concerned, for the basic theses advanced by the advocates of the interpretation under consideration are untenable. If therefore the interpretation were correct, we would have to conclude that Marx's thought is deeply incoherent. We may eventually come to this conclusion, but we must first explore if he can be read in a manner both less damaging to him and faithful to his writings. Such a manner of reading him is proposed below. It is inevitably brief and sketchy, and only intended to illustrate the broad direction in which a more satisfactory interpretation of Marx could be found.

Basically it maintains that, although the two are integrally connected and similarly grounded, we must, for analytical convenience, distinguish between Marx's political support of the proletariat, and his epistemological appreciation of its point of view.[15] His political support of it was derived from his belief that it was the only class capable of promoting the interests of mankind. He was first and foremost a humanist, and only derivatively a supporter of the proletariat. As a scientist Marx was not a class theorist, but a 'free agent of thought'. He aimed to study the capitalist mode of production and human history from the most comprehensive and self-critical point of view possible. Accordingly he studied them not from the proletarian point of view, but from the standpoint of the social whole, critically constructed out of all the standpoints available to him, including the proletarian.

IV

For Marx Hegel, the classical economists and others became the apologists of their society because, among other things, they accepted its ideological self-image. As we saw, Marx's investigations into the structures of their thought convinced him that they discussed the law, state, constitution, the economy, history, technology, civilisation, human needs, etc. entirely from the perspective of the dominant class, and never asked how these affected and looked from the standpoint of the dominated classes. Their standpoint was 'narrow' and 'partial'. They viewed society from the perspective of one of its parts, and hence they could not but remain ideological, uncritical and partisan. Marx was convinced that, in order to study society critically, he must investigate it not from a partial and narrow, but the widest point of view available to him, from the 'standpoint of the whole' as he called it. A limited point of view necessarily rests on unexamined assumptions, and can never be fully critical. Accordingly Marx went on to develop the most comprehensive and self-critical point of view possible. For him the standpoint of the species alone offers the widest perspective; anything short of it is, by definition, partial and potentially partisan.

For Marx man is the highest being for man. God is a human fantasy, and nature only exists to subserve man. Marx made this clear at the start of his intellectual career, and continued to subscribe to it until the end of his life. He observed, 'To be radical is to grasp the matter by the root. But for man the root is man himself.'[16] In all his works, including *Capital*, he evaluated the social institutions and practices on the basis of how they affected the human well-being.

In Marx's view many a vulgar socialist to their credit evaluated the capitalist society by this standard. However, they defined human well-being in abstract and ahistorical terms, that is, in terms of abstract moral principles or their subjective conceptions of an ideal society. As a result, their criticisms bore no relation to the prevailing social order, were not grounded in concrete human needs, showed no appreciation of the inner workings of capitalism and, for the most part, remained sentimental and irrelevant. In Marx's view the human well-being must be defined historically. This means two things. First, it must be defined in terms of the needs and capacities that men have already developed at a specific point in time. Given its privileged position, some needs and capacities are likely to have been developed only by the dominant class; for example, the cultural and aesthetic needs and capacities. Some other needs and capacities are likely to have been developed by the dominated classes; for example, the social and productive needs and the capacities for co-operation, solidarity, concerted action and technical versatility. Marx reflects upon the needs and capacities developed by the different classes, and formulates a conception of what men are capable of becoming. Rather half-heartedly he recognises that men are also likely to have developed 'inhuman' needs and capacities. He explains them in terms of the distortions human beings undergo in the class-divided society, and teases out by means of 'criticism' the real needs expressed in such a pathological manner. Needless to say, Marx's personal preferences profoundly shape his views on what needs are 'real' and 'human' or 'illusory' and 'inhuman'.

Second, Marx investigates the inner nature and the direction of the development of capitalism, uncovers its productive potentialities, shows what human needs it frustrates and is capable of satisfying, how its crises arise, and how it can be superseded.

On the basis of the already developed and developing human needs and capacities, as well as the prevailing level of technological development, Marx formulates a vision of the historically immanent society, and uses it as a standard with which to criticise the prevailing social order. He exposes the evils of the latter, and demonstrates that these can be eliminated in a differently structured society which is both possible and necessary. In other words he confronts the capitalist society with an image of its own possibilities. His criticisms of it are not abstract but historically grounded, not superficial but radical, not dogmatic but based on a realistic assessment of its potentialities, not sentimental and moralistic but based on the actual needs of men, and not external but based on what is historically both possible and necessary.

Marx turned to what he called the 'negative class' for the realisation of the historically maturing possibilities. He borrowed Hegel's 'great insight', that the progress in history is achieved by the 'principle of negativity', that is by a determined and concerted attempt to challenge and go beyond the established body of ideas and institutions.[17] As Marx puts it, 'It is the bad side that produces the movement which makes history, by providing a struggle.'[18] Although Marx's later writings modify his earlier romantic view of the negative class, basically he meant by it a social group that was capable of acting as a *class* and *negating* the established society in favour of one more conducive to human well-being. The negative class is not *outside* society in a way that the beggars, prostitutes, the lumpenproletariat and drop-outs are, but is its integral and essential part. It sustains the society and bears its burdens, but does not benefit much from its achievements. Its common 'conditions of existence' generate common interests and needs, which it can only promote by constituting itself and acting as a self-conscious class. The negative class is 'compelled' by its very conditions of existence to negate the established social order, and replace it with a better one which it is *both* possible and necessary for it to create.

Marx assigns the negative class a crucial historical role, and considers it 'higher' than the dominant class for the following reasons. First, unlike the dominant class, it is a universal class in the sense that it represents in its struggles the sufferings and aspirations of the whole society. Second, unlike the dominant class, which is only interested in perpetuating its domination, the negative class is concerned with human liberation, that is with the further development of the productive forces and the gratification of the unfulfilled human needs. Third, unlike the dominant class, which is happy in and unaware of its alienated existence, the negative class is acutely aware of its subhuman existence, and likely to wish to do something about it. As Marx puts it, the worker 'stands here from the very first on a higher level than the capitalist' because, unlike him, he is deeply conscious of and wishes to rebel against his 'enslavement'.[19]

In Marx's view the bourgeoisie were once a negative class and played an emancipatory historical role; their mantle had now passed to the proletariat. He made it repeatedly clear that the proletariat had a historical role to play not because it was a *suffering* class, but because it was a *negative* class, that is a universal class which had the ability and power to create a new civilisation and to further human wellbeing. For Marx its historical importance was derived from the fact that it represented the true interests of mankind and a higher level of humanity.

He observes that 'only in the name of the general rights of society' can the proletariat lay claim to general domination. He says, again, that only 'a class in which the revolutionary interests of society are concentrated' has a right to historical supremacy. Again, the emancipation of workers is important not because 'their emancipation alone is at stake but because the emancipation of the workers contains universal human emancipation'. The proletariat's historical mission is not to establish its own rule, but to abolish the classes altogether and replace them by a unified humanity. The proletariat is 'the bearer of human development', the 'agent' of human progress and the 'general representative of mankind.[20] Marx stresses the role of the proletariat because, and to the extent that, its interests coincide with those of mankind. Not that the proletariat is a mere means, although Marx sometimes comes close to saying so; rather its short-term interests *qua* proletariat may clash with its own long-term human interests, and then he urges that they should be sacrificed. For Marx the interests of the species are served by the fullest development of the productive forces; if these require that the proletariat should suffer for a while, the price must be paid. As he observes in a strongly Hegelian paragraph:[21]

> To assert, as sentimental opponents of Ricardo's did, that production as such is not the object, is to forget that production for its own sake means nothing but the development of human productive forces, in other words the *development of the richness of human nature as an end in itself*. To oppose the welfare of the individual to this end, as Sismondi does, is to assert that the development of the species must be *arrested* in order to safeguard the welfare of the individual, so that, for instance, no war may be waged in which at all events some individuals perish (Sismondi is only right as against the economists who *conceal* or deny this contradiction). Apart from the barrenness of such edifying reflections, they reveal a failure to understand the fact that, although at first the development of the capacities of the *human* species takes place at the cost of the majority of human individuals and even classes, in the end it breaks through this contradiction and coincides with the development of the individual; the higher development of individuality is thus only achieved by a historical process during which individuals are sacrificed, for the interests of the species in the human kingdom, as in the animal and plant kingdoms, always assert themselves at the cost of the interests of individuals, because these interests of the species coincide only with the *interests of certain individuals*, and it is this coincidence which constitutes the strength of these privileged individuals.

The idea of representation is crucial to Marx's political thought. For him a class capable of raising mankind to a higher level is progressive, and has a right to rule.[22] For example, he admired the leadership the French bourgeoisie provided to the French Revolution on the ground that they 'represented the whole of modern society against the representatives of the old society, royalty and aristocracy'. In 1848 Marx, assuming that the social conditions in Germany were similar to those in France in 1789, favoured a liberal revolution led by the bourgeoisie. He observed:

> In the mouth of the people the word revolution has this meaning: You bourgeoisie are the 'Committee of public safety' into whose

hands we have placed the government, not so that you will combine with the crown in your own interest; but so that you will champion our interests, the interests of the people, against the crown.

Marx supported the Paris Commune because it was 'the true representative of all the healthy elements of French society', and therefore 'the truly national government'. For Marx mankind realises itself in and through the classes, even as Hegel's *Geist* realises itself through the world-historical nations. Mankind does not exist independently of the classes, but it is not fully exhausted in any of them either. Mankind becomes an abstraction if detached from the classes; but equally the classes lack general significance unless they represent mankind. In essence Marx views the progressive class as a concrete universal. It is not a vehicle but a representative or agent of mankind. It has its own independent moral claims, but these are defined in larger human terms. For Marx in a class-divided society one cannot pursue human interests in the abstract. Humanism must necessarily take sides, as otherwise it becomes abstract, sentimental, indeterminate, aiming for the lowest common denominator, afraid to fight and hurt, and politically naïve.

It is because Marx takes the proletariat to be capable of promoting the historically defined human interests that he politically aligns himself with it. He fights with and for it, and promotes its interests. He does so not because he has made a commitment to the proletariat, but because he is convinced, on the basis of the essentially Hegelian philosophy of history and his analysis of capitalism, that it alone represents the universal and emancipatory interests of mankind. Further, it is because he takes such a wider view that he appreciates the great historical achievements of the bourgeois, integrates them with the needs and capacities developed by the proletariat, and constructs a wider view of the true interests of mankind. It is this broader conception that enables him to take a *critical* view of the proletarian perception of its interests, and to expose its narrow class view of its political and historical role. Marx aims to stand on the shoulders of *both* the bourgeoisie and the proletariat, catch a glimpse of the immanent new order, and use it to criticise both. In short, Marx views the proletariat against a wider humanist perspective. He is not its narrow and partisan champion. His first and ultimate loyalty is to the well-being of the species; his support of the proletariat is grounded in and derived from it.

V

The scientific importance of the proletariat in Marx's thought is broadly the same as the political, and is similarly grounded. Even as Marx stresses the political role of the negative class, he stresses its epistemological role. In his view it is epistemologically privileged in a way that the established class is not. It is, as we saw, a universal class and interested in human liberation. Besides, it is a national and organised class, and hence capable of viewing society as a totality. Further, it is at the receiving end of the social order, and therefore sees its ugliness in all its fullness. And it has distinct experiences which reveal aspects of the social order that remain opaque to the dominant class.

Marx argues that, because of all this, it is compelled by its conditions of existence to ask questions which the dominant class cannot or will not.[23] It has a distinct pool of negative experiences, and the consequent interests and needs. As such it asks disturbing questions, challenges the basic assumptions underlying the dominant universe of discourse, questions the prevailing social arrangement, and wonders if there are no better alternatives. Since its experiences and interests are different, it does not share the biases of the dominant class. It is therefore particularly sensitive to the biased assumptions of the current views of man and society and forms of inquiry. As such it finds problematic what the dominant class takes for granted. It asks how private property is justified, why there should be classes, why society collectively cannot regulate production, why production should be for profit rather than the satisfaction of human needs, why some should work when others do not, why one should respect the established authority when it preserves a social order unable to guarantee one even a decent livelihood, and so on. These and other fundamental and subversive questions directly grow out of its experiences and are a matter of life and death to it. By continuously raising them in one form or another, the proletariat places new items on the intellectual and political agenda, extends the limits of the dominant horizon of thought and opens up a whole new way of looking at man and society. Unlike the proletariat, the dominant class is not compelled by its conditions of existence to ask radically novel questions. It has created the social order in its own image, and shares its basic biases. As such it is inherently incapable of raising fundamental questions about it. What is more, it is necessarily impatient and suspicious of such questions, and positively discourages them. Its questions or, more accurately, its queries are therefore mostly superficial, formal and 'academic'.

As a social scientist concerned to understand capitalism, Marx derives a profound theoretical benefit from the questions asked by the proletariat. They offer him new insights and a fresh perspective which he cannot gain elsewhere. Further, since the proletariat is an integral part of capitalism, its experiences constitute a large segment of social reality. Hence Marx analyses and uses them to explore the inner structure of the capitalist mode of production. Again, since he is persuaded that the proletariat is the agent of historical progress and stands on a 'higher level' than the bourgeoisie, its experiences, questions and interests have a particular significance for Marx. He pays close attention to them, joins it in examining the sources of its suffering, derives intellectual energy from and grounds his critique in its praxis, and so on.

While profoundly benefiting from the questions asked by the proletariat, Marx cannot remain its theorist for at least three important reasons.[24] First, there are many questions about capitalism that do not get asked from the proletarian point of view. Contrary to the view advanced by Lukács and Althusser, Marx does not think that the proletarian experiences represent the whole of social reality or that capitalism is *only* about the exploitation of the proletariat. There are areas such as the international trade, colonisation and the intra-bourgeois competition in which the proletariat is not the principal subject and which are not reducible to its experiences. Further, although the relations between the bourgeoisie and the proletariat are, for Marx, the basis of capitalism, such important forms of relation as those between the bourgeois 'fractions' and between the landed classes and the agricultural workers are not fully 'visible' from the proletarian point of view. Although more comprehensive than the bourgeois point of view, the latter is still partial and cannot be considered the 'standpoint of the whole'. This explains why, on Marx's own testimony, his work on capitalism was designed to consist of various parts, each looking at it from the conflicting standpoints of the capitalist, the worker and the landed aristocrat.[25]

Second, like all partial points of view, the proletarian point of view suffers from several characteristic limitations. The proletariat is not generally able to see through the ideologically constituted social world, and asks for such things as fair wages rather than the very abolition of the wage slavery. Further, as we saw, it tends to stress immediacy and ignore mediation. For it the human subject is 'everything'; the objective world counts for little; and the 'living' not the 'stored up' labour is the sole creator of wealth. The proletariat has a tendency to concentrate only on the evils of capitalism, ignore its great material and cultural achievements, reject luxury and individuality, and champion an ascetic and regimented society.

Third, even when profoundly illuminating, the questions asked by the proletariat are not scientific, and must be transposed into the scientific language before they can be accepted as genuinely theoretical questions. In the process of transposition some of its questions get rejected, and others refined and redefined.

Given these and other limitations, Marx cannot be content to look at capitalism from the proletarian point of view. No doubt, he is profoundly sympathetic to it, regards it as more illuminating than the bourgeois point of view, and benefits from its questions and their underlying experiences and anxieties. However, he finds it partial, inadequate and somewhat partisan. Accordingly, he supplements and criticises it in the light of the insights offered by the bourgeois point of view. As we saw, Marx carefully examines the thought of the bourgeois economists and aims to incorporate and build on their achievements. While benefiting from their questions and answers, he also, however, criticises them in the light of the insights gained from the proletarian point of view. Thanks to his knowledge of both the bourgeois and the proletarian points of view, he is able to notice and criticise the partialities and exaggerations of each. To be sure, the two points of view are *not* equal. For Marx the proletarian point of view is theoretically richer and more penetrating. However, it has its own limitations. What is more, the bourgeois point of view, as Marx himself says, offered profound insights and got 'very close' to the heart of capitalism. It is therefore of more than marginal importance. Accordingly, Marx aims to stand on the shoulders of *both*, and construct a most critical and comprehensive point of view possible, the 'standpoint of the whole' as he called it. It is the highest point of view available to him from which he can hope to grasp the full truth of capitalism.

What Marx said of Proudhon is illuminating in this context.[26] As a 'man of science' he wants to 'soar above the bourgeoisie and the proletarians'. He can be 'superior' to both only if he can 'rise above' and can 'criticise' them. Since Proudhon is unable to do so, he is 'continually tossed back and forth' between, and remains 'inferior to both'. Marx suggests here that between the bourgeois and the proletarian points of view, the latter is higher, but that higher still is a point of view which can criticise and rise above both. This is precisely what he aimed to do. Although politically allied to and scientifically appreciative of the proletariat, Marx is not a proletarian thinker, but a 'free agent of thought'. While locating himself on the proletarian standpoint, he examines and benefits from whatever other standpoints seem illuminating to him, and freely constructs a point of view most adequate to the understanding of capitalism.

It is because, among other things, Marx intended to rise above and combine the achievements of the different points of view that the dialectical method became extremely important to him. It offered him the Archimedean location from which to keep the contradictory class standpoints in view, and examine each without losing sight of the rest. It also enabled him to see the limitations and strengths of each, and both avoid its partiality and preserve its achievements. It helped him to appreciate that only that class or point of view is higher which can consolidate, build on and go beyond the achievements of the others, and that, in rejecting them, it diminishes its own moral and historical claims. In short the dialectic offered him the methodological lever he needed to criticise and rise above the various class points of view.

The extent of Marx's preoccupation with method has not been sufficiently appreciated. His critique of the apologetic bodies of thought convinced him that he needed a method capable of comprehending the richness, complexity and totality of the social whole without distortion. And as he often made clear, he needed such a method at each of the three levels of theorising, namely thinking about his subject matter, analysing and investigating it, and presenting his findings to the general public.[27] After suitably modifying and de-mystifying it, Marx took over Hegel's dialectical method and used it for all three purposes. Above all, it was for him, as it was for Hegel, a way of *thinking*, a method of conceiving his subject matter. In contrast to the 'either — or' approach of the positivist, the dialectical manner of thinking holds the conflicting points of view *together*, examines each *in relation to* the rest, sets up a dialogue between them, uses one to illuminate the strengths and limitations of the others, and helps the thinker resist being overwhelmed by any one point of view. As Marx observed, it is 'impossible to *think* critically' except by means of the dialectic.

VI

Let us briefly sum up the interpretation of Marx offered above. Marx saw himself as a 'free agent of thought'. He developed his theories of historical materialism and capitalism as a scientist thinking freely, and not from within a class point of view. As such, they can claim the attention of and be understood and criticised by all, not just the proletariat. Both as a scientist and a political activist, Marx was committed to human well-being, and not only to that of the proletariat. His investigations revealed to him that in a class-divided society, human well-being is class-mediated and promoted by the critique and praxis of the negative class. Accordingly he stressed the role of the negative class in every historical epoch. During the early decades of capitalism the bourgeoisie were the negative class and represented the interests of mankind. When they became a narrow class *as against* others, they forfeited their moral claim to universal support, and their historical mantle passed to the new negative class, the proletariat.

Both in his political analysis and epistemology Marx assigned the negative class a crucial role. As the representative of the universal interests of mankind, it is a 'higher' class. However, it is higher because it is capable of promoting the universal interests of mankind; and hence its interests must be defined and its praxis criticised in the light of the latter. Even as it is politically and historically higher, its epistemological perspective on society is higher and free from many of the biases and blindspots characteristic of the established class. However, it is not free from its own characteristic limitations, and therefore, although higher, it does not represent the highest point of view. As such it must be criticised, enriched by the insights offered by the bourgeois and other points of view, and sublated into the most critical and comprehensive point of view possible. Marx anchored himself in, but also went beyond the proletarian point of view.

Marx aligned himself with the proletariat both politically and scientifically; politically because it was for him a more progressive class, scientifically because it represented a higher point of view. However, he was not *its* spokesman or theorist. He criticised the proletariat politically from a wider human point of view, and scientifically from a more critical, impartial and comprehensive scientific point of view. As a scientist Marx was not a 'class-theorist', but a 'free agent of thought'.[28] His scientific inquiries profoundly benefited from, but were not undertaken from, the proletarian point of view. He systematically explored capitalism from a scientific point of view constructed from, among others, the proletarian point of view. He criticised the classical economists from a scientific not a proletarian point of view.

8 MARX'S THEORY OF TRUTH

Marx nowhere systematically discusses the nature and criteria of truth. Not surprisingly, this has encouraged some of his commentators to ascribe strange and implausible views to him. Some argue that he was not at all interested in truth but only in human well-being, and judged social theories according to whether or not they promoted it. For some others he was interested in truth, and defined it as whatever serves the interests of the progressive class, accords with the laws of history or promotes the classless society. For others he held that, since all knowledge is class-determined, the traditional concept of objective truth is incoherent and must be replaced by that of class truth. For yet others Marx subscribed to the traditional concept of objective truth, but despaired of attaining it in a class-divided society, and thought that the only relevant criterion here was whether a theory promoted the cause of the proletariat. For some Marx held that the objective truth was the highest ideal of theoretical knowledge and that, although difficult, it was not impossible to attain in a class-divided society.[1]

The textual evidence does not support any of these interpretations save the last. As we shall see, Marx criticised the traditional discussion of the nature of truth, and introduced several new ideas. However, they enrich the traditional conception of truth, and do not amount to its rejection.

I

As with most aspects of Marx's thought, his theory of truth can be best seen against the background of his critique of idealism. In his view much of the traditional discussion of truth has taken place within the idealist framework, and suffered from the limitations characteristic of the latter.

For Marx the pursuit of knowledge is a three-dimensional activity. It involves the knowing subject, the object to be known, and the activity of pursuing knowledge. A theory of knowledge and of truth, its *telos*, cannot therefore be developed except on the basis of a systematic discussion of the nature of its three dimensions.

As we saw, Marx takes the view that the knowing subject is not God, but a human being who is necessarily embodied, has specific interests and needs and is a member of a specific society at a specific period in history. The object of knowledge, too, especially when it relates to man and society, is necessarily historical; it is subject to historical change and is shaped and even constituted by human praxis. And the activity of knowing occurs within a specific social structure and the framework of an intellectual discipline possessing a definite character born out of its basic assumptions and tradition. The pursuit of knowledge is therefore an activity in which a socially and historically shaped being, actively engaged in satisfying his historically created needs, aims to understand a historically shaped object within the overall framework of a historically developing intellectual discipline.

In Marx's view idealism, for reasons considered earlier, took an abstract and ahistorical view of the pursuit of knowledge. It de-historicised and de-socialised the knowing subject and treated him as pure reason or, with the empiricists, as a blank slate who is in no way affected by his interests, desires, needs, social background, the stage of historical development, and so on. It similarly de-historicised the object of knowledge. As we saw, it abstracted away its historical specificity and either concentrated on its formal features or aimed to comprehend it 'as such'. Idealism de-historicised also the activity of knowing. It conceived knowing as an unmediated encounter between the subject and the object, and ignored the mediating influences of the intellectual discipline involved, the socially dominant ideology and the forms of thought characteristic of the historical epoch in question.

By de-historicising the pursuit of knowledge, idealism removed its inherently conditional nature. It conceived the knowing subject not as a historical and conditioned being but as a transcendental and unconditioned being, that is as an Absolute Subject or God. For it the essence of an object consists in, and therefore the only form of knowledge worth seeking is the knowledge of its historically invariant, immutable and Absolute nature. And it conceived the activity of knowing as if it occurred in an intellectual and historical vacuum and were in no way socially and historically shaped. For idealism, then, the pursuit of knowledge is an activity in which an Absolute subject aims to know an Absolute object in an Absolute manner. The *telos* of knowledge is taken to be what Plato and others called Absolute truth, or what Hegel called Absolute knowledge.

For Marx much of the traditional discussion of the nature and criteria of truth has taken place within this framework. Since it accepted the idealist absolutisation of the subject, object and the process of knowledge, it absolutised truth as well and defined it in appropriate terms. For it the truth worth seeking must be immutable or historically unchanging, final or not liable to revision, unconditional or true under all conditions, pure or uncontaminated by any form of error and objective or unalterable by human praxis. It is sought not for crude, mundane or practical reasons but because men love truth or have a disinterested desire to understand the world. Since Marx takes the view that the acquisition of knowledge is profoundly historical in the sense outlined earlier, he takes a very different view of the nature of truth.

II

Marx locates the concept of truth within the larger context of human existence. For him man is first and foremost a creature of needs. He has basic as well as historically created material, social, cultural, intellectual and other needs. His satisfaction of them involves praxis in the form of interaction with nature and with other men. He engages in material praxis in order to conquer and humanise nature, and in social and political praxis in order to create a social order most capable of satisfying his needs. For Marx the satisfaction of needs constitutes human well-being. Sometimes he says that human well-being ultimately consists in freedom. By freedom he means self-determination, the ability to define, shape and satisfy one's needs as one thinks proper. When so defined, freedom involves liberation from both the external and internal constraints imposed by nature, and from the economic, political and other forms of human domination. We could therefore say that, for Marx, human well-being or freedom is the *telos* of praxis.[2]

Men cannot successfully undertake material and political praxis without understanding nature and society. They cannot conquer and humanise nature without a full knowledge of its inner structure; and they cannot create or maintain a desirable social order without understanding its inner nature. In other words men pursue truth because it is the *sine qua non*, initially, of successful praxis and, ultimately, of human well-being. For Marx the pursuit of truth is materially grounded. Men do not pursue it because they have an allegedly innate love of truth or a disinterested desire for knowledge, for both these are historically derived and not inherent in human nature. Rather they pursue truth because they are needy beings who must engage in successful material and political praxis in order to satisfy their needs. If men had no needs, or did not care whether or not they satisfied them, or were able to satisfy them by waving a magic wand, they would accept the world as it is and not endeavour to know and control it. Marx admits that as men engage in material and political praxis, they may and do, over time, develop the love of truth and a disinterested desire for knowledge. His point is that the pursuit of human well-being is ontologically prior to and materially underpins the pursuit of truth.[3]

In locating the pursuit of truth within the context of human praxis, Marx does not wish to say that it is not autonomous, nor that the praxis or its results constitute the criterion of truth. Although the pursuit of knowledge owes its origin and continuing impetus to the human pursuit of well-being, once it gets under way it acquires autonomy and raises its own distinct problems. The attempt to solve a particular practical problem may generate others that may have no relevance to the initial practical concern. In this way a whole cluster of problems may grow up with no practical relevance at all. While admitting all this, Marx wishes to argue that the pursuit of knowledge does not take place in a social vacuum, but is shaped by practical concerns. The very pursuit of knowledge springs from and is sustained by the practical desire to live well. Further, new theoretical disciplines arise in response to the newly developed human interests; within each, new problem areas arise or acquire unprecedented importance when men acquire new interests and needs; and the different branches of knowledge undergo accelerated development and rise and fall in response to the change in human interests and needs. Let us take Marx's example of the natural sciences.

For a long time the natural sciences developed very slowly. Men had limited needs, and therefore a limited knowledge of nature was sufficient for their purposes. When commerce and trade underwent unprecedented expansion with the emergence of the bourgeoisie, and the human needs expanded dramatically, the intensity and extent of man's interaction with nature increased tremendously. This accelerated the growth of the natural sciences, whose development became a pressing social need. Although their growth was unplanned and occurred in fits and starts, it followed a recognisable pattern. Physics developed first in response to the theoretical problems thrown up by the requirements of modern industry. Chemistry developed later in response to the new areas of production like metallurgy, dyeing, textile and pharmaceutical industries. Trigonometry developed in response to the great maritime discoveries of the modern age; and the calculation of probabilities became an urgent matter when the international trade developed during the colonial period.

The fact that the pursuit of knowledge occurs within the wider context of human praxis does not mean that it lacks an independent character and *telos*. Although owing its impetus to and profoundly shaped by the human praxis, the realm of theoretical knowledge is guided by its own independent criteria. Practical problems throw up theoretical problems, but do not by themselves become theoretical unless suitably redefined and transposed into a theoretically appropriate language. Further, the theoretical inquiries have their own standards of truth, methods of investigation, and so on, and their independence is not affected by the fact that they occur within a practical context. A theory is true if it satisfies the criteria of truth. Within the realm of theoretical knowledge, truth is the sovereign value. Human praxis shapes the areas and problems selected for theoretical investigation. However, once the theoretical investigation gets under way only the truth, as scientifically defined, matters. To put the point differently, human praxis shapes the truths men seek, but not what counts as or constitutes truth. Men *pursue* truth because they desire freedom, but freedom is not itself truth nor even the criterion of it. For Marx, therefore, a theory cannot be judged true or false by the criterion of praxis or by its practical results. The human well-being is the *telos* of truth, but truth is the *telos* of knowledge. Within the field of knowledge praxis cannot replace truth. To make praxis the criterion of scientific knowledge is to establish an immediate or unmediated identity between the two and ignore the mediation of the concept of truth.[4]

For Marx, then, the pursuit of knowledge does not occur in a historical vacuum, but within the context of, and derives its inspiration and energy from, man's material and political praxis. Men pursue knowledge, and pursue certain kinds of knowledge in the first instance because they wish to understand, and ultimately because they wish to control and shape the world in the light of their needs. This may not be easily evident in the theoretical investigations by specific men in specific areas, which may be better accounted for, at least in the first instance, in terms of the professional pressures, the history of the discipline, the personality of the researcher, and so on. However, in Marx's view, it is amply evident in such larger phenomena as the pursuit of knowledge itself, the rise and fall of specific disciplines, the direction of the development of knowledge, the development of new areas of investigation, and the clusters of problems upon which the bulk of the researchers concentrate.

In the natural sciences there is an almost universal consensus as to what practical interest informs the pursuit of knowledge. Marx agrees that different social classes do, no doubt, take different attitudes to nature, exploit it in different ways and different degrees, and that their social conflicts spill over into their relations with nature. However, he insists that, by and large, men struggle against nature as a united species, and their technological achievements are, albeit in different degrees, available to all men and constitute a common human heritage.

In the social sciences the situation is very different. The conflicts of interest between the classes profoundly shape and inform their pursuit of knowledge. As seen earlier, men engaged in the pursuit of knowledge are also members of a specific society, belong to specific groups, are engaged in practical struggles, find their interests preserved or threatened by other groups, and so on. Unless they are fully conscious of and strive to rise above their social biases, the latter inescapably inform their theoretical pursuits. Men do not forget or escape their conflict-ridden social being simply because they are engaged in the theoretical rather than practical pursuits.

According to Marx the interests informing the pursuit of knowledge about society are of two types. A student of society may be in favour of class 'domination' embodied in the prevailing social order, or in favour of human 'emancipation'. In one case his interests are 'apologetic', in the other 'critical'. For Marx all social thought is informed and underpinned by one of these interests. Interest-unrelated social thought is inherently impossible. As usual Marx takes an extremely narrow view of the attitudes one can take to the existing social order, and argues that one either wishes to preserve or overthrow it. As a result a large number of views get either left out or misrepresented.[5]

For Marx society, the object of knowledge of the social theorist, is conflict-ridden. What is more, the theorist is himself involved in and affected by the conflicts. In Marx's view he cannot therefore avoid taking a view of and sides in the conflicts. The object cannot be studied without some view of its contradictory nature; it *requires* a response. Simply because a social theorist believes in pure theory and refuses to take a view, he cannot avoid taking one. If he does not consciously choose one, he will only end up adopting one dictated by his unarticulated social biases. For Marx every social theorist has a more or less clearly defined view of the social contradictions constituting the very identity of his subject matter. He takes sides, or imagines that the class conflicts do not exist, or proposes recipes for resolving them. Given his narrow and dualistic framework, Marx argues that the latter two positions are 'naive', unrealistic and ultimately lead to an apologia for the established social order.

For Marx, then, the body of knowledge offered by a social theorist is either apologetic or critical. The apologetic and critical dimensions are not a matter of how the knowledge once arrived at is subsequently used; rather they are embedded in the knowledge itself. As we saw, an apologetically inspired social theory has a strong tendency to de-historicise society, employ ahistorical and abstract categories, ask systematically biased questions, and so on. Consequently, the theoretical knowledge offered by it is inherently apologetic, and cannot be used to criticise and change the social order. This was why Marx thought that the Left Hegelians and the vulgar socialists were wrong to imagine that they could 'use' Hegel's philosophy and the theories of the classical economists respectively to criticise the contemporary society. A critically orientated theoretical knowledge is very different. It not only explains the social order, but also interrogates and criticises it. It explores not only the manner in which a social order is held together, but also its internal contradictions, its historically maturing potentialities, the needs and capacities it realises or frustrates, and the way it could be changed. As such the critical knowledge offered by it not only explains, but also judges, accuses and points a way out. As he says of his own work, it is 'the system of bourgeois economy critically presented. It is a presentation of the system and, simultaneously, through this presentation, a criticism of it.'[6]

For Marx, then, the pursuit of knowledge is not a disinterested and contemplative activity. A definite interest inspires and energises it.[7] It is because an interest, a practical impulse, lies at its basis that the knowledge offered by a social theory has practical implications. Obviously the kind of interest lying at its basis determines the nature of the implications. For Marx a body of knowledge contains its own imperatives and recommendations. Theory and practice, thought and action, reason and will, etc. cannot be disjoined and compartmentalised. They are interdependent moments of a single whole and, when separated, become incomprehensible abstractions. Marx argues that, since all thought, including the most abstract and theoretical, is necessarily informed by a practical impulse, a social theorist must *decide* what view he will take of the fundamental structure of his society. Pure theory is an illusion. He who believes in it fails to notice and counter his pre- and para-theoretical biases, and is doomed to become a most insidious and dogmatic apologist.

Of the two types of interest informing the pursuit of knowledge, Marx argues that only the emancipatory interest is justifiable. Although he nowhere clearly states them he seems to take this view for two reasons. First, only the emancipatory interest is consistent with the *telos* of truth. As we saw, the pursuit of truth is ontologically grounded in the pursuit of human well-being or freedom. Men seek truth so that they can liberate themselves from the natural and social restraints. To pursue truth for domination is to pervert its inspiring principle. Second, only the emancipatory interest is capable of attaining the truth, the *telos* of knowledge. As we saw, Marx takes the view that the pursuit of knowledge in the interest of domination leads to ideological distortion. Such a pursuit is biased towards the dominant class and locked within a system of assumptions which prevent it from asking searching questions and probing the innermost nature of the social order. Marx's detailed investigation into the thought of Hegel and the classical economists was designed to show how this is so.

Like all rationalist philosophers Marx establishes, or rather assumes, a fundamental harmony between truth and freedom. For him the interest in freedom is a fundamental precondition of truth. Only the theorist interested in human freedom is capable of attaining the truth, whereas one interested in or indifferent to class domination is doomed to remaining an ideologist. Conversely, truth is the necessary precondition of freedom. Only the truth liberates man from the slavery to nature and to other men. Further, for Marx the love of truth and of freedom are inseparable. A social theorist who loves freedom is necessarily led to pursue the truth; and one interested in pursuing the truth is led to criticise the established pattern of domination and pursue human freedom. As we saw, it was one of the important implications of Marx's analysis of the classical economists that the more honest seekers after the truth among them increasingly rose above their bourgeois biases and came to appreciate the historical and contradictory nature of capitalism.

III

Truth has often been taken to be immutable, unalterable by human praxis and existing independently of what men think and do. While accepting this view at one level, Marx questions it at another.

As we shall see, Marx takes the view that truth consists in conformity to reality. He argues that, in human affairs, reality is created and altered by human praxis. It consists of social relations, which are not given by nature but created by men. This means that, as men alter the social reality, they *make* true what was once false, and vice versa. At one point in time a theory might be true, that is conform to social reality. At another point in time when the human praxis has changed the social reality, the statement or the theory in question becomes false. It is not only *falsified* by reality, as happens when a hypothesis is refuted or *proved false* by a fact; rather it has been *made false* by men. In the same way, by changing social reality men *make true* a theory that once was false. In short, in human affairs men can *create* truth and falsehood.[8]

Marx's point would become clearer if we took an example. It was widely believed in the eighteenth and nineteenth centuries that the working classes were inherently or naturally inferior to their masters. Acting on that belief, their masters treated them as such, and confined them to menial jobs. For their part the working classes internalised the image others had created of them, aimed low, rarely stretched themselves and over the years became inferior. As a result of constant propaganda, the subtle indoctrination and the institutionalised inequalities, what was once no more than a prejudice later *became* a truth, a fact. Thanks to the decades of working-class struggles, the changes in the social climate, and the expansion of the educational and other opportunities, the picture is beginning to alter. And it is not beyond the bounds of imagination that the truth of today might become a total falsehood tomorrow.

This happens in all areas of life. Men were once in superstitious awe of nature; they are no longer so today. They were once not greedy; they are so today. And so on. The facts about men are created and destroyed by the human praxis. The social and political theories are not only *proved* but *made* true or false. Indeed men may act on a completely false theory, change the social reality appropriately, and make the theory true. In such cases the theory creates its own truth, or rather makes itself true by bringing the world into harmony with itself. A theory does not helplessly attend upon reality and passively await its judgement; it enters and shapes the world, and participates in the determination of its own truth and falsity.

While Marx rightly highlights the mutability of social facts and the complex relationship between truth and human praxis, he nowhere makes clear how far he intended to push the view and what lessons he wished to draw from it. This has led some of his commentators to put an untenable volitionalist gloss on his views. According to them, for Marx truth is *entirely* a product of the human will, men create truth as they please, human praxis is the *criterion* of truth, whatever they may mean, and so on. There is no evidence to support such an interpretation.[9]

In saying that men can and do alter social reality, Marx does not seem to wish to challenge the traditional conception of the nature and criteria of truth. He only wishes to highlight what, in his view, has not been sufficiently appreciated, namely that the facts about man and society and, in some cases, about nature are historically mutable, that even the fundamental human capacities, needs and men's relations with nature undergo drastic changes in different historical epochs, and that men are capable of reshaping their social relations and creating new social truths. However, none of these entails a radical revision of the traditional view that truth is objective and independent of human will.

Men were once in awe of nature. They are not so today. This does not alter the fact that they were *once* in awe of nature. *This* truth is immutable. Feudalism was once a social reality. Thanks to human praxis, it is no longer so today. This does not in any way alter the fact that it was a determinate structure of social relations, and that the theories about it are true or false according to whether or not they give a faithful account to it. Again, capitalism is today a social reality. And although it may one day be replaced, this does not alter the fact that it is a definite mode of production with its own nature and dynamics, of which one may give an objectively true or false account. Praxis creates new reality, but can never be the criterion of truth. Only the reality is the criterion of truth. For Marx, further, there are limits to what human praxis or will can achieve. It cannot alter man's physical constitution, nor such fundamental facts as human mortality. Even a social order, although ontologically constituted of human relations, has its own distinct and autonomous 'nature'. For Marx this is especially so in a class-divided society, in particular capitalism where, thanks to the lack of collective human control, the social relations become independent and are governed by their own laws. As such human praxis can alter a social order only by comprehending and acting in harmony with its inherent tendencies.

IV

Following Aristotle many philosophers have drawn a fairly rigid distinction between truth and falsehood. For them a statement or a theory is either true or false, and cannot be both or neither. Hegel challenged this view, and Marx follows him. To avoid misunderstanding, it needs to be said that Marx is primarily interested in the truth or falsity of theories and not individual statements.

Hegel denied the sharp distinction between truth and falsity, and rejected the view that a theory or a form of consciousness must be either true or false. Since we cannot here outline his complex theory, we shall take an example to illustrate his basic point. Hegel argued that, like philosophy, religion aims to comprehend the true nature of reality. However, given its basic assumptions and structural limitations, it is unable adequately to represent the rational nature of the *Geist*. Unlike philosophy, which is a rational form of consciousness and can fully comprehend and express the *Geist*'s rational nature, religion can only comprehend and articulate it in symbolic terms. As such it is an 'inadequate' and 'imperfect' representation of the *Geist*. Its account of reality cannot be considered true, but nor is it false. In Hegel's view it would be wrong to say that philosophy gives a true, and religion a false knowledge of the Absolute, or that the Absolute is a true notion and God a false one. He thought it more accurate to say that religion is an 'approximation' to or an 'inadequate' or 'imperfect' representation of the ultimate reality.

Marx's view is not dissimilar. As we saw earlier, Hegel's philosophy and classical political economy are, for him, neither wholly true nor wholly false. They do, no doubt, contain some ideas which are wholly true or false. However, taken in their entirety, they do not fall into either category. In Marx's view this is generally the case with all social and political theories. He seems to think that this is so for four reasons.

First, a theory might be true, but not the manner in which it is expressed. This is what Marx thought of Hegel. For him Hegel's basic thesis, that man creates himself by means of labour, shapes his historical destiny himself, and develops his capacities by means of the dialectically superseded acts of self-externalisation, was true. However, he presented it as the mystical story of the *Geist*, and this was false. Taken at its face value Hegel's account of human history is mystical and fallacious. Its inner core, however, is perceptive and accurate.

Second, for Marx a theory is a highly complex body of thought. It may contain true and profound insights which, however, its structural assumptions might not allow it fully to articulate and develop. Further, it might distort its insights, interpret them wrongly, put them to questionable theoretical uses or combine them with false ideas. In short a theory is made up of truths, half-truths, quasi-truths, distorted truths, and so on, which are all integrally connected and cannot always be isolated and individually judged. What is more, a theory has an immanent dimension. It points beyond itself, says far more than it intends to, and sometimes contains a criticism and even a refutation of its basic premises. For these and other reasons the theory as a whole cannot be neatly categorised as true or false. As we saw, this is what Marx thought of both classical political economy and Hegel's philosophy. And hence he neither accepted nor rejected them *in toto*, but subjected them to a critique designed to distil their insights and preserve their immanent truth.

Third, a theory might offer a true account of the surface of society but not of its inner structure, and be true at one level and false at another. For Marx this was the case with the liberal social and political theory. It takes the individual as its ultimate unit. While this is a true account of the ideologically constituted social world under capitalism, where only the individuals are generally recognised as the subjects of rights and obligations, it ignores the deeper reality of the classes and their mediation of interpersonal relations.

Fourth, as we saw, social reality is amenable to human praxis, and subject to historical change. A theory which gives a true account of its subject matter at one time or in one context might give a false account of it at another time or in another context. For example, as we saw, a theory which says that a man's property is a product of his labour is true of a society in which all men engage in labour, but false when applied to the advanced capitalist society in which those owning the means of production do not themselves labour, and derive their property from *others'* labour. The theory is true at the earlier, but false at the later stage of capitalism; hence it cannot be judged true or false in the abstract. Within a specific context, it is true; extended outside, it is false.[10] As we saw, this is one of the basic theses of Marx's theory of ideology.

For Marx, then, social and political theories are structurally too complex to be judged true or false, and their truth is context-dependent. He did not, however, spell out the implications of his analysis for his theory of truth. Engels did, and did so in a work written during Marx's lifetime. He argued that the categories of truth and falsehood were too crude to be useful in any area other than mathematics. He argued, further, that the traditional view of truth was too puristic to do full justice to the nature of thought or to constitute a realisable ideal. He repeatedly criticised the concept of 'pure' truth, and contended that truth and error were inseparably connected. He put these points well in the following paragraph which deserves to be quoted at length.[11]

> Truth and error, like all concepts which are expressed in polar oppo-
> sites, have absolute validity only in an extremely limited field . . .
> As soon as we apply the antithesis between truth and error outside
> of that narrow field which has been referred to above, it becomes
> relative and therefore unserviceable for exact scientific modes of
> expression . . . Let us take as an example the well-known Boyle's
> law, by which, if the temperature remains constant, the volume of
> gases varies inversely with the pressure to which they are subjected.
> Regnault found that this law did not hold good in certain cases. Had
> he been a philosopher of reality he would have had to say: Boyle's
> law is mutable, and is therefore not a pure truth, therefore it is not
> a truth at all, therefore it is an error . . . But Regnault, being a man
> of science, did not indulge in such childishness, but continued his
> investigations and discovered that Boyle's law is in general only
> approximately correct, and in particular loses its validity in the case
> of gases which can be liquefied by pressure, as soon as the pressure
> approaches the point at which liquefaction begins. Boyle's law
> therefore was proved to be correct only within definite limits.
> But is it absolutely and finally true even within those limits? No
> physicist would assert that this was so. He would say that it holds
> good within certain limits of pressure and temperature and for
> certain gases; and even within these more restricted limits he would
> not exclude the possibility of a still narrower limitation or altered
> formulation as the result of future investigations. This is how things
> stand with final and ultimate truths in physics for example. Really
> scientific works therefore as a rule avoid such dogmatic and moral
> expressions as error and truth.

Engels interspersed his essentially Hegelian account of truth with
such mechanistic metaphors as 'grain' or 'elements' of truth and the
'sandhill' of error, of which Marx would have disapproved. However,
his general view, which is supported by Marx's own passing remarks,
is a fairly faithful account of the latter's thought.

To avoid the misunderstanding to which some of Marx's commentators are prone, Marx's view does not imply that he rejected the concept
of truth altogether. To say that a theory applies to one area and not
another, or that it applies to a particular object at one time but not
at another, or that it is true under certain conditions but not others
is not relativism. The theory in question is not said to be true *for* some

and not others, but rather true with respect to a particular subject matter or under specific conditions. Its truth is objective, open for all to check by means of the commonly agreed procedures and criteria, and claims the allegiance of all. Again, in saying that the social theories are too complex to be called true and false *sans phrase*, Marx is not rejecting the concept of objective truth. He is only arguing that a theory has various levels and dimensions and sometimes points beyond itself, and that therefore judging it is an extremely complex activity requiring subtler conceptual tools than simple truth and falsity.

V

Sometimes the philosophers have introduced the notion of what Engels calls 'final truth', and maintained that it is possible to know or understand one's subject matter in a manner that is definitive, incorrigible and beyond further revision.[12] For Marx the traditional preoccupation with the absolute truth and Hegel's claim to offer absolute knowledge are examples of this. Marx rejects the concept of 'final' or 'absolute' truth, especially in matters relating to man and society, on several grounds.

First, we can attain full knowledge of a social order only after it has ceased to exist. A social theorist aims to discover the inner nature and absolute limits of a social structure or mode of production, and these cannot be known so long as it is in existence. As Engels puts it, we know societies 'only . . . when [they] are already out of date and are nearing extinction'. We cannot, therefore, hope to attain the full truth about our own society or historical epoch. Further, the inner nature of a social order becomes fully transparent only when the crucial operative factors become separate and clear. As Marx puts it, the importance of the economy could not be grasped until it came into its own under capitalism. This means that a social theorist in the pre-bourgeois societies could not have known the full truth about his society, and would have been mistaken to think that he had. It also means that we have ourselves no means of knowing what new factors the future might highlight, and what new explanatory insights it might offer.

Second, even when a social order is long dead, new information and interpretations can never be ruled out. As Marx observed, the job of writing *Capital* is 'making very slow progress because problems . . . constantly exhibit new aspects and call forth new doubts'.[13] The knowledge of society and indeed of anything else is subject to constant revision, increases over time and can never be said to be final. As Engels observes, even in the mathematical and natural sciences, no truths 'are so securely based that any doubt of them seems . . . to amount to insanity'. The 'crop' of final truths is 'extremely rare' and 'small'. In the historical sciences 'our knowledge is even more backward'. Engels goes on, the history of human thought'[14]

> should make us extremely distrustful of our present knowledge, inasmuch as in all probability we are but little beyond the beginning of human history, and the generations which will put *us* right are likely to be far more numerous than those whose knowledge we − often enough with a considerable degree of contempt − are in a position to correct . . . all previous experience shows that without exception such knowledge always contains much more that is capable of being improved upon than that which cannot be improved upon or is correct.

Third, all human knowledge is subject to the socially imposed limitations. As Marx says, there is a 'certain judicial blindness' in all of us so that we sometimes do not notice the obvious. He goes on:[15]

> Human history fares like palaeontology. Even the best minds *absolutely* fail to see − *on principle*, owing to a certain judicial blindness − things which lie in front of their noses. Later, when the moment has arrived, one is surprised to find traces everywhere of what one has failed to see . . . *we all* labour under this judicial blindness.

Besides, all men are subject to the assumptions and forms of thought characteristic of their age. Thanks to 'the peculiar condition of the society in which he lived', even a 'genius' like Aristotle could not form the concept of abstract labour and explain how the qualitatively different objects could be rendered commensurable and exchanged.[16] Further, unless one is extremely careful and sometimes not even then, the social assumptions of one's class continue to shape one's thought and are only noticed by others later. As Engels says, truth is known 'only step by step' and requires the co-operation of the 'endless succession of generations of mankind'.[17]

Since Marx rightly rejects 'final' truths, he cannot consistently claim that his own thought represents the last word on history or capitalism.

He cannot deny that his ideas are limited by the horizon of his age. Nor can he deny that even as the bourgeois society highlighted the importance of the economy, the future society may highlight some other factor and go beyond him. Nor, finally, can he say that he had discovered the essence of capitalism when it was very much alive in his time, although he conveniently assumed that it was nearing extinction. Marx's claim to have discovered the innermost essence of capitalism or of history is disallowed by his own theory of truth, and he was wrong to make it. He did no doubt, penetrate into their nature much deeper than many of his predecessors. However, he was nowhere near offering the full and final truth about them.

VI

We outlined above Marx's major criticisms of the traditional views on the nature of truth. As we observed, the criticisms make several interesting points which need to be incorporated in our discussion of the subject. None of them, however, entails a rejection of the concept of objective truth, nor its demotion from the pride of place it has enjoyed in the history of philosophy. Although Marx locates the pursuit of truth within the context of human praxis, he does not make praxis the criterion of truth, nor does he deny that truth is the *telos* of the pursuit of knowledge and supreme in the field of theoretical thought. Again, the human praxis alters social reality; and makes false what was once true, and vice versa. However, this does not in any way affect the objectivity of truth. Finally, as we saw, neither Marx's Hegelian concept of the 'partial' truth, nor his rejection of the so-called 'final' truth implies rejection of the concept of objective truth. In short for Marx truth remains the highest theoretical ideal.

For Marx, then, a scientific theory must be judged by its ability to give a true account of its subject matter. His discussion of the criteria of truth is sketchy and inchoate. It is relatively easier to see where, for him, the truth of a theory does *not* lie than where it does.

Marx rejects the view that a theory is true if in accord with common sense. As we saw, a theory aims to elucidate the inner structure of reality, whereas common sense catches only the 'delusive appearance of things'. By definition the conformity to common sense cannot be the criterion of scientific truth.

Marx also implicitly rejects the coherence theory of truth. One can distinguish two versions of the coherence theory: the positivist and the critical. Marx rejects the former, and is sympathetic to the latter. The positivist version of the coherence theory maintains that a theory is true if in harmony with the generally accepted body of theoretical knowledge on the subject. In Marx's view the generally accepted theories may be wrong or superficial. Indeed he felt that, in the social sciences, the general acceptance of a theory is often the sign that it rests on assumptions conducive to the continuance of the established social order, and is ideological in nature. For Marx the ideas conducive to the interests of the ruling class tend to become the ruling ideas in society. The coherence theory of truth therefore basically represents the demand that new theories should continue to operate within the framework of the established structure of thought, and has a built-in ideological bias. While it allows revision and reform it disallows radically new departures, and is essentially conservative. Marx also took the view that the scientific knowledge grows dialectically, at first by gradual and incremental reforms, and then, when the changes have reached a certain point, by a revolutionary conceptual overhaul. Adam Smith and Ricardo almost totally revolutionised the discipline of economics, and Marx aimed to do the same. The coherence theory of truth would have made such radical advances impossible. We shall return to the critical version of the coherence theory later.

Although Marx never discussed the pragmatist theory of truth, he said enough to indicate that he would be unsympathetic to it. In his view a theory is not true because it works; rather it works because it is true. In an alienated society religion works, in the sense that it consoles the wretched and sustains the social order. However, this does not detract from the fact that, for Marx, God is a fantasy, and the happiness offered by religion 'illusory'. Similarly the radically new ideas might not work if tried out under inhospitable conditions; however, this does not mean that they are therefore false. Further, the pragmatist theory of truth determines the workability of a theory within the framework of the established social order, whose own workability it either never questions, or defines in extremely narrow terms. It has therefore a built-in ideological bias.[18]

Contrary to the widespread belief among some of his critics, Marx also rejects the view that a theory is true if it serves the interests of a progressive class or promotes human well-being. As we saw, he considers it 'mean' and 'vulgar' to 'accommodate it [science] to a point of view which is not derived from science itself', but 'borrowed from extrinsic interests'. Further, as we saw, human well-being is, for Marx, the *telos*, but not the criterion of truth. It indicates what kinds of truth deserve to be pursued, not what constitutes truth. Like most rationalist philosophers, Marx assumes that truth is conducive to human well-being, but he nowhere says that whatever promotes human well-being is true. Again, for Marx, neither the interest of the progressive class nor human well-being can be the criterion of truth, since these are themselves a matter of theoretical determination. It is one of the purposes of Marx's analysis of capitalism to determine which class is progressive, and the satisfaction of which needs constitutes human well-being.

Basically Marx seems to subscribe to a modified version of the correspondence theory of truth. For him a theory aims to reproduce 'as in a mirror' the inner structure of its subject matter. It is true if its conceptual structure 'reproduces' the inner nature of its subject matter. The inner nature is not, however, a matter of empirical observation, and hence the question arises as to how we can ascertain whether or not a theory faithfully reproduces it. Marx seems to resolve the difficulty in the following way.

A theorist uses his knowledge of an entity's inner structure to explain why it behaves in a particular way and displays specific forms. If he has correctly comprehended its inner structure, he should be able to offer a 'correct' explanation of its behaviour. This means that, if his explanation is correct, we are entitled to conclude that his theory corresponds to the inner structure of the entity in question. In other words, although the correspondence cannot be directly verified, it can be verified indirectly.

This raises the question as to what counts as a correct explanation. Although Marx is not entirely clear, he seems to think that an explanation is correct if it shows that the behaviour of the entity in question is not a chance occurrence, but a necessary consequence of its inner constitution. For Marx a scientific theory explains the behaviour of an entity in terms of its inherent tendencies or, what he also calls laws, and explains these, in turn, in terms of its inner nature or constitution. For Marx a scientific explanation has the following logical form.

(1)　An entity A is constituted in a specific way or has a specific inner structure;

(2)　as such it has tendencies O, P and Q, and must behave in a manner M;

(3)　the tendencies become manifest under conditions X, Y and Z;

(4)　the conditions were present at time T;

(5)　hence A behaved in the manner M at time T.

Although Marx's usage is not entirely consistent, he thinks that (1) is a theoretical statement, and (2) a statement of tendencies or laws; (2) is grounded in (1), and is 'proved' or 'demonstrated' by showing that it follows from it 'with logical necessity'. Thus Marx said that he had offered a 'proof' of the law of the declining rate of profit when he showed that it followed with logical necessity 'from the nature of the capitalist mode of production'.[19] He said that, as against Ricardo, he intended to 'prove theoretically' the possibility of absolute rent. The concept of proof is central to Marx's theory of science, and is a recurrent theme in his criticisms of other writers. For him it is not enough to explain the behaviour of an entity in terms of general laws. The laws must themselves be demonstrated, and shown to be inherent in its inner nature. The primary task of a scientific theory is not so much to establish general laws as to articulate the inner nature or constitution of its subject matter.[20]

On the basis of his theoretical knowledge of the inner nature of an entity, a scientist specifies how, left to itself, it *must* behave, as well as what kinds of factor can frustrate the realisation of its tendencies, in what ways, and within what limits.[21] For Marx the scientific prediction is of the following form: under conditions X, Y and Z, an entity A must behave in a manner M, unless the factors D, E or F intervene, and then it must behave in a manner C.

Marx does not expect a scientific theory to provide a list of all possible countervailing influences. A new factor may arise which the scientist may not have foreseen. This does not by itself discredit his theory, provided that he is able to account for its ability to influence the behaviour of the entity concerned within the framework of his analysis of the latter's inner nature. If the scientist is unable to do so, his explanation must be judged inadequate. For example, according to Marx the capitalist society must eventually collapse because of its internal contradictions. He specifies a set of countervailing tendencies such as the increase in the intensity of exploitation, the lowering of wages below the value of labour power, relative overpopulation and foreign trade, but concludes that these must eventually reach their limits, leaving capitalism no means of escape. Since Marx's death, a new countervailing tendency has appeared of which he took little account. The state has increasingly undertaken welfare functions and prevented the wage labourer from falling below the minimum level of subsistence. In so doing it has stabilised the capitalist system and prevented its predicted extinction. If Marx were able to explain the welfare state within the framework of his analysis of the inner nature of the capitalist mode of production, his failure to foresee it would in no way impugn his theory. On the contrary, it would increase its theoretical appeal. If, on the other hand, he were unable to account for it, we would have to say that his theory of capitalism does not accurately 'reproduce' its inner structure.

For Marx, then, a scientist is concerned to elucidate the inner structure of his subject matter and, in its light, to articulate its inherent 'tendencies' and the manner in which, left to itself, it must behave. The tendencies refer to a pattern of behaviour. By their very nature they express themselves over a period of time, and are manifested not in an isolated instance but a class of instances. As such a single counter-example cannot constitute the refutation of a theory. As Marx puts it, a theory cannot be 'immediately' verified or falsified for it is not 'directly identical' with the facts.[22] It asserts how an entity has a *tendency* to behave, not how it *will* behave. It is possible for a tendency to be frustrated by the unexpected but subsequently accountable factors.

Marx, however, does not wish to say, as Lukács and others have taken him to say, that the 'immediate reality' or singular facts do not matter. For Lukács only the 'history' can deliver judgement on Marx's theory of capitalism, and the 'immediate reality', however much it may contradict it, does not in any way impugn its truth. This is a mistaken interpretation of Marx. For Marx the tendencies are not transcendental entities, but immanent in the behaviour of the entity in question. Therefore, although a scientist does not regard every fact as incorrigible and absolute in authority as the positivists maintain, he cannot entirely ignore them either. He cannot be frightened away by inconvenient facts, but nor can he be contemptuous of them. He must pay scrupulous attention to them and explain in each case why the tendency failed to realise itself. Discussing Adam Smith's and Ricardo's analyses of the law of value, Marx makes some pertinent remarks. He argues that Smith confers absolute authority on individual facts and loses his confidence in a law when it is contradicted by some of them. By contrast, Ricardo ignores the inconvenient facts altogether. Marx criticises *both* attitudes.[23]

> It is his [Smith's] theoretical strength that he feels and stresses this contradiction, just as it is his theoretical weakness that the contradiction shakes his confidence in the general law. Even for simple commodity exchange . . . Ricardo is ahead of Adam Smith in that these apparent contradictions — in their result real contradictions —

do not confuse him. But he is behind Adam Smith in that he does not even suspect that this presents a problem, and therefore the *specific* development which the law of value undergoes with the formation of capital does not for a moment puzzle him or even attract his attention.

VII

Although Marx does not himself put it this way, he seems to think that a theory gains in plausibility if it can be shown to represent the immanent truth of other theories. Hegel had already sketched the outlines and stressed the importance of the immanentist theory of truth. After suitable modifications, Marx seems to have adopted it.

For Hegel thinking is an activity by which reason interprets, appropriates and comes to terms with the world. A thought is the product of reason; more accurately, it is the way reason exists for itself. As such, however confused it might be, every thought embodies reason. What is true of the ordinary man's thoughts is even more true of the philosopher's. Being products of highly rational minds, philosophical systems represent the highest manifestations of reason. However much it may be limited in its vision, exaggerate its insights or confuse a partial truth for the whole, a philosophical system represents reason's attempt to understand and appropriate the world, and cannot be *wholly* false or mistaken.

On the basis of this view of reason, Hegel argues that philosophy is a single and continuous inquiry. As he says, there are no philosophies, there is only philosophy. Each philosopher articulates a mode of understanding the world upon which the others build. Each corrects the limitations of his predecessors and preserves their partial truths. In this way Reason develops an increasingly comprehensive and coherent view of the world. Since philosophy is a continuous inquiry, it necessarily involves a historical critique. A philosopher examines the thoughts of his predecessors, shows why they are inadequate, elucidates their insights, and demonstrates how his own system of thought both consolidates and goes beyond them.

Although Hegel does not put it this way, he seems to think that such a historical critique is a form of philosophical legitimisation. In showing that his philosophy embodies and enriches their insights and represents their truth, and indeed that they themselves point towards it, the philosopher turns his rivals into his allies and uses them as the independent sources of confirmation of his own philosophy. This may perhaps explain why Hegel rarely dismisses his predecessors, and shows great intellectual generosity towards them. Since his strategy consists in chartering his rivals into his service, the greater the truth he can demonstrate in their systems, the more he confirms his own, and the more does his thought appear as the grand summation of all the truth hitherto known to man.

For convenience I shall call Hegel's immanentist theory of truth the principle of critical coherence.[24] It is a principle of *coherence* because it requires that a theory must cohere with the other theories of the subject; and it is a principle of *critical* coherence because it requires that a theory must not uncritically conform to others, but criticise them, expose their limitations, extract and take over their rational insights and show that it represents their immanent truth.

Marx rejected the positivist version of the coherence theory discussed earlier, but seems to have subscribed to what we have called the principle of critical coherence.[25] Like Hegel, he devoted considerable attention to the earlier economists, both major and minor, and subjected their ideas to a careful critique. Like Hegel and unlike the positivist historians of ideas, he did not approach his predecessors with the dogmatic conviction that he had discovered the truth and that they were all muddle-headed fools. Rather, he examined their thoughts in order better to understand the nature of the capitalist mode of production. Further, like Hegel, when he examined his predecessors he did not debunk or dismiss but criticised them, exposed their limitations, abstracted and highlighted their insights, and showed how they sometimes almost got close to the truth but could not fully articulate it.

Marx's historical critique served several important theoretical purposes. It enabled him to show first, that the available theories of capitalism were inadequate, and a new one was needed; second, that his own theory was free from the defects he had pointed out in others; and third, that his theory was an organic continuation of its rivals, corrected and completed them, and incorporated their immanent truth. In this way, like Hegel, Marx used the rival theories as independent corroborations of his own, and hoped to demonstrate that his theory was superior to theirs. As we saw, he claimed that his theory of history represented the immanent truth of Hegel's, and that his theory of capitalism represented and built upon the immanent truth of classical political economy. Indeed he seems to have thought that only a theory which offers a critique of the previous theories and shows why a 'break' with them is necessary can ever be fully satisfactory.[26]

VIII

In Marx's view a theory should not only be true, but also give 'theoretical satisfaction'. A theory is an intellectual 'product'; and as of any other product, we are entitled to demand that it should possess certain qualities. At one place Marx lists nearly all the qualities he expects in a satisfactory theory. He observes that the first part of Ricardo's *Principles of Political Economy and Taxation* gives 'theoretical satisfaction . . . because of [its] originality, unity of basic conception, simplicity, concentration, depth, novelty and comprehensive conciseness'.[27] Evidently Marx attached considerable importance to these. A reader of the three volumes of the *Theories of Surplus Value* is struck by the fact that many of Marx's criticisms of the classical economists are directed not at their inconsistencies or their inability to explain specific economic phenomena, but their lack of conceptual tidiness, clumsy presentations, the absence of analytical rigour and their messy theoretical structures.

Although Marx does not analyse and relate the overlapping qualities he expects in a theory, his comments on various writers give a fairly clear indication of what he meant by them. Originality or novelty is a straightforward concept. A theory which does not develop a new concept, insight, or a 'striking train of reasoning' makes no contribution to knowledge, and is intellectually redundant. Marx judges a thinker's originality on the basis of the range and penetration of his theoretical insights. A theorist who offers a totally new way of defining and understanding his subject matter is a 'genius', a 'mighty thinker'. Marx considered Hegel, Adam Smith and Ricardo belonged to this category. At a lower level a thinker might develop several new concepts and establish inner connections among a wider range of phenomena than before. Marx placed Richard Jones, McCulloch and a few others in this category. At yet a lower level a theorist might contribute no more than a new concept, or find a word which a concept may have hitherto lacked, or distinguish the phenomena hitherto confused. Marx placed James Steuart and a number of other minor economists in this category.

The second requirement of a theory is the unity of its basic conception. By this Marx seems to mean that a theorist should view his subject matter from a single and coherent point of view, and not keep 'passing from one kind of explanation to another' as Adam Smith had done.[28] For Marx, J.S. Mill's thought was 'eclectic' and lacked a unity of conception. By simplicity Marx seems to mean that a theory should have a tidy and easily intelligible logical structure. In his view this is achieved if it develops a few clearly defined and internally related basic concepts, and deduces the rest from them. It is difficult to guess what he means by concentration. Presumably he has in mind an economical development of thought unencumbered by irrelevant digressions. In his view a theory which lacks concentrated analysis, goes 'off into details', and lacks focus and clarity of exposition is 'boring and difficult to concentrate on'.

For Marx depth, or what he also calls 'critical' or 'dialectical' depth, is one of the most important requirements in a theory, and the hallmark of a genuinely theoretical level of analysis.[29] In Marx's view the theoretical depth can be ranged on a spectrum. At one end, a theory does not go beyond the ordinary modes of thought, is vulgar and not a theory in the true sense of the term. At the other end, it penetrates the innermost structure of its subject matter, and articulates it in terms of the most basic categories imaginable. For Marx the deeper a theory's penetration into its subject matter, the greater is its explanatory power. A theory which penetrates deeper than another is able *both* to reduce a wider range of phenomena to a common inner structure, and establish more rigorous connections among them. Marx considered it to be the great merit of the Physiocrats and, especially, Quesnay to have reduced such diverse phenomena as the wages, rent and profit to the surplus value produced in agriculture. He thought that Ricardo reduced an even wider range of phenomena to a common inner structure. Marx believed that he himself penetrated yet deeper, and explained the entire structure of the capitalist economy in terms of the inner dialectic of commodity.

By the last quality, namely comprehensive concisenesss, Marx seems to mean that a theory should offer 'a consistent and comprehensive theoretical view of the abstract general foundations' of its subject matter.[30] In his view a theory which lacks such a comprehensive view has a messy and ill-coordinated conceptual framework. The phenomena it leaves out cannot be left unexplained, especially when they affect the behaviour of those explained, and consequently it is forced to offer *ad hoc* explanations of them. Since these explanations are not integrated into its general explanatory framework, the latter lacks coherence. In Marx's view this was the case with Adam Smith whose narrow initial framework prevented him from explaining 'the influence of the fluctuations of wages, profit, etc., on the price of commodities'.[31] In his study of prices Smith did not take full account of all the relevant factors, and kept introducing them as they came to his attention. As a result, his economic theory remained a collection of unrelated explanatory patterns.

IX

For Marx, then, a scientific theory should be judged by three criteria: its explanatory power or truth, the principle of critical coherence, and its logical structure. A theory that meets all three is the most satisfactory, and deserves acceptance. Marx seems to think that the first two criteria coincide. A true theory, by definition, represents the partial truths of the other theories on the subject. For Marx the importance of the second criterion seems to be twofold: first, it offers an independent and additional confirmation of a theory and, second, it shows that a theory is not only satisfactory but also *more* satisfactory than the others. The third criterion is of a different order. It judges the logical *structure* of a theory and has no bearing on its truth. However, it is striking that all those writers such as Hegel and Ricardo who, in Marx's view, almost got to the heart of their subject matter also produced logically elegant theories.[32] They offered *both* truth, albeit of a somewhat limited and distorted nature, and theoretical satisfaction. For Marx the discovery of truth requires a correct method of investigation, and the latter generally leads to a well-structured and well-presented theory. As he says, the 'faulty architectonics' of a theory is 'not accidental, rather it is the result of . . . and . . . expresses the scientific deficiencies of the method of investigation itself'.[33] This seems to suggest that, for Marx, a true theory is, as it were, compelled by the very force of its 'deep insight' to develop an elegant conceptual structure. One wonders if, like Plato, Marx believed in the harmony between truth and beauty. If he did, his thought would seem to endorse the familiar rationalist belief in the harmony of truth, goodness (which Marx also calls freedom) and beauty.

9 SOME REFLECTIONS

In the previous chapters we outlined the logical structure and epistemological basis of Marx's theory of ideology. It would be useful briefly to highlight its important insights and limitations.

I

Marx's theory of ideology can perhaps be best understood as a product of the marriage between the Western philosophical tradition and his socially orientated epistemology. As we saw, he accepts several basic doctrines of the Western philosophical tradition. He agrees that man is capable of knowing the world, that knowledge liberates man from the natural and social constraints, that truth is the *telos* of knowledge, and that the truth can only be attained from a point of view which is fully self-conscious, self-critical, adequate to its subject matter and does not rest on unexamined assumptions. He agrees also that, being based on unexamined assumptions, every narrow point of view offers a biased and distorted knowledge of its subject matter, and has an inherent tendency to set itself up as an absolute. Its limits can only be determined, and its absolutist claims deflated from a wider standpoint capable of locating and examining it in a larger context.

Marx applies these and other philosophical doctrines to the study of society, his primary area of interest. He argues that the truth about society can only be attained by studying it as a whole, as a totality, and doing so not from a narrow point of view, but from the standpoint of the whole. A narrow social point of view is structurally limited by its conditions of existence and characteristic assumptions. As such it necessarily perceives the social world in a partial manner. Unaware of its limitations and unwilling for reasons of self-interest to abandon them, it claims universal or 'absolute' validity for its forms of experience and thought, and offers a partisan and distorted understanding of the social whole. Only a fully self-conscious and self-critical study of the social whole can identify the limits and deflate the claims of the narrow social points of view. Needless to say, Marx's approach to the study of society, and his basic categories — such as point of view, presupposition, assumption, the standpoint of the whole, the partial point of view, objectivity, distortion and critique — are all derived from the Western philosophical tradition. By applying them to the area to which they had rarely before been applied, he enriches and affirms his allegiance to it.

While subscribing to some of the basic doctrines of the Western philosophical tradition, Marx also challenges it in several crucial respects. He rightly rejects its dualist view of man, and insists upon the inherently social and historical nature of the knowing subject. He argues that men are not Gods inhabiting mortal bodies, but human in their innermost being. They are socially and historically constituted, and their faculties and modes of thought are socially shaped. The human reason is not a transcendental faculty immune to the influences of time and space, but socially structured and closely intertwined with passions, sentiments and interests. The pursuit of knowledge is not a cerebral or even mental, but a human activity in which the total human being is engaged. It is integrally related to and profoundly influenced by the pre- and para-theoretical world of practice. The individual who theorises is also a member of a specific society. He grows up within it, imbibes its values, traditions and ways of understanding man and society. By the time he learns to theorise, he is already shaped by his society. While he is engaged in the theoretical pursuits, he does not cease being involved in the non-theoretical pursuits. The theorising self cannot be abstracted from the rest of his personality, and reflects its characteristic tensions, anxieties, preferences and prejudices. In short a social theorist brings to his study a body of socially derived assumptions and forms of thought which mediates his approach to and shapes the selection, organisation and interpretation of his subject matter. Marx was right to bring down human reason to the earth and locate it firmly and securely in the social world. By insisting upon the inherently social and historical nature of the knowing subject, he stressed the social character of the pursuit of knowledge and paved the way for a socially orientated epistemology. Not the sociology of knowledge, which is Mannheim's brain-child, but the socially grounded epistemology, a very different concept, is Marx's principal concern and contribution.[1]

In challenging the dualist view of man, Marx also challenged the various interconnected forms of dualism generated or inspired by it. He questioned the neat disjunction between the pursuits of truth and human well-being, theory and practice, reason and will, knowledge and action, etc., and suggested stimulating ways of relating them without destroying their autonomy. As he said on many occasions, he was concerned to establish the 'mediated unity' of the interdependent extremes, and not their immediate identity. His much understood unity of theory and practice brings out the point well. It does not imply that theory is itself a form of practice, or that practice is merely an execution of a theory, or that a theory is to be judged by practice, but something very different.

Marx argues that theory and practice appear to be, and indeed are, totally distinct as long as theory is understood in the untenable contemplationist or spectatorial sense, and practice in the equally untenable atomic and utilitarian sense. When properly analysed they turn out to be interdependent notions partaking of a common nature and entailing each other. This is precisely what he sets out to do. As we saw, he analyses the nature of the theoretical thought, and argues that it is informed by a practical impulse. A social theory not only explains, but also interrogates and criticises. Indeed it is only when it is rigorously critical that it can fully understand the innermost nature of its subject matter. A social theory is therefore necessarily a *critique*, a theoretical form of active engagement with the world. Marx also re-examines the nature of social and political action. He argues that an action occurs within a specific context, which is not insulated from, but an integral part of, and shaped and limited by the social whole. The social whole is not a contingent collection of institutions and practices; it has a determinate character, is structured in a certain manner and characterised by specific tendencies. As such, an action, especially a political action which aims to influence the social whole, requires *both* a detailed knowledge of the specific context, and a general understanding of the structure and tendencies of the social whole. In other words a political action necessarily requires both the detailed practical and the general theoretical knowledge. A political actor may not be aware of the way his action presupposes and involves the general knowledge of his society. However, if his action were to be carefully scrutinised, a whole body of general ideas about his society would seem to lurk in the background. Since this is so, Marx argues that a political action is more effective if the general knowledge of the social whole were not intuitively derived, but based on a careful theoretical investigation. He calls such a theoretically informed action praxis. When the theory is understood as a critique, and the action as a praxis, they are no longer qualitatively different. A critique is a theory informed by and half-way towards praxis; and a praxis is an action informed by and half-way towards a critique. When so defined, they turn out to be complementary. Each contains an immanent impulse to move towards and 'calls for' the other. Their unity is now not only possible but also necessary.

Marx, then, borrowed some of the basic epistemological doctrines of the Western philosophical tradition, and integrated them with his socially grounded epistemology. The result was his theory of ideology. From the philosophical tradition he borrowed the insight that every narrow point of view offers a limited and distorted knowledge of its subject matter, and has an inherent tendency to universalise its assumptions and categories of thought. His socially grounded epistemology implied that the knowing subject is a socially situated being who perceives the world from a specific social position characterised by specific conditions of existence and forms of thought. When the two were combined, it followed that every knowing subject has an inherent tendency to take for granted and universalise or absolutise a specific body of assumptions and forms of thought. Being unaware of its limitations, every social point of view claims universal or absolute validity. As we saw, this is basically what Marx means by ideology.

For him an ideology is a body of thought systematically biased towards a specific social group. It turns the latter's requirements into universal norms, its needs and interests into the sole criteria of human well-being, its view of reason into the sole criterion of rationality, the limits of its world into those of the world itself, and so on. In so doing, an ideology is forced to commit a number of logical fallacies, employ an abstract and ahistorical mode of reasoning, de-historicise the historically specific categories and give a biased and distorted account of its subject matter. What is more, it is guilty of moral arrogance. In setting up a particular group's conditions of existence as the absolute which the rest of society (or mankind) is expected to subserve, an ideology treats the latter as a mere means. In attempting to shape the entire society (or mankind) in the image of the group, it denies the integrity of other forms of experience and thought.[2]

While appreciating the importance of the socially derived biases, Marx to his credit continued to uphold the traditional concept of objective truth. Indeed it was precisely because he was concerned with the objective truth that he was interested in the phenomenon of ideology. As we saw, he examined a host of writers in order to elicit the highly complex ways in which their socially derived assumptions entered and shaped their thought. He uncovered the forms of reasoning, the methods of investigation and the types of concept that concealed from them the influences of their assumptions. He also explored the ways in which a social theorist could attain full self-consciousness, develop a most comprehensive and self-critical point of view, and overcome his socially derived biases.

For him truth is the highest ideal in the field of theoretical truth, and it is either objective or not truth at all. As we saw, he entered into a sustained debate with the classical economists, and aimed to show why their account of the capitalist society was mistaken. No doubt, he was sometimes not wholly fair to them. The point, however, is that he did not dismiss their economic theories as bourgeois, nor said that they were only true *for* the bourgeoisie. He criticised them, appealed to the universally valid empirical and logical criteria, and accepted whatever in their thought seemed true to him. Similarly he did not dismiss the liberal conceptions of individuality, liberty, equality, etc. as true only *for* the bourgeoisie. He critically examined them, explored their basic assumptions, demonstrated their bias, showed that they were incoherent, abstracted what he thought was true in them, and offered an alternative way of understanding man and society. Some of his criticisms are perhaps unpersuasive, and his own alternative is not free of grave difficulties. The relevant point, however, is that he was interested in assessing their truth in terms of the universally accepted criteria.

The profound significance of Marx's theory of ideology can hardly be exaggerated. Its greatest contribution consists in discovering the ideological dimensions of thought and heightening our epistemological self-consciousness. By pointing out that human beings uncritically take for granted and universalise their characteristic forms of experience and thought, Marx highlights an important and rarely noticed source of bias and distortion. He shows how the ideas and forms of thought, in terms of which we perceive and judge the world, can contain deep biases and involve an attempt to shape others in our own image.

As Marx rightly points out, this is evident in the way in which the dominant ideology in the modern society seeks to mould its members in the bourgeois-individualist image, and denies the authenticity of other forms of thought. The systematic social bias is evident also in the way in which the struggles of the three-quarters of mankind to improve their material conditions are described. The 'new' nations are considered to belong to the ethereal realm of the 'third' world; judged as 'undeveloped', 'underdeveloped' or 'developing'; said to be engaged in 'modernising' or 'Westernising' themselves; awarded high or low marks according to whether they are 'pro-' or 'anti-West' and preserve or reject 'liberal' institutions; are deemed to suffer from the handicap of 'traditionalism' or 'old-fashioned' values; and so on. The ideological presuppositions of this vocabulary and the implied standards of judgement need hardly be spelt out. The bias is evident in a perhaps less obnoxious form in the ways in which America, Australia and New Zealand are said to have been 'discovered' by the Europeans, the underlying assumption being that, although people had long been living in these countries, the latter did not *really* exist until the Europeans saw them with their own eyes. Since the Europeans did not *know* of them, they did not *exist*; and when they did come to know of them, the latter miraculously sprang into existence. As Marx rightly observes, every ideology aims to shape the world in the image of a specific social group, and in so doing invests the latter with the power the religions have traditionally reserved for God.

As Marx shows, a systematic unconscious bias permeates not only the thoughts of ordinary men, but also those of the highly sophisticated and theoretically self-conscious philosophers and social scientists. When their philosophical and scientific forms are peeled away, they seem to rest on the conventional prejudices of their society or class. Their elegantly presented and well-argued theories rest on certain basic assumptions which they never critically examine and, on careful analysis, turn out to be uncritical reproductions of the most commonplace beliefs of the ordinary members of their society or class. In arguing that our philosophical tradition has too heavily concentrated on the analyses of abstract concepts and the epistemological, ontological and other assumptions, and almost entirely ignored the ways in which the social assumptions can be brought into the open and critically investigated, Marx makes a point of the highest importance.

Marx not only discovers a new phenomenon, but also offers a useful analysis of its nature, structure and origin. As we shall see, his achievements in this area are considerably limited. However, some aspects of his analysis are valid. He is right to argue that the ideological thought owes its origin to the lack of social self-consciousness and self-criticism, and the consequent unwitting acceptance of the characteristic forms of thought of one's own social group. He is equally right to argue that certain types of concept, method of investigation and form of analysis, for long regarded as unproblematic, in fact prevent an individual from detecting or admitting the social bias of his assumptions. Further, Marx carefully identifies some of the illicit logical transitions involved in presenting the historical as the natural, the contingent as the necessary, and the socially specific as the universally valid.

In stressing the social nature of the knowing subject, the object known and the pursuit of knowledge, Marx highlights the fact that the forms of inquiry do not operate in a social vacuum. They rest on specific assumptions about man and society, which are derived from their cultural milieu and mediate and distort their interpretations of the social world. Their assumptions, concepts, methods of analysis, etc. must therefore be subjected to a critical scrutiny if we are not to remain imprisoned within a limited and biased framework of thought. Again, by articulating the complex relationship between a body of social and political thought and its social context, Marx's theory of ideology emphasises the fact that the former derives a large part of its appeal not from its allegedly intrinsic intellectual merit, but from its unarticulated social presuppositions, and that its theoretical merit is not its intrinsic natural property, but socially grounded. The philosophical arguments based on the doctrines of the atomic individual, natural rights, negative liberty and man's limitless desires, which seemed so obvious to Hobbes and seem so convincing to us, would have appeared unpersuasive and even incomprehensible to the ancient Athenian whose social and political experiences and forms of thought were so very different. All these are important and original insights and deserve to be incorporated in our social and political epistemology.

If our account of Marx's theory of ideology is correct, some of the criticisms levelled against it are misplaced. It is contended that the theory denies the autonomy of ideas, refuses to take them seriously, replaces the concept of the objective with class truth, makes men playthings of unconscious forces and, in general, subverts the very foundations of the Western intellectual tradition. If the charges were true, the theory would be totally unacceptable. As we saw, there is little evidence to support them. True, some of Marx's polemical remarks are open to such a construal. However, as we have shown, his general position is very different. Marx does take ideas seriously, insists that they must be judged in their own terms and not dismissed on the bases of their creator's social background, acknowledges that they are influential provided that they do not go counter to people's needs and the immanent tendencies of the social order, and rejects the concept of relative truth. Again, Marx says little to support the widespread view that, for him, ideas are the epiphenomenal products of the unconscious promptings of interests and wishes. It is a mystery how the concepts of unconscious determinism and false consciousness should have come to be fathered upon him, for he rarely uses the terms in any of his writings. He does, no doubt, make remarks, especially in the *German Ideology*, which are open to such a construal. However, the general thrust of his argument is very different.

When Marx says that an individual may be unconscious of his real intentions, he means one of two things. First, since men are not generally self-conscious, they take certain things 'for granted', 'merely assume' them, so that their thought rests on 'unarticulated assumptions'. Their assumptions delimit their horizon, prevent them from noticing certain aspects of their subject matter, focus their attention upon some others, and so on. This is a familiar and straightforward philosophical notion, and neither implies determinism nor detracts from the fact that men are autonomous beings capable of freely forming their beliefs. Part of the controversy surrounding Marx's theory of ideology would be eliminated if the term 'unconscious', with its psychological overtones, were to be replaced by the term 'unaware'.

Second, men often tend to talk about themselves and their society in general terms. The content of what they wish to say is specific, although they express it in general terms. Marx insists that it is easy to be misled by the general form, and ignore its limited and specific content. For example, in his view the bourgeoisie are primarily interested in the *economic* freedom. For them *this* is the most important constituent of freedom, and hence they claim to be fighting for *freedom itself*. Now if we are to understand their demands, we must not concentrate on the general term freedom, for freedom can be understood in several different ways and, since different types of freedom cannot all be attained, they must be hierarchically graded. Marx therefore asks to know *what* the bourgeoisie mean by freedom, and what *type* of freedom they most cherish such that they would sacrifice other types of freedom if they were to conflict with it. He concludes that they define freedom in negative terms, and prize the economic freedom above all others. In support of this, he points to the cases where the bourgeoisie clamoured for the restriction of the civil and political liberties when these posed a threat to their economic freedom. In other words when Marx asks what an individual (or a group) *really* wants, he intends to know not his (or its) real motive or will, but the *essential* content of his (or its) general and abstract demand. This in no way implies unconscious determinism. What is more, there is nothing improper in saying that a group, claiming to be fighting for freedom, is really interested in the freedom to undertake a particular kind of activities, *so long as* one is able to demonstrate this by reference to its utterances and, especially, its actual choices and actions.

Marx's theory of ideology then makes an important contribution to the social and political thought. It highlights a novel phenomenon with its own distinct nature and structure. In so doing, it opens up a whole new dimension of human thought, and a whole new area of inquiry. The phenomenon is significant, pervasive and elusive, and must be theorised and distilled into a distinct concept if we are not to lose sight of it. Thanks to Marx, it has already been conceptualised and named. It would therefore be a pity if we were to lose our theoretical grip on it, by extending the term ideology to mean every organised body of beliefs, or employing it as a crude slogan to discredit inconvenient ideas, or by refusing to accept it on the ground that it has 'Marxist' overtones. The last reaction, fairly widespread in some circles, is particularly objectionable, since it damns a concept on the basis of its creator, precisely the charge the critics level against Marx! Although Marx formulated it, the concept of ideology grows out of the Western philosophical tradition itself. As we saw, the latter has always emphasised the inherent bias and limitations of a narrow point of view; the concept of ideology carries the argument further and suggests that the point of view could also be social.[3]

II

Although Marx says a good deal that is perceptive and illuminating, his theory of ideology is open to several objections. For analytical convenience I shall set these out in a somewhat schematic form. Each objection relates to a specific feature of it, or to a claim made on its behalf.

First, Marx nowhere carefully analyses any of the basic categories in terms of which his theory of ideology is structured and articulated. As we saw, such concepts as presupposition, point of view, social position, bias, distortion, class, conditions of existence, forms of thought, criticism, universalisation and apologia are its constitutive categories. Each of them raises acute problems. Since Marx does not analyse and define them, nor deals with the problems raised by them, the theory lacks a precise and unambiguous formulation. We attempted in the second chapter to analyse some of its basic categories. However, our analysis was necessarily brief and sketchy, and only showed how much work needs to be done before Marx's theory can be taken as more than a cluster of brilliant insights.[4]

Second, Marx confuses the concept of ideology with several other related but essentially distinct concepts, from which it must be clearly distinguished if we are adequately to theorise its nature. Marx discovered the phenomenon of ideology within the general framework of his materialist conception of history, and his identification and analysis of it suffers from some of the limitations of the latter. As a historical materialist, idealism was his *bête noire*, and a constant frame of reference. Accordingly he defined it very widely and subsumed all sorts of very different doctrines under it. Although idealism and ideology are connected, the connection is not as close as Marx imagined, and must be clearly separated. As we shall see, historical materialism is in no way immune to the ideological virus. Further, as we saw, Marx tended, from time to time, to confuse ideology with the sociological inquiry into the social origin of knowledge. Although the two are related, their relationship is not conceptual, and hence they need to be clearly distinguished. Again, as a historical materialist Marx tended to concentrate on the class as the source of systematic bias. As we saw, he did recognise the importance of the other social groups as well and defined the class fairly broadly. It is therefore important to state his theory in a manner that liberates the concept of ideology from the narrowly defined class orientation.

Third, Marx's theory of ideology raises several general problems to which he gave little attention. As he rightly says, in order to de-absolutise a body of thought and demonstrate its partiality, a social theorist must be able to study society as a whole and from the standpoint of the whole. Marx, however, says little concerning the nature of the social whole, how it can be grasped as a whole, how a social theorist can develop a fully self-conscious and self-critical point of view, whether the standpoint of the whole is constructed independently of or by integrating the narrow points of view and the acute difficulty involved in each, whether the standpoint of the whole merely limits or also corrects and criticises the narrow social points of view, and so on. Since Marx studied only the capitalist mode of production and not a specific society in any detail, it is difficult to say how he would have answered these questions. Again, he rightly says that most systems of thought have both scientific and ideological dimensions, but does not examine in any detail how the two are structurally related, nor explains why the truth always wins over ideology as we saw him argue in connection with Hegel and the classical economists. Again, he rightly criticises Hegel and the classical economists for assuming that the modern bourgeois society represents the end of history, but does not take account of the obvious rejoinder that it might well be the end of history, that the basic principles of social organisation have already been evolved, and that the remaining question of eliminating poverty is only a matter of time. Marx's thesis that the bourgeois society *cannot* be the last word in history is intuitively plausible, but he cannot substantiate it, although his critics cannot substantiate their opposite claim either. Marx's criticism rests on, among other things, the validity of his forecast, and obviously he cannot criticise them for declining to accept it.

Fourth, Marx stresses the social at the expense of other kinds of assumption, and either ignores the latter altogether or establishes no clear connection between the two. A body of thought rests on the epistemological, methodological, ontological and other kinds of assumption which cannot all be explained in terms of its social assumptions. Marx himself acknowledges that both Kant and Hegel shared their social assumptions, and yet their ontological and methodological assumptions could not have been more different. Further, the non-social assumptions shape a theorist's approach to his subject matter, and exercise an *independent* influence which may and, in a long-established discipline, generally does run counter to that of his social assumptions. Marx generally ignores the complex interplay between the two. Since each influences the other, the resulting point of view of a social theorist is never an exact reflection of his social assumptions. The social point of view, although influential, is mediated, redefined and reduced to a moment in a wider point of view where its influence cannot be easily ascertained.

Further, the influence of social assumptions is considerable when one is dealing with a socially relevent subject matter. As one moves to a different level of reflection, their influence diminishes. Plato's political thought reveals an unmistakable social bias; but this could not be said of his theory of Ideas. Marx was therefore wrong to suggest that the social point of view is equally reflected at all levels of a body of thought. It is not surprising that, in his analysis of Hegel, he was able to demonstrate the social bias in his social and political thought, but had great difficulty concerning his concept of the *Geist* or the dialectical method. Not surprisingly he was reduced to saying such strange and conflicting things as that the *Geist* was an idealisation of the modern man or the forces of the world market, the anthropomorphisation of the ideas of reason dominant in his class, society or historical epoch, and the rationalised version of the Christian God.

Fifth, Marx says that an ideology universalises the forms of thought of a particular social group. However, he has great difficulty specifying what assumptions, conditions of existence and forms of thought characterise which social groups. He subsumes such different men as Bentham, Kant, Proudhon, Hegel and the Left Hegelians under the capacious category of the petty bourgeoisie. It is difficult to see what they all share in common, and how it is reflected in their very different bodies of thought. This is not to say that some of the groups that Marx calls petty-bourgeois do not share certain assumptions and views in common; despite their limitations Marx's analyses of Proudhon and Stirner, for example, are insightful. The point is that the term 'petty bourgeoisie' is so indeterminate and covers such motley groups as shopkeepers, independent farmers, men living on their modest savings and craftsmen that it is extremely difficult to identify their common point of view and shared assumptions. Further, on Marx's own account, the dominant ideology shapes the thought of the entire society, and therefore the different social groups fail to generate their own distinctive forms of thought. The relationship between the dominant and subordinate forms of thought gives Marx considerable difficulty, which he does nothing to resolve. Thus he began by arguing that Proudhon was a petty-bourgeois thinker, but ended by showing that he generalised the categories of thought and was an apologist of the bourgeois society. As we saw, he also traces the basic assumptions of Hegel, the Left Hegelians and the classical economists to their society rather than their social groups. He never specifies what the characteristic assumptions of the proletariat are, and how they are reflected in the writings of its theorists. Marx is much more successful in uncovering the basic social assumptions of a body of thought than in demonstrating their social origins. And he is far more successful in showing that the social theorists uncritically accept the basic assumptions and forms of thought of their society or historical epoch than that they accept those of their class.

Sixth, although Marx rightly stresses the inherently social nature of the knowing subject, he rather naively imagines that, once an individual becomes conscious of the influence of his class and society, he can *fully* overcome them. As we saw, he talks about the epistemological potential of the different social points of view, and freely choosing the one most appropriate. He says that, although difficult, the fullest social self-consciousness is within man's grasp. Marx has been frequently criticised for not appreciating the human capacity to transcend the social and class influences. In fact, he is open to the opposite criticism that he exaggerated the human capacity to do so. He was too deeply rooted in the Western philosophical tradition to appreciate the full force of his socially grounded epistemology. In conferring upon self-consciousness the power to transcend the deepest influences of class and society, he remained an 'idealist'.

If an individual is socially constituted and social in the innermost depths of his being, as Marx rightly insists, it is simply not possible for him ever to become fully self-conscious.[5] He lacks the necessary Archimedean standpoint where he can locate himself and lay bare the layer after layer of his socially constituted being. He can examine his assumptions and forms of thought only by means of the socially derived conceptual and methodological tools, and hence part of his social being necessarily eludes him. A complete social self-consciousness must therefore remain an unrealisable ideal. Marx's own thought offers ample evidence of this. Despite his determined effort to become fully and critically self-conscious, his ideas bear the unmistakable fingerprints of their creator. His enormous emphasis on technology and the economy was inspired by the contemporary bourgeois society in which they had acquired unprecedented importance and independence. He was wrong to universalise the bourgeois categories of thought, and argue that the economic could be easily distinguished from the other social relations in the pre-bourgeois societies. Further, the central importance he attached to labour in the creation of civilisation and his persistent underestimation of the capitalist's contribution to the creation of wealth seem to reflect the working-class bias. Again, he was not himself free from the belief in the end of history which he castigated in Hegel and the classical economists. While they ended history with the bourgeois society, Marx ended it with the communist. He naively imagined that the bourgeois society was the *last* class-divided society, the proletarian was the *last* revolution, the communist society will conclusively put an end to the human pre-history, and that no new post-communist form of social organisation was possible. Contrary to Marx's claim, his historical materialism did not save him from developing a body of thought with a fairly large ideological content. He universalised the categories of the bourgeois society and did not wholly avoid a systematic bias towards the proletariat.

If what we have said is true, science and ideology cannot be too neatly separated. All thought retains an ideological component. No doubt, some systems of thought may be less biased, make genuine attempt to examine their assumptions, endeavour to view their subject matter from as many different points of view as possible, and so on. However, they cannot be entirely free from the social biases, and are not entitled to put themselves on a qualitatively different plane. The only justifiable qualitative distinction is that between what Marx calls base and genuinely disinterested writers. As for the latter, the difference between them is at best one of degree. What is more, no writer, however self-conscious and self-critical, can ever *know* what biases still remain in his thought; only the posterity can identify them. Hence, although he may *in fact* be less biased than those he criticises, he has no means of knowing this. He can, at best, only know that he is free from *their* biases, but not that he is free from *other* biases. There is therefore no epistemological ground upon which Marx can claim that while the others are ideologists, he is a non-ideological scientist.

Seventh, Marx contrasts the ideological approach or thought with the critical, and insists that unless a social theorist takes a critical view of his society, he cannot avoid becoming its apologist. There is a good deal of truth in this for, unless a writer distances himself from his society and epoch, he cannot hope fully to understand it. And unless he is concerned with human well-being and has the breadth of moral imagination to explore sympathetically the needs and capacities frustrated, truncated or mutilated in his society, he would not be able to rise beyond the conventional platitudes and prejudices. Marx is right to argue that, unless one is sensitive to human suffering, loves one's fellow-men and wishes to help them grow and live, one is bound to find one's society 'more or less perfect'. On such a basis one can hardly avoid becoming its uncritical spokesman.

Marx's concept of criticism is, however, too extreme and Manichean to be satisfactory. For Marx anyone not interested in overthrowing the established social order is an apologist. Such a fierce and narrow view of criticism indiscriminately lumps together men and groups who take very different attitudes to their society. It is totally wrong to say that both Malthus and Ricardo or Burke and J.S. Mill were alike apologists of the bourgeois society. A theory that requires us to say this is inherently deficient. Further, Marx argues that the genuine criticism of a social order must transcend its fundamental assumptions or horizon of thought. Since, as we saw, no individual can fully transcend the prevailing horizon of thought, Marx's concept of criticism is incoherent. What is more, it presupposes that the constitutive characteristics of the prevailing horizon of thought can be unambiguously and fully identified, and this is a highly questionable assumption. For example, Marx identified the pursuit of value, the extraction of the surplus value, the austere conception of the individual, etc. as the defining characteristics of the bourgeois society. Tolstoy, Ruskin, Gandhi and many a theologian would disagree. In their view Marx's analysis is superficial, since it is the preoccupation with material abundance, the multiplication of desires, the infatuation with the technological development, the loss of the transcendental dimension of human existence and the concern with individuality, all of which Marx cherishes, that are the basic features of the modern society, and must be rejected. Marx might dismiss them as archaic and atavistic, but that is not an argument, and only goes to show that, like the ideologists he castigates, he takes for granted a certain conception of good life and disallows those that fall outside it. Further, Marx needs to show why his criticism of the bourgeois society is more penetrating and 'critical' than others, and this is not easy to show. In the ultimate analysis Marx's theory of criticism rests on a definite conception of human well-being. Even if Marx had stated and defended his conception better, it is, by its very nature, incapable of conclusive demonstration. The human well-being can be defined in several different ways, some more persuasive than others, but none capable of demonstration. Every social theory involves elements of personal preference, and in that sense retains a subjective dimension.

Marx's theory of criticism is further handicapped by the fact that he wishes to do two different and incompatible things. He aims both to transcend the bourgeois horizon of thought, and preserve the 'great' bourgeois technological and cultural achievements. It is not easy to see how the bourgeois achievements could be abstracted from and retained without at least partially remaining within the bourgeois horizon of thought. The cultural achievements of the bourgeois society are made within and informed by the bourgeois assumptions about man and society, and cannot be abstracted from the latter. Even the bourgeois productive forces which, on Marx's own definition, include the technical and organisational skills and the forms of industrial organisation, cannot be easily abstracted from the bourgeois horizon of thought. Further, it is not clear how Marx proposes to distinguish between the features of the bourgeois civilisation that must be transcended and those that deserve to be preserved. Is the complex bourgeois conception of the individual to be preserved? Transcended? Or some of its constituent elements preserved, and the rest rejected? Marx offers no criteria. Those he does offer, such as the 'universal', 'all-round' and 'rich' individual, are extremely vague and point in several different directions. Marx shows little awareness of the infinitely complex problems raised by the whole discussion.

Eighth, some of what Marx says about the nature of concept, the method of abstraction and the legitimate epistemological objectives of the social theorist is persuasive, and opens up whole new areas of debate and inquiry. The concepts cannot be defined in the abstract and then imposed upon the relevant subject matter; they must be teased out of a careful analysis of the latter. Besides, some of them have a historically derived content, and are therefore historically specific. Even the universally valid concepts are historically mediated and cannot be *directly* applied to a historically specific subject matter. Further, although he did not himself always manage to avoid Hegel's two-tier method of analysis, Marx's criticisms of it are well taken. He was right to suggest that the traditional ambition to offer a universally valid knowledge about man and society needs to be radically reconsidered. While all this is well said, it raises several problems of which Marx took little account.

Marx argues that, since all content is historically specific, all significant concepts are historically specific. This is simply not true of such philosophical concepts as substance, causality, space, time and existence. Further it is not entirely true of the social and political concepts either. However much the social conditions may change, certain fundamental features of human existence that have so far remained constant are likely so to remain, for they are either grounded in the *minimal* capacities which men cannot lose without ceasing to be human, or in the general patterns of relationship between men and nature or among them. For example, men are capable of initiative and unpredictable action, think for themselves, have different personal preferences, disagree, retain a core of incommunicable experiences, cannot always be or do what they would like to be or do, must make and remain responsible for their choices, must somehow come to terms with themselves, learn to reconcile themselves to their own mortality and that of those they love, and so on. The concepts designed to articulate and interpret the experiences, problems and forms of consciousness generated by these and other features of the human condition are not historically specific, but transcend the historical boundaries and retain a perennial appeal. As Marx himself admits, the bourgeois conception of the solitary individual, although profoundly different, was prefigured by the early Christians, and beautifully articulated by St Augustine. Some of the basic categories of the bourgeois economic life were also anticipated by Roman law.

While acknowledging that some forms of social consciousness have remained historically constant, Marx argues that this was so only because all post-tribal societies have been class-divided. This is not entirely correct, for even the tribal societies shared such ideas as transcendence, individuality and social differences. It is simply ignorant and a Eurocentric bias to say that the Asiatic society was merely a 'bee-hive' and its members lacked a sense of individuality. In any case, whatever the explanation, the fact remains that not all forms of consciousness, experience and thought are historically specific, and therefore not all concepts can be entirely historical. Indeed, if they were, we would lack the ability to understand men in other historical epochs than our own. This means that Marx was wrong to link idealism and ideology too closely, and to argue that any attempt to make a substantive universal statement is inherently ideological, and that all concrete concepts claiming universal validity are the vehicles of ideology. One cannot indiscriminately reject all universal concepts and statements, but must show in detail what specific concepts and statements of a social theorist can and cannot be universalised.

Although Marx's distinction between rational or legitimate and infantile or illegitimate abstraction is illuminating, his underlying criterion is questionable. He says that a rational abstraction is one which, among other things, takes full account of historical specificity. The difficulty with this is that historical specificity can be conceived so very differently. Marx maintains that the bourgeois society and its legal, political and other institutions are historically specific. He takes this view because he defines and classifies the historical epochs in terms of their modes of production; and he does so because he believes that the mode of production is the basis of society and shapes its entire character. In other words his classification of the historical epochs and his definition of historical specificity are grounded in the materialist conception of history. The historical specificity is not objectively given and easily recognisable, but a theoretical construction. Someone holding a different theory may therefore classify the historical epochs differently, and take different social relations and experiences as historically specific. What is a rational abstraction for Marx may be an infantile abstraction for him. This is, for example, what many of his critics have felt about his concept of the mode of production. They have argued that the mode of production is integrally connected with the rest of the social structure and cannot be understood in abstraction from it. For them British capitalism is not capitalism as articulated in Britain, for this implies that there is something called capitalism which gives itself different national forms, a point that Marx himself rightly criticised. Rather, it is a distinctively British way of constituting capitalism. British and American capitalism are not two different *forms* of the self-same capitalism whose 'essence' remains unaffected by one being British and the other American. Rather, although they share certain features in common, they are distinct *types* of capitalism with different 'essences' derived from the fact that each is a part of a distinct political and social structure with a distinct history, set of values, national character, and so on. Some of Marx's critics have asked if we can even meaningfully talk about capitalism, for that implies a belief in 'capitalism as such', precisely the kind of concept Marx so rightly rejects. While these and other objections are not unanswerable, they do make the relevant and telling point that the distinction between the rational and infantile abstraction can only be made within the framework of a larger social theory, and is not based on a theory-independent and universally valid criterion. Marx's way of distinguishing it is grounded in, and not binding upon, those rejecting his historical materialism.

III

Our tentative examination of the basic insights and limitations of Marx's theory of ideology would seem to entail the following conclusions. Marx discovered a novel intellectual phenomenon, namely that a body of thought may universalise the conditions of existence and forms of thought of a specific social group, and be systematically biased towards it. Such a structurally embedded and pervasive social bias is to be found in the body of ideas dominant in a specific society, as well as in the much more sophisticated systems of thought developed by the writers on man and society. While appearing to be self-evident and impartial, the established structure of moral and political discourse can contain a deep bias. And although, like the Athenian Gods, the philosophers, the social theorists, the novelists, the poets and others who deal with man and society may seem to occupy the Olympian heights, they do not avoid taking sides in the battles of the market place. Unlike the original sin, the social bias does not totally corrupt their thought, but distorts and limits it within a narrow range. It can be identified, criticised and overcome, and the achievements of the writer preserved.

Marx's greatness consisted in identifying and baptising the pervasive but elusive intellectual phenomenon, and exploring its internal structure, intellectual roots, forms of reasoning, characteristic fallacies and the ways of countering its influence. His limitations lay in not analysing it with sufficient rigour, giving an inadequate and sometimes misleading sociological account of its nature and origin, failing to notice its ubiquitous presence, including in his own thought, drawing too neat a distinction between science and ideology, not distinguishing it sufficiently sharply from other similar phenomena, and failing to appreciate that its range of influence extends to social and political thought, but not necessarily much further.

NOTES

Introduction

1.   For an excellent discussion of the difficulties involved in interpreting Marx, and of the various levels at which he wrote, see Alvin W. Gouldner, *The Two Marxisms* (Macmillan, London, 1980), Part III.
2.   H.B. Acton, *The Illusion of the Epoch* (Cohen and West, London, 1955), p. 271.

Chapter 1

1.   Marx uses the term in several senses. In the course of reacting against Hegel, the young Hegelians, and indeed the entire philosophical tradition, Marx used the term to mean almost everything of which he disapproved. He used it to mean illusion (*German Ideology* — hereafter *GI*), false ideas, (*GI*), any organised body of beliefs (1859 Preface), and even (*Theories of Surplus Value*, vol. 1, pp. 285, 301) the unproductive occupations. Those we have chosen for analysis are, however, the most common and important; the rest are sporadic usages.
2.   For a detailed discussion, see Chapter 3.
3.   In the Foreword to *Holy Family* (hereafter *HF*), Marx says that speculative idealism, which he also calls spiritualism, is the most 'dangerous enemy' of humanism.
4.   The Preface to the *GI* contains a remarkable battle cry.
5.   *Collected Works* (Lawrence and Wishart, London, 1975), vol. 5, p. 24; vol. 4, pp. 33, 123. See also *Capital* (Lawrence and Wishart, London, 1970-71), (hereafter *C*), vol. 1, p. 648 where Marx calls de Tracy a 'bourgeois doctrinaire'. The *Collected Works* are hereafter cited as (*CW*).
6.   *CW*, vol. 5, p. 24.
7.   *CW*, vol. 5, pp. 254ff, 153; *CW*, vol. 3, p. 159; *CW*, vol. 4, pp. 83, 85.
8.   *CW*, vol. 5, pp. 153f.
9.   *CW*, vol. 6, 197f; *Selected Correspondence* (Moscow, 1975) (hereafter *SC*), pp. 36, 143f; *CW*, vol. 5, pp. 468f.
10.   *Grundrisse* (Penguin, Harmondsworth, 1973), (hereafter *G*), pp. 86, 88.
11.   *CW*, vol. 5, p. 456.
12.   Ibid., pp. 236, 456. See also Marx's 'Marginal Notes on Wagner', in *Value: Studies by Marx* (New Park Publications, London, 1976), pp. 201ff for a very useful discussion of the whole subject.
13.   *CW*, vol. 5, 446f. Marx shows how in his view language becomes an 'independent realm', and the linguistic analysis replaces theoretical investigation.
14.   *CW*, vol. 5, pp. 431f.
15.   Ibid., pp. 30, 424f.
16.   *SC*, pp. 31f; *CW*, vol. 5, pp. 55f; *A Contribution to the Critique of Political Economy* (Lawrence and Wishart, London, 1971), p. 215, where Marx contrasts 'idealistic historiography' with 'realistic historiography'. This work is hereafter cited as *CPE*.
17.   *CW*, vol. 5, p. 236.
18.   Ibid., pp. 91f; see also *Anti-Duhring* (hereafter *AD*), p. 152.
19.   *CW*, vol. 5, pp. 29, 232, 237, 287, 341, 379, 420, 447, 456, 469.

20. Ibid., p. 447.
21. Ibid., p. 456.
22. Ibid., p. 420.
23. Ibid., p. 232.
24. *CW*, vol. 6, pp. 170, 165.
25. *CW*, vol. 5, p. 29.
26. *Selected Works* (Moscow, 1962), vol. 1, pp. 140, 161, 179, 185, 208, 209; the two volumes of *Selected Works* are hereafter referred to as *SW*.
27. *G*, pp. 322, 890; *Theories of Surplus Value* (Moscow, 1968) (hereafter *TSV*), vol. I, p. 281.
28. *G*, pp. 164f. See also *CPE*, p. 22 where Marx uses the term ideology to mean idealism.
29. *C*, vol. I, p. 373.
30. *SC*, p. 400.
31. Ibid., p. 435.
32. Ibid., p. 443.
33. Ibid., p. 434; 'wrong' could also be translated as 'false'.
34. Ibid., italics added.

Chapter 2

1. This essentially sound view of the nature of philosophy was first articulated by Socrates, systematically formulated by Plato and has been held by nearly all the philosophers since, including those such as the logical positivists and the linguistic philosophers who otherwise reject a large part of the philosophical tradition. It was explored at great length and defended with great skill by Hegel. One of its clearest modern statements from which I have greatly benefited is to be found in Michael Oakeshott, *Experience and its Modes*, (Cambridge University Press, London, 1934). I have discussed it at length in my 'The Nature of Political Philosophy' in P.T. King and B.C. Parekh, (eds.), *Politics and Experience* (Cambridge University Press, London, 1968).

2. *CW*, vol. 5, pp. 406, 417; *G*, p. 162; *TSV*, vol. I, pp. 50, 60, 61, 88 and 281; *TSV*, vol. II, p. 237, 238, 239 and 527; *TSV*, vol. III, pp. 260, 453, 456; *C*, vol. II, p. 231; *SC*, pp. 97, 147, 198f. For Marx a theory offers an interpretation of its subject matter, and is always constructed from a specific point of view. See *CW*, vol. 5, p. 410; *CW*, vol. 6, p. 124; *TSV*, vol. III, pp. 172, 260, 265; *TSV*, vol. II, pp. 238f; *C*, vol. I, p. 508. Marx equates the concepts of interpretation and point of view at *CW*, vol. 5, p. 406. For Engels's view on the nature of assumption, see *SC*, p. 397.

3. *CW*, vol. 3, p. 205. It is translated here as a 'point of view of the whole'. Like Easton and Guddat I have translated it as 'the standpoint of the whole'. See also *G*, pp. 100, 108, 196, 197, and *C*, vol. II, p. 436, where Marx talks about the 'point of view of society' and society 'viewed as a totality', and *CW*, vol. 1, pp. 333f, where Marx first explores how to develop a standpoint of the whole. For him a point of view determines what one sees. From the bourgeois point of view 'the origin of surplus value is entirely withdrawn from view' and the reality of exploitation is 'buried at one stroke', *C*, vol. II, pp. 229, 223.

4. *TSV*, vol. II, pp. 168, 238, 239, 527; *CW*, vol. 5, pp. 28, 31, 36, 37, 236, 416, 417, 435; *CW*, vol. 6, p. 202; *C*, vol. III, p. 182; *SC*, p. 99; *G*, pp. 254f, 474f, 490f.

5. *CW*, vol. 3, p. 199; *SC*, pp. 97, 147.

6. *CW*, vol. 3, pp. 197f; *C*, vol. II, pp. 120, 123; *TSV*, vol. II, 237; *TSV*, vol. III, 259, 260, 453, 456, 467; *G*, 334, 404, 410, 421, 541; *CW*, vol. 5, pp. 334,

404, 410, 421, 541.
 7. *C*, vol. I, p. 542; *CW*, vol. 3, p. 205.
 8. *G*, p. 265: 'Society does not consist of individuals, but expresses the relations within which these individuals stand. To be a slave, to be a citizen, are social characteristics, relations between human beings.'
 9. For a good discussion, see Marx's analysis of Proudhon; *SC*, pp. 30f.
 10. *C*, vol. II, p. 231 where Marx talks about the 'point of view of a bank clerk', and *CW*, vol. 5, pp. 218f where Stirner is seen to represent the standpoint of a 'petty handicraftsman', John Plamenatz is one of the few writers to appreciate the importance of Marx's idea of social point of view. See his *Ideology* (Macmillan, London, 1970), pp. 50f.
 11. For good discussions of the shifts in Marx's views, see the works by McLellan, Ollman, Nicolaus and Draper listed in the bibliography.
 12. Marx uses the term even in the uncompleted discussion in *C*, vol. III, pp. 885, 886.
 13. *CW*, vol. 5, pp. 30f, 60f, 78f, 85f, 301; *CW*, vol. 4, pp. 274ff; *CW*, vol. 3, pp. 273ff; *C*, vol. I, pp. 269, 278, 283, 295, 339, 341, 399, 484, 506.
 14. *SW*, vol. I, pp. 272, 215.
 15. *TSV*, vol. III, pp. 55, 84, 129, 130, 259, 402, 428, 429; *C*, vol. I, pp. 14, 81; *TSV*, vol. II, p. 529; *C*, vol. III, p. 830.
 16. *SW*, vol. I, p. 275. I have slightly amended the translation; 'explicitly' here means 'deliberately' or 'on principle'.
 17. See *TSV*, vol. I, pp. 175, 285, 287, 300, 301 and Chapter 3 below.
 18. Marx observes that 'all our history books, dictated as these are, for the most part by bourgeois prejudices' give a distorted account of the middle ages. 'It is very convenient to be "liberal" at the expense of the middle ages', *C*, vol. I, p. 718.
 19. Marx's use of such terms as 'legitimise', 'defend', 'apologise for', 'apologia', 'speak for' and 'justify' indicates that he has only the social bias in mind.
 20. For Marx every philosophical system universalises the socially limited forms of thought and becomes what he pejoratively calls 'moral philosophy'. See *CW*, vol. 5, pp. 247, 254, 269, 274, 285, 290, 292, 375f, 407. Even as an ideology involves moralising, Marx thinks that all moralising is inherently ideological. One moralises in order to get others to do what they otherwise could not. It is because Marx regards moralising – though not necessarily morality itself – as ideological that he insists that the communists 'do not preach morality at all', *CW*, vol. 5, pp. 247, 255.
 21. *CW*, vol. 5, pp. 417, 418, 420.
 22. This point is well brought out by Istvan Meszaros in his 'Ideology and Social Science' in V.K. Roy and R.C. Sarikwal (eds.), *Marxian Sociology*, (Ajanta Publications, Delhi, 1979) vol. 1, pp. 1-61.
 23. *CW*, vol. 3, p. 181.
 24. Marx's concepts of 'transcript' and 'conditions of existence' are considerably vague. His meaning will become clearer in section IV of this chapter.
 25. *TSV*, vol. II, p. 238; *SC*, p. 99.
 26. I have both elaborated Marx's arguments and added some of my own in order to bring out his complex points.
 27. *CW*, vol. 5, pp. 64f.
 28. Ibid., pp. 342f, 90f.
 29. *G*, pp. 164f, 172, 325, 471ff, 491ff, 650f; *CW*, vol. 5, pp. 424f, 436f.
 30. *G*, pp. 494f.
 31. Ibid., p. 650f.
 32. For Marx's view of 'materialist freedom', see *CW*, vol. 5, pp. 301f and 310f.

33.   The idea that the government should leave the individuals alone in almost all areas of life is central to Marx's vision of the communist society.

34.   *CW*, vol. 7, pp. 204, 430, 483; *Value: Studies by Marx* (New Park Publications, London, 1976) p. 192. (This work is cited as *Value*); *G*, pp. 240ff, 649f.

35.   *SW*, vol. I, p. 275; I have amended the translation.

36.   *TSV*, vol. II, p. 169.

37.   He devoted several hundred pages to the refutation of Stirner and nearly a hundred to that of the Utopian socialists. That his views on several important matters changed as a result of his close examination of Stirner is an interesting example of how seriously Marx took his opponents while claiming to reject them.

38.   *SC*, p. 145; emphasis added.

39.   Marx devotes scores of pages to the critical examination of Smith, Ricardo and other economists.

40.   The distinction between the two is mine, but there is evidence for it in Marx's writings. In his discussion of Stirner, Hegel, Smith, Ricardo, Proudhon and others, Marx almost always concentrates on the elucidation and critique of their basic social assumptions; he says little about their social background, except *en passant* and without giving any importance to it.

41.   This view, of course, goes against the bulk of the writing on Marx's theory of ideology, which starts with the thesis of the social determination of knowledge and interprets Marx's theory of ideology within that framework. I suggest that the latter can be independently defined.

42.   Nationalism, racialism, etc. have all the logical properties we earlier saw to be characteristic of ideology.

43.   *CW*, vol. 7, p. 378.

44.   *TSV*, vol. III, pp. 453, 501.

45.   See *CW*, vol. 4, pp. 267f, where he scathingly criticises Friedrich List for attacking the motives of his opponents, and *C*, vol. I, p. 10.

46.   *TSV*, vol. III, p. 399, where Marx says that 'what has been lacking in all English economists since Sir James Steuart . . . [is] a sense of the *historical* differences in modes of production . . . a correct distinction of historical forms'.

Chapter 3

1.   *TSV*, vol. II, pp. 119, 117.

2.   *SC*, p. 147.

3.   *TSV*, vol. III, p. 172.

4.   *TSV*, vol. II, pp. 117f.

5.   Ibid., p. 120.

6.   Some of Marx's commentators have argued that since the essence and appearance in social life coincide in the communist society, science as a distinct form of inquiry must disappear. See, for example, Kosta Axelos, *Marx, Penseur de la technique* (Paris, 1961); Adolfo Sanchez Vazquez, *The Philosophy of Praxis* (Merlin Press, London, 1977); and recently G.A. Cohen, *Karl Marx's Theory of History: A Defence* (Clarendon Press, Oxford, 1978) Appendix I.

7.   *TSV*, vol. III, pp. 168, 453, 485, 522-3; also *C*, vol. I, pp. 81, 538.

8.   *C*, vol. I, p. 217.

9.   *TSV*, vol. III, pp. 521-3.

10.   *C*, vol. I, pp. 734ff.

11.   *CW*, vol. 6, pp. 433, 434; *CW*, vol. 4, p. 234.

12.   *TSV*, vol. I, pp. 285, 287, 300, 301. It is for this reason that Marx

calls them 'ideological professions'.

13. *C*, vol. I, p. 741, where Marx refers to the British parliament as the 'permanent Trades' Union of the capitalists' and says that its laws confine the 'struggle between capital and labour within limits comfortable for capital'.

14. For a useful discussion, see John McMurtry, *The Structure of Marx's World-View* (Princeton University Press, New Jersey, 1978) pp. 145f.

15. This view is taken by Althusser, Paul Hirst and J. Mepham in his otherwise excellent article 'The Theory of Ideology in Capital' in *Radical Philosophy*, vol. II, no. 2 (1972). cf. Marx's remarks in the *Communist Manifesto* and *C*, vol. I, p. 766, where he shows how 'the ideologist's apologetic armour crumbles off, bit by bit, like rotten touchwood'.

16. *C*, vol. III, p. 209.

17. *C*, vol. I, pp. 72f.

18. *C*, vol. I, pp. 83, 86, 92; *C*, vol. II, p. 229.

19. *G*, pp. 243f. As Marx observes at *CW*, vol. 5, p. 78, the individuals do not 'cease to be persons', but 'their personality is conditioned and determined by quite definite class relations'.

20. *G*, p. 247. For a good discussion see, *CW*, vol. 10, pp. 589f.

21. *G*, p. 248; *CW*, vol. 10, p. 590.

22. *C*, vol. I, p. 568.

23. *TSV*, vol. III, p. 483. For an excellent discussion of the whole subject, see Norman Geras 'Marx and the Critique of Political Economy' in Robin Blackburn (ed.), *Ideology in Social Science* (Fontana, London, 1972).

24. *TSV*, vol. III, pp. 260, 261, 267, 453, 456, 467, 472, 485, 523; *G*, pp. 247; *SC*, p. 36 and *CW*, vol. 5, p. 413. Marx's discussion of vulgar socialism is worth comparing with his discussion of 'true' socialism in vol. 5, pp. 455ff.

25. *SC*, p. 36; *CW*, vol. 5, p. 413.

26. *TSV*, vol. III, p. 456; *SW*, vol. I, pp. 221f; *SC*, p. 34.

27. *SC*, p. 106.

28. *TSV*, vol. III, pp. 456, 467.

29. Ibid., p. 523.

30. *SC*, pp. 34, 38; also *CW*, vol. 5, p. 410.

31. *SW*, vol. I, p. 222; *SC*, pp. 36, 106.

32. *SC*, p. 36.

33. *TSV*, vol. III, p. 261.

34. Ibid., pp. 267, 275.

35. Ibid., pp. 260, 276.

Chapter 4

1. For excellent discussions of the Right and Left Hegelians' attitudes to Hegel, see David McLellan, *The Young Hegelians and Karl Marx* (Macmillan, London, 1969) and Sidney Hook, *From Hegel to Marx* (University of Michigan, Ann Arbor, 1971).

2. *CW*, vol. 1, pp. 84-5.

3. *CW*, vol. 3, pp. 333.

4. Hegel, *The Science of Logic*, Miller (trans.) (Allen and Unwin, London, 1969), pp. 154f.

5. *CW*, vol. 3, pp. 7f, 23f.

6. *CW*, vol. 4, p. 139. The same point is made with a different emphasis at vol. 5, p. 98.

7. *CW*, vol. 4, pp. 57f.

8. *CW*, vol. 3, pp. 16f, 23f.

9. Ibid., p. 23.
10. Ibid., p. 11.
11. Ibid., p. 12.
12. Ibid., p. 14.
13. *CW*, vol. 5, p. 283.
14. *CW*, vol. 3, p. 12.
15. Ibid., pp. 343f.
16. Ibid., p. 16.
17. Ibid., p. 14.
18. Ibid., p. 91.
19. Ibid., p. 48.
20. Ibid., p. 15.
21. Ibid., p. 21.
22. Ibid., p. 39.
23. Ibid., pp. 23, 342f.
24. Ibid., p. 39.
25. *CW*, vol. 5, p. 175.
26. *CW*, vol. 4, p. 179.
27. *CW*, vol. 3, pp. 177f.
28. Ibid., pp. 39, 42, 91.
29. Ibid., p. 88.
30. Ibid., pp. 88-9. The paragraph is not entirely clear and it would be wrong to claim that my interpretation is the only one possible.
31. Ibid., p. 88.
32. *G*, pp. 331-2; see *C*, vol. I, p. 744, where Marx links the concept of mediation with the role of the 'middleman'.
33. J.J. O'Malley, R.W. Algozin, H.P. Kainz and L.G. Rice (eds.) *The Legacy of Hegel* (Martinus Nijhoff, The Hague, 1973), p. 69.
34. *CW*, vol. 3, pp. 340f.
35. *CW*, vol. 5, p. 446f. Here and elsewhere Marx says much that is reminiscent of the later Wittgenstein. For a stimulating discussion, see Ted Benton, 'Wittgenstein and Marx', *Radical Philosophy* (Spring 1976).
36. For Marx the mechanical materialism of the eighteenth- and nineteenth-century philosophers rested on idealism. It either needed to postulate God to explain motion, or had so to define matter that it could only be ideal in nature. Engels expresses the point well in *Dialectics of Nature*, Appendix 1 B entitled 'On the mechanical conception of Nature'. *Contra* Colletti, Engels takes a dialectical view of nature, not of matter. His dialectical naturalism (not materialism) is, of course, no less objectionable.
37. *CW*, vol. 6, pp. 164, 165. The entire second chapter entitled 'The Metaphysics of Political Economy' makes interesting reading. For Marx Hegel's method is common to the political and moral theorists as well; see *CW*, vol. 5, p. 410.
38. *CW*, vol. 3, p. 333.
39. Ibid., p. 332.
40. Engels takes a similar view; see *SC*, p. 381. The logic of this view is well-explored by Ernst Fischer, *Art against Ideology*, (1961) and T. Eagleton, *Marxism and Literary Criticism* (Methuen, London, 1976), pp. 47f and 57f.

Chapter 5

1. *C*, vol. I, p. 14; italics added.
2. *C*, vol. I, pp. 573, 14; also *C*, vol. II, p. 223.
3. *C*, vol. I, p. 438; *CPE*, p. 61, where Marx agrees with Lord Brougham

that Ricardo had 'as if . . . dropped from another planet'.

4. *TSV*, vol. II, p. 529.
5. *SC*, pp. 64, 37.
6. Ibid., p. 32.
7. *CW*, vol. 6, p. 174.
8. *TSV*, vol. II, p. 529.
9. *CW*, vol. 6, p. 174; *C*, vol. I, p. 81.
10. *G*, p. 105.
11. *TSV*, vol. II, p. 165.
12. *CW*, vol. 3, p. 290.
13. *TSV*, vol. III, p. 429.
14. *C*, vol. III, p. 830.
15. *G*, p. 249.
16. *TSV*, vol. III, pp. 265, 272, 274, 448.
17. *TSV*, vol. II, p. 501.
18. *Value*, p. 99; also *G*, pp. 257-8.
19. *G*, pp. 105, 249.
20. *TSV*, vol. III, p. 52.
21. *TSV*, vol. II, p. 529.
22. *C*, vol. I, p. 80.
23. *C*, vol. I, p. 538.
24. *TSV*, vol. II, p. 529; *TSV*, vol. III, pp. 88, 101.
25. *C*, vol. I, p. 80.
26. *TSV*, vol. III, p. 138.
27. *C*, vol. I, pp. 80-1.
28. *TSV*, vol. III, p. 88; *TSV*, vol. II, pp. 498, 520, 527.
29. *TSV*, vol. II, pp. 528-9.
30. *G*, p. 852.
31. *TSV*, vol. III, p. 85.
32. *TSV*, vol. II, p. 521.
33. *TSV*, vol. I, pp. 301, 175.
34. Ibid.
35. *CW*, vol. 5, p. 469.
36. *TSV*, vol. III, p. 90.
37. Ibid., pp. 88f and *G*, p. 322.
38. *G*, p. 250.
39. *TSV*, vol. II, p. 501.
40. *TSV*, vol. III, p. 495.
41. Ibid., p. 315.
42. *C*, vol. I, p. 114. Marx here outlines what he takes to be the 'two methods characteristic of apologetic economy'.
43. *TSV*, vol. I, p. 92; *TSV*, vol. III, p. 460.
44 *TSV*, vol. I, p. 81.
45. Ibid., p. 89.
46. Ibid., p. 92.
47. *G*, pp. 339, 888; *TSV*, vol. III, pp. 500f.
48. *TSV*, vol. III, p. 500.
49. *TSV*, vol. II, pp. 164f, 493, 497f, 505f.
50. *TSV*, vol. III, p. 501.
51. Ibid.
52. Ibid., p. 329.
53. Ibid., pp. 258-9. The two examples discussed indicate what Marx meant by unconscious influences. As the examples indicate, he had in mind not some kind of psychological determinism, but the structural influence of the basic

assumptions of the classical economists.
54. Ibid., p. 259.
55. *TSV*, vol. II, p. 166.
56. *TSV*, vol. III, p. 429.
57. Ibid., p. 328.
58. *C*, vol. I, p. 542.
59. *TSV*, vol. III, p. 501.
60. *C*, vol. III, p. 830.
61. *TSV*, vol. III, p. 501.
62. *G*, p. 884; *TSV*, vol. III, p. 260.
63. *C*, vol. I, p. 17; italics added. The words are Marx's, not the Russian commentator's.
64. *C*, vol. I, p. 75.
65. *CW*, vol. 5, pp. 60f. Marx observes at ibid., p. 61 (in the marginal note) that in the early years of the bourgeois society 'the illusion of the *common* interests . . . is true'.
66. *TSV*, vol. III, pp. 329, 331.
67. *C*, vol. II, p. 395; see also *SC*, p. 401.
68. *TSV*, vol. II, p. 519.
69. *G*, p. 106.
70. *C*, vol. I, p. 14.
71. For a good discussion see *TSV*, vol. III, pp. 500f; *C*, vol. I, pp. 14f. Whether much of the contemporary literature on political and social theory falls into these four categories is an interesting question.
72. *CW*, vol. 5, p. 293.
73. *C*, vol. I, p. 15.
74. *TSV*, vol. III, p. 502.
75. Ibid., p. 84.
76. *C*, vol. III, p. 786.
77. *C*, vol. I, p. 14.
78. *G*, p. 883.
79. *TSV*, vol. III, p. 502.
80. *TSV*, vol. II, pp. 497, 499, 501, 520, 529.
81. Ibid., p. 519. See also ibid., p. 499, where Marx says that the classical economists 'deny' the existence of a phenomenon because it 'contradicts existing prejudices'.
82. *TSV*, vol. III, 258f; *C*, vol. II, p. 461; *TSV*, vol. I, p. 89; *C*, vol. I, pp. 539, 542, 590; *C*, vol. II, pp. 223, 367.
83. See, for example, *CW*, vol. 3, pp. 12, 75, 78; *C*, vol. I, pp. 516, 537, 538, 590; *TSV*, vol. II, p. 499, 520; *C*, vol. II, 367, 368, 382. See also *C*, vol. I, p. 590, where Marx criticises J.S. Mill who 'in spite of his *Logic*' overlooks an elementary fallacy.
84. *C*, vol. I, pp. 537, 538. This is how Marx explains the classical economists' use of such terms as the 'rewards of labour' and the 'price' or 'cost of production' of labour, and the questions formulated in terms of them.
85. *G*, p. 883.
86. *TSV*, vol. III, pp. 259, 331. Colletti confuses the two when he says that 'Political economy . . . is born with capitalism and dies with it'. See his 'Marxism: Science or Revolution?' in Robin Blackburn (ed.), *Ideology in Social Science*, (Fontana, London, 1972).
87. See, for example, *C*, vol. II, p. 438; and *TSV*, vol. III, p. 331, where Marx talks of 'empty tradition'. Such remarks occur often in *TSV* and *C*.
88. *TSV*, vol. II, pp. 164f; *TSV*, vol. III, pp. 500f; *G*, pp. 106f, 307f; *C*, vol. I, pp. 13f.

89. *C*, vol. I, pp. 13f; *TSV*, vol. III, p. 501.
90. Ibid., pp. 501f and 519f.
91. *SC*, p. 148.
92. *G*, pp. 472-503 and 408f, where Marx suggests that when nature holds full sway, the dialectic is absent; when it is conquered but without collective control, the dialectic fully comes into its own. Thus the dialectic first emerges in ancient Athens and gathers momentum under capitalism.
93. See Lukács, *History and Class Consciousness* (Merlin Press, London, 1971), pp. 83ff, and Alfred Schmidt, *The Concept of Nature in Marx* (New Left Books, London, 1971) pp. 165ff. For a further discussion see my 'Marx and the Hegelian Dialectic' in V.K. Roy and R.C. Sarikwal (eds.), *Marxian Sociology* (Ajanta publications, Delhi, 1979), vol. I, pp. 83-104.

Chapter 6

1. *CW*, vol. 5, p. 293; ibid., p. 482, Marx calls them logical lapses.
2. *CW*, vol. 10, pp. 305f; *Value*, pp. 98f.
3. *CW*, vol. 6, p. 432.
4. *CW*, vol. 5, p. 425; *TSV*, vol. III, p. 259; *Value*, pp. 105f, 145; *C*, vol. II, p. 229.
5. *TSV*, vol. III, pp. 55, 84, 259, 429. If we so wished, we might give this fallacy a name, such as naturalising the social, or even perhaps a naturalistic fallacy!! All the other fallacies can be similarly baptised.
6. *TSV*, vol. III, pp. 276, 322.
7. *CW*, vol. 5, pp. 422, 294f.
8. *C*, vol. I, p. 713.
9. *C*, vol. I, pp. 714f. For Marx the personal qualities are products of social conditions, and therefore material in their origin. See *CW*, vol. 5, pp. 375f.
10. *CW*, vol. 10, pp. 306f; *CW*, vol. 5, p. 375.
11. *C*, vol. I, p. 765.
12. *Value*, p. 192.
13. *SC*, pp. 157f; *C*, vol. III, pp. 869, 872.
14. *CW*, vol. 5, pp. 230f, 245f, 277; see also *CW*, vol. 10, pp. 306f.
15. The distinction between the pre- and para-theoretical influences is mine. The former refers to the way an individual is shaped before he begins to theorise, and includes his upbringing and professional socialisation. The latter refers to the influence of the practical activities in which he continues to engage while remaining a theorist.
16. *C*, vol. I, p. 10.
17. Ibid., p. 15.
18. Ibid., p. 14.
19. Ibid., p. 17.
20. *CW*, vol. 5, pp. 47f. The idea that an individual should be free to develop his own authentic form of life and individuality, and that he should therefore be freed from the natural or socially imposed patterns of behaviour runs right through Marx's thought. Note, for example, the way the term individual is used in *German Ideology*, ibid., pp. 80, 81, 82, 85, 86, 87, 88.
21. *CW*, vol. 6, p. 125. Marx observes, 'To put the cost of manufacture of hats and the cost of maintenance of men on the same plane is to turn men into hats'; ibid.
22. *CW*, vol. 1, pp. 204f. Marx observes, '*Everything existing* serves him as an *argument* . . . In short a rash is just as positive as the skin itself.' Ibid., p. 205.
23. *CW*, vol. 3, p. 177.

24.   D. Fernbach (ed.), *Surveys from Exile* (Penguin, Harmondsworth, 1973), p. 144.
25.   *C*, vol. I, p. 505.
26.   *G*, pp. 85f, 100f, 249f.
27.   *SC*, p. 98; *G*, 251.
28.   *G*, pp. 331, 852.
29.   *G*, pp. 303, 332, 512f.
30.   *CW*, vol. 6, p. 163.
31.   *CW*, vol. 5, p. 37.
32.   *CW*, vol. 6, 164f; *SC*, p. 34.
33.   *G*, p. 85.
34.   *G*, p. 88; *C*, vol. I, p. 114.
35.   *C*, vol. I, p. 114.
36.   *CPE*, p. 20.
37.   *SC*, p. 294.
38.   Ibid., p. 393.
39.   *G*, p. 249; *CW*, vol. 5, p. 456.
40.   *G*, p. 86.
41.   *CW*, vol. 5, pp. 236, 456, 475.
42.   Ibid., p. 449.
43.   *C*, vol. II, p. 230; *G*, p. 249; *CW*, vol. 5, pp. 478, 481.
44.   *TSV*, vol. III, p. 128. See also 'Marginal Notes on Wagner' in *Value*, where Marx subjects Wagner's abstract analysis of the concept of 'value as such' to a searching critique, and insists that he should have begun with 'the simplest economic *concretum*', or 'the simplest social form' of the capitalist mode of production rather than the concept of value.
45.   *SC*, p. 99.
46.   *CW*, vol. 5, p. 129.
47.   *SC*, p. 32; emphasis added; see also ibid., p. 34; *G*, pp. 85f.
48.   *CW*, vol. 5, pp. 53f.
49.   *TSV*, vol. III, p. 500; *G*, p. 105, where Marx says that the concepts 'possess their full validity only for and within' the specific historical relations. See also *G*, p. 106 and Ollman, *Alienation: Marx's Concept of Man in Capitalist Society* (Cambridge University Press, Cambridge, 1971), pp. 12f.
50.   *CW*, vol. 5, p. 236.
51.   *C*, vol. I, p. 372.
52.   *G*, p. 105.

Chapter 7

1.   For references see Lenin, *Collected Works* (Foreign Languages Publications, Moscow, 1960), vol. 1, pp. 362, 385, 388, 394, 416, 421, 503f; Lukács, *History and Class Consciousness* (Merlin Press, London, 1971), pp. 68ff; Gramsci, *Selections from the Prison Notebooks* (Lawrence and Wishart, London, 1971), pp. 368, 392, 445f; L. Althusser, *Lenin and Philosophy and Other Essays* (New Left Books, London, 1971), pp. 16, 68f, 73f, 95f, 119f, and also *Elements of Self-Criticism* (New Left Books, London, 1976), p. 161; Karl Korsch, *Marxism and Philosophy* (New Left Books, London, 1970), pp. 42f; Ernst Bloch, *On Karl Marx*, (Herder and Herder, New York, 1971), pp. 143, 147ff.
2.   Lukács, *History and Class Consciousness*, pp. 68f, 163f.
3.   Gramsci, *Selections*, pp. 445f.
4.   Althusser, *Lenin and Philosophy*, pp. 95f. For a good discussion of Althusser, see Alex Callinicos, *Althusser's Marxism* (Pluto Press, London, 1976)

and Norman Geras, 'Althusser's Marxism', *New Left Review* (January-February 1972).

5.   Adam Schaft, *History and Truth* (Pergamon Press, London, 1976), p. 246; see also pp. 234ff.

6.   Lucio Colletti, 'Marxism: Science or Revolution?' in Robin Blackburn (ed.) *Ideology in Social Science* (Fontana, London, 1972), pp. 375ff.

7.   *CW*, vol. 5, pp. 457, 469.

8.   *CW*, vol. 6, p. 177.

9.   *C*, vol. I, p. 21 and *SC*, p. 106.

10.   For the composition of *German Ideology*, see *CW*, vol. 5, pp. 586f.

11.   The theoretical weight of a remark depends upon the amount of theoretical burden it is made to carry within a given system of thought. It is determined by inquiring what other remarks depend upon it for their validity, and how much the whole system would suffer if it were to be questioned.

12.   *G*, p. 406.

13.   *C*, vol. I, p. 16; emphasis added.

14.   *TSV*, vol. II, p. 126, 119

15.   See *SC*, p. 251, where Marx draws a distinction between himself as a political activist and a scholar.

16.   *CW*, vol. 3, p. 182.

17.   Ibid., p. 332.

18.   *CW*, vol. 6, p. 174.

19.   *Value*, p. 92.

20.   *CW*, vol. 4, pp. 281, 282; *CW*, vol. 3, pp. 184f.

21.   *TSV*, vol. II, pp. 117. See also *G*, p. 173, where Marx observes that 'the demands placed on the representing subject are contained in the conditions . . . of that which is to be represented'.

22.   *Surveys*, pp. 73, 45.

23.   The subject was discussed at length in Chapter 5.

24.   For Marx to be a theorist of the proletariat is to interpret the bourgeois society and human history from its point of view and within the limits of its assumptions and horizon of thought. A proletarian theorist cannot therefore be fully self-conscious and self-critical, and hence Marx cannot aim to be one. It is striking that Marx rarely, if ever, talks of taking the proletarian point of view, or even uses the phrase.

25.   For a painstaking account of this, see Joseph O'Malley, 'Marx's Economics and Hegel's *Philosophy of Right*', *Political Studies*, vol. XXIV, no. 1 (March, 1976).

26.   *CW*, vol. 6, p. 178; *SC*, p. 145.

27.   *C*, vol. I, p. 19.

28.   *The First International and After*, David Fernbach (ed.) (Penguin, Harmondsworth, 1974), p. 259.

Chapter 8

1.   For the statements of these and other views, see the works of Popper, Acton, Seliger, Sanchez Vazquez, Hook and Milton Fisk cited below. One of the best statements on the subject still remains Leszek Kołakowski, 'Karl Marx and the classical definition of Truth' in his *Marxism and Beyond* (Pall Mall Press, London, 1969).

2.   For a careful discussion of Marx's moral theory, see Helmut Fleischer, *Marxism and History* (Penguin, Harmondsworth, 1973).

3.   For Marx no impulse or desire comes into being and becomes effective

unless it is materially both possible and necessary. For an interesting discussion of why greed was materially impossible in the pre-capitalist society, see *G*, pp. 163, 223f. One of the fundamental ambiguities in Marx's materialist conception of history lies in the fact that he is sometimes content to say that a social practice cannot come into being unless it is materially possible, but on other occasions insists that it cannot come into being unless it is materially necessary. Marx's accounts of the state, religion, morality, ideology, etc. oscillate between the weaker and the stronger versions.

4. Some of Marx's commentators fail to appreciate that the concept of mediated unity, that is uniting two things while retaining their autonomy, is the most basic principle of his thought, and that no interpretation of him that ignores this can ever be satisfactory.

5. This is the general limitation of Marx's thought, and explains why Marxism has difficulty coming to terms with the non-revolutionary radicalism.

6. *SC*, p. 96.

7. Habermas, in *Knowledge and Human Interests* (Heinemann, London, 1972), brings out the point well. His concept of interest, however, is rather vague; his threefold classification is neither exhaustive nor based on a clear criterion; and his proposed relationship between interest and the pursuit of knowledge remains vague. Marx would have disagreed with his attempt to establish an 'identity' (p. 197), rather a mediated unity of the two.

8. The distinction between 'proving' and 'making' true or false is mine, but it captures Marx's point.

9. A number of distinguished Marxists have either advocated or come close to advocating praxis as the criterion of truth, largely on the basis of a dubious interpretation of Marx's second thesis on Feuerbach. The thesis proposes praxis as the test of reality, and not of truth. For those who make praxis in one form or another the criterion of truth, see Garaudy, *Marxism in the Twentieth Century* (Collins, London, 1970) pp. 83f; Mao Tse-Tung, *Selected Works* (Peking, 1967) vol. 1, p. 297; Vazquez, *Philosophy of Praxis*, chs. 3-5. Gramsci, too, comes close to taking this view.

10. For a useful statement, see *AD*, p. 101.

11. *AD*, p. 101. See *C*, vol. II, p. 443, where Marx talks about the 'partial correctness' of a theory.

12. *AD*, vol. II, pp. 98, 100.

13. *SC*, p. 96.

14. *AD*, p. 96.

15. *SC*, p. 189. Translation amended.

16. *C*, vol. I, p. 60.

17. *AD*, p. 101.

18. Sidney Hook takes Marx to be a pragmatist largely on the basis of a strange interpretation of his fifth thesis on Feuerbach. See Hook, *From Hegel to Marx*, pp. 294, 299; Kolakowski, offers a good critique of the pragmatist interpretation.

19. *SC*, pp. 124f, 196; *C*, vol. III, pp. 190, 213, 244, 828; *TSV*, vol. II, pp. 509, 512f. Marx insists that a scientific theory is concerned to explain how and under what conditions an event is logically possible, as well as why and when the possibility becomes a reality. He observes: 'If one asks what its cause is, one wants to know why *its abstract form*, the form of its possibility, turns from possibility into actuality', *TSV*, vol. II, p. 515. The whole section is useful on Marx's concept of causality.

20. *C*, vol. III, p. 213; *CW*, vol. 6, p. 124. Those who argue that Marx is only or even primarily interested in the *laws* of capitalism do him a grave injustice.

21. *C*, vol. I, p. 644. Those who argue that Marx is only or even primarily

interested in prediction seriously misrepresent his thought. Marx is primarily concerned with explanation, and only incidentally with prediction.
22.   *SC*, p. 197.
23.   *TSV*, vol. I, p. 88.
24.   Cf. Karl Popper who calls it a 'principle of correspondence' at *Conjectures and Refutations* (Routledge and Kegan Paul, London, 1963), pp. 202f.
25.   Marx does not explicitly say so, but it underlies his historical inquiry and his dialectical critique of the classical economists.
26.   *TSV*, vol. II, p. 169.
27.   Ibid. Translation amended.
28.   *TSV*, vol. I, p. 71.
29.   *Value*, p. 39; *TSV*, vol. III, p. 123.
30.   *TSV*, vol. I, p. 88.
31.   Ibid., p. 97, 102, 103.
32.   *TSV*, vol. II, p. 167, 169. Marx praises the first two chapters of Ricardo's book in which his 'entire . . . contribution is contained' (p. 169), and criticises the next for 'faulty architectonics' (p. 167).
33.   Ibid., pp. 166, 167.

Chapter 9

1.   The Marxist and neo-Marxist literary critics have been greatly sensitive to this crucial distinction. Although they do not formulate it in these terms, the distinction is implicit in some of the work of the Frankfurt School. For perceptive discussions, see Raymond Williams, *Marxism and Literary Criticism* (Oxford University Press, London, 1977), and T. Eagleton, *Marxism and Literary Criticism* (Methuen, London, 1976).
2.   The strength of Marx's moral revulsion against the assimilationist thrust of ideology should not be underestimated.
3.   Marx's proposal that a social theorist must endeavour to look at society from different points of view and inquire how the same phenomenon could appear to different groups is profoundly significant, and deserves to be given a methodological articulation.
4.   There is a good deal of theoretical work to be done by the Marxists if Marx's theory of ideology is to receive the attention it deserves.
5.   For a further discussion, see my 'Social and Political Thought and the Problem of Ideology' in R.T. Benewick, R.N. Berki and B. Parekh (eds.), *Knowledge and Belief in Politics* (Allen and Unwin, London, 1974). I should like here to retract the mistaken comment that Marx was guilty of 'naïve economism'.

BIBLIOGRAPHY

Major Editions of Marx's and Engels's Works

Marx. K. and Engels, F. *Historisch - Kritische - Gesamtausgabe. Werke - Briefe-Schriften*, D. Riazanov (ed.) (Marx-Engels Institute, Frankfurt and Moscow, 1927-36)

Marx, K. and Engels, F. *Marx-Engels Werke* (Dietz Verlag, Berlin, 1956-68)

Marx, K. and Engels, F. *Collected Works* (Lawrence and Wishart, London, 1975)

Individual Writings in English not yet published in the *Collected Works*

Capital, A Critique of Political Economy, Samuel Moore and Edward Aveling (trans.) (Lawrence and Wishart, London, 1970)

Capital, (2 vols. Lawrence and Wishart, London, 1971)

A Contribution to the Critique of Political Economy (Lawrence and Wishart, London, 1971)

The Ethnological Notebooks (1880-2). Studies of Morgan, Maine, Phear and Lubbock, transcribed and edited, with an introduction by L. Krader (Assen, 1972)

The First International and After, David Fernbach (ed.) (Penguin, Harmondsworth, 1974)

Grundrisse: Foundations of the Critique of Political Economy, translated with a foreword by M. Nicolaus (Penguin, Harmondsworth, 1973)

Selected Correspondence (Moscow, 1975)

Selected Works (2 vols. Moscow, 1962)

Theories of Surplus Value (3 vols. Moscow, 1968)

Value: Studies by Marx, Albert Dragstedt (trans. and ed.) (New Park Publications, London, 1976)

Engels, F. *Anti-Duhring* (International Publishers, New York, 1972)

Commentaries: Books and Articles

Acton, H.B. *The Illusion of the Epoch* (Cohen and West, London, 1955)

Althusser, Louis, *Reading Capital* (New Left Books, London, 1970); *Lenin and Philosophy* (New Left Books, London, 1971)

Avineri, S. *The Social and Political Thought of Karl Marx* (Cambridge University Press, London, 1968)

Axelos, K. Marx, *Penseur de la Technique* (Paris, 1961)

Benewick, R.T., Berki, R.N. and Parekh, B. (eds.) *Knowledge and Belief in Politics* (Allen and Unwin, London, 1974)

Benton, T. 'Wittgenstein and Marx' *Radical Philosophy*, vol. VI (Spring 1976)

Blackburn, R. (ed.) *Ideology in Social Science* (Fontana, London, 1972)

Bloch, E. *On Karl Marx* (Herder and Herder, New York, 1971)

Bober, M.M. *Karl Marx's Interpretation of History*, 2nd edn rev. (Harvard University Press, Cambridge, Mass., 1962)

Callinicos, A. *Althusser's Marxism* (Pluto Press, London, 1976)

Cohen, G.A. *Karl Marx's Theory of History: A Defence* (Clarendon Press, Oxford, 1978)

Colletti, L. *From Rousseau to Lenin: Studies in Ideology and Society* (New Left Books, London, 1972)

Cutler, A., Hindess, B., Hirst, P. and Hussain, A. *Marx's Capital and Capitalism To-day*, (vols. I and II, Routledge, London, 1977 and 1978)

Draper, H. 'The Concept of the Lumpenproletariat in Marx and Engels', *Cashiers de l'Institute de Science Économique Appliquée* (December, 1972)

Eagleton, *Marxism and Literary Criticism* (Methuen, London, 1976)

Evans, M. *Karl Marx* (Allen and Unwin, London, 1975)

Findlay, J.N. *The Philosophy of Hegel* (Collier Books, New York, 1966)

Fisk, M. *Ethics and Society* (Harvester Press, London, 1980)

Fleischer, H. *Marxism and History* (Penguin, Harmondsworth, 1973)

Garaudy, R. *Marxism in the Twentieth Century* (Collins, London, 1971)

Geras, N. 'Althusser's Marxism', *New Left Review*, no. 72, (January-February, 1972)

Gouldner, A.W. *The Two Marxisms: Contradictions and Anomalies in the Development of Theory* (Macmillan, London, 1980)

Gramsci, A. *Selections from the Prison Notebooks* (Lawrence and Wishart, London, 1971)

Habermas, J. *Knowledge and Human Interests* (Heinemann, London, 1972)

Hegel, G.W.F. *The Science of Logic*, A.V. Miller (trans.) (Allen and Unwin, London, 1969)

Hirst, P.Q. 'Althusser and the Theory of Ideology', *Economy and Society*, vol. 5 (1976)

Hook, S. *From Hegel to Marx* (University of Michigan, Ann Arbor, 1971)

Hyppolite, J. *Studies on Marx and Hegel* (Heinemann, London, 1969)

Jakubowski, F. *Ideology and Superstructure in Historical Materialism* (Allison and Busby, London, 1976)

Jordan, Z.A. *The Evolution of Dialectical Materialism* (Macmillan, London, 1967)

King, P.T. and Parekh, B.C. (eds.) *Politics and Experience* (Cambridge University Press, London, 1969)

Kolakowski, L. *Marxism and Beyond* (Pall Mall Press, London, 1969)

Korsch, K. *Karl Marx* (New Left Books, London, 1938)

— *Marxism and Philosophy* (New Left Books, London, 1970)

Lefebvre, H. *The Sociology of Marx* (Vintage Books, New York, 1969)

Lenin, V.I. *Collected Works* (Foreign Languages Publication, Moscow, 1960)

Lichtheim, G. *Marxism: An Historical and Critical Survey* (Routledge and Kegan Paul, London, 1961)

Lifshitz, M. *The Philosophy of Art of Karl Marx* (Pluto Press, London, 1973)

Lukács, Georg, *History and Class Consciousness* (Merlin Press, London, 1971)

Mao Tse-Tung, *Selected Works* (Peking, 1967)

McLellan, D. *The Young Hegelians and Karl Marx* (Macmillan, London, 1969); *The Thought of Karl Marx* (Macmillan, London, 1971); *Karl Marx: His Life and Thought* (Macmillan, London, 1973)

McMurtry, J. *The Structure of Marx's World-View* (Princeton University Press, Princeton, New Jersey, 1978)

Mepham, J. 'The Theory of Ideology in Capital', *Radical Philosophy*, vol. 11, no. 2 (1972)

Mepham, J. and Ruben, D.H. *Issues in Marxist Philosophy* 3 vols. (Harvester Press, London, 1979)

Nicolaus, N. 'Proletariat and Middle Class. Hegelian Choreography and the Capitalist Dialectic', *Studies On the Left*, vol. 7 (1967)

Oakeshott, M. *Experience and its Modes* (Cambridge University Press, London, 1934)

Ollman, B. *Alienation: Marx's Concept of Man in Capitalist Society* (Cambridge University Press, London, 1977); 'Marx's use of "class" ', *American Journal of Sociology*, vol. 73 (1968)

O'Malley, J. 'Marx's Economics and Hegel's *Philosophy of Right*', *Political Studies*, vol. xxiv, no. 1 (March, 1976)

O'Malley, J., Algozin, K., Kainz, H. and Rice, L. *The Legacy of Hegel* (Martinus Nijhoff, The Hague, 1973)

Philosophical Forum, vol. VIII (1978) The entire issue is devoted to Marx and the Left Hegelians

Plamenatz, J. *Man and Society. A Critical Examination of Some Important Social and Political Theories from Machiavelli to Marx* (2 vols. Longmans, London, 1963)

— *Ideology* (Macmillan, London, 1970)

Popper, K. *Conjectures and Refutations* (Routledge and Kegan Paul, London, 1963)

Rotenstreich, N. *Basic Problems of Marx's Philosophy* (Bobbs-Merrill, Indiana, 1965)

Roy, V.K. and Sarikwal, R.C. *Marxian Sociology* (Ajanta Publications, New Delhi, 1979)

Schaff, A. *History and Truth* (Pergamon Press, London, 1976)

Schmidt, A. *The Concept of Nature in Marx* (New Left Books, London, 1971)

Seliger, M. *The Marxist Conception of Ideology*, (Cambridge University Press, London, 1971)

Taylor, C. *Hegel* (Cambridge University Press, London, 1975)

Tucker, R.C. *Philosophy and Myth in Karl Marx* (Cambridge University Press, London, 1961)

Vazquez, A.S. *The Philosophy of Praxis* (Merlin Press, London, 1977)

Walker, A. *Marx: His Theory and its Context* (Longman, London, 1978)

Williams, R. *Marxism and Literature* (Oxford University Press, London, 1977)

INDEX